W9-CKM-383

The New York Bartender's Guide

The New York Bartender's Guide

1,300 ALCOHOLIC
AND NON-ALCOHOLIC DRINK RECIPES
FOR THE PROFESSIONAL
AND THE HOME

Sally Ann Berk

GENERAL EDITOR

Copyright © 1997, 2009 Black Dog & Leventhal Publishers, Inc.

All rights reserved. No part of this book may be reproduced in
any form or by electronic or mechanical means including information
storage and retrieval systems without written permission
of the publisher.

Published by Tess Press, an imprint of
Black Dog & Leventhal Publishers
151 West 19th Street
New York, NY 10011

Manufactured in China

Interior design: Scott Citron, Scott Citron Design
Design production: NICI von Alvensleben, SPELL
Contributor: John Glenn

Photo Credits:
Getty Images: pp. 6-7
Foodpix/PictureArts: p. 17
Luk Thys/PhotoAlto: pp. 9, 10, 12, 14, 18, 21, 22, 24, 27, 28, 30, 33, 34, 37,
38, 41, 42, 44, 46, 50, 51, 52, 62, 86, 130, 161, 169, 203, 220, 228, 240
George G. Weiser, Jr.: All other photos.

ISBN-13: 978-1-60376-165-9
         g f e d c b a

Library of Congress Cataloging-in-Publication data on file
at Black Dog & Leventhal Publishers, Inc.

Contents

Introduction

Since this book was first published in 1995, New York City has been through many changes. In that time, New Yorkers have experienced events that none of us could ever imagine. But what shines through is the enduring spirit of New Yorkers who continue to celebrate life every day. And that means enjoying the good things that New York City has to offer...including the nightlife of this fabulous city. Just like the Empire State Building and the Chrysler Building, both classics with style, perfection, and grace, many of the cocktails in this book are timeless masterpieces. As quintessential as the Flatiron Building, these cocktails—the Martini, the Manhattan, and the Cosmopolitan—are sensuous icons of the ineffableness that is Manhattan (and the outer boroughs, too!). This revised and reorganized edition of *The New York Bartender's Guide* is a tribute to that heart and soul, to the indomitable spirit of New York City.

The New York Bartender's Guide gives you the tools to make the perfect drink, and with more than 1,300 alcoholic and some classic non-alcoholic recipes for traditional and popular new cocktails, you'll never be stumped for a new drink idea. In addition to all the drink recipes you will ever need, *The New York Bartender's Guide* contains time-tested tips from famous New York bartenders. Why New York? Because, after all, if you can't find it in New York, you probably can't find it anywhere! Here is some of the collected wisdom of our favorite bartenders—good advice for anyone wanting to learn about bartending, entertaining, or just creating a good drink.

Margarita from Mesa Grill

Favorite Drinks

Nicholas Mellas, Gallagher's Steak House: "My all-time favorite drink to make is a classic dry Martini with beautiful, extraordinary olives. Martinis have been drunk forever."

Mark Fleckenstein, Gotham Bar & Grill: "I enjoy making classic cocktails and enticing people to try them. A perfectly proportioned Manhattan made with a light, blended rye such as Crown Royal is a charming elixir. I also like to take an old standard and tweak it a little, such as making a vodka gimlet with Hangar One Kaffir Lime vodka and fresh lime juice."

Michael Lagnese, Union Square Cafe: "My favorite cocktail depends on the season. During the summer months it can be either a dry Tanqueray martini up with a twist, or a dry Stoli martini up with a twist. In the winter, I would have to say first is a Tanqueray Negroni, classic."

Jack Kennedy, Delmonico's Steakhouse: "Tastes in cocktails swing in New York. Right now, I'm making a lot of green and red apple martinis. I enjoy making the classic cocktails as well as the current favorites, but my drink of choice is vodka and Coke."

Billy Steel, '21' Club, Hudson River Club, Mesa Grill: "The most poured drink at '21' was anything on the rocks, mostly Scotch. My favorite drink to make there was a classic Martini, with a little more vermouth than usual. At '21' they are into making drinks the way they should be made."

Peter Mellett, Au Bar, Mesa Grill: "I have watched the old standards fade from popularity, ordered only by folks of a certain age, only to be brought back into vogue. I saw a resurgence of the Martini as early as the late eighties, along with variations of it such as the Cosmopolitan, made famous at Odeon, in New York City."

On Bartending at Home

Peter Mellett: "There is a big difference between mixing drinks at home and doing in at work. But in both instances people love to watch a bartender in action."

Mark Fleckenstein: "Don't buy cheap triple sec for your home bar, it can make a good drink go very bad."

Jack Kennedy: "When I train new bar staff, I always tell them, 'Don't let the crowd absorb you.' The same rule applies in your home. Whether you have two guests or customers or two hundred, give each guest and each drink the same level of attention."

Michael Lagnese: "Whether bartending at work or at home, I try to make sure everyone always has a full glass in their hand. When someone is taking care of you with a cocktail in hand it helps to make the pain of your day go away."

Tips From the Pros

Peter Mellett: "All the up drinks are fun to make, Margaritas, Martinis, Gibsons, etc. It's interesting to note that if one person is drinking them, most of the bar will follow suit. They look fun to drink."

Martini with Dubonnet and a Twist (from Hi-Life Bar Grill)

Jack Kennedy: "The best way to make sure you serve great cocktails is to begin with great ingredients and then mix them the same way every time. Experimentation is fun—adding a new ingredient to an old standard—but consistency is the key. Once you've figured out the right balance of ingredients, you want your customers to recognize the drink you put in front of them, to trust that it will be exactly like the excellent martini you made for them last week."

Michael Lagnese: "This is your stage—make the most of it. Engage in conversation with everyone. Something can always come out of it . . . like meeting your wife, as I did."

Sarah Fearon, Hi-Life Bar and Grill: "Every party needs a host to make sure things flow well. As a bartender you have to host a killer party every night. The first step to making this experience incredible is inviting your clients to feel welcome."

Bar Etiquette and Oddities

Billy Steel: "Bartenders at '21' would come in wearing a suit and tie, carrying a briefcase with their bartending tools in it. They don't let you behind the bar there until you have trained for about five months, no matter what your background. This is real old-school, where bartending is a respected art."

Mark Fleckenstein: "If you find yourself in a busy bar and you are with a group of friends, before you give in to the compulsion to start waving at your bartender, make sure everyone in your group knows what they want to drink."

Jack Kennedy: "The rule of bartending is 'Service first, your tip will come.' I think that's about right. And setting the right mood for your customers begins as soon as they walk in the door. Even if you can't serve them right away, acknowledge them immediately. When you're working you should be neat, tidy, well groomed, and polite. It also doesn't hurt to be good with gentle one-liners, a bit of conversation to help customers relax but without being intrusive."

Billy Steel: "The strangest thing I had to do as a bartender was at my first job, in this Mafioso bar called Paul's Lounge. I used to act as the middleman for bookies and the bar clientele. They would place the bets and make the payoffs through me. Bartending really goes beyond pouring a drink."

Michael Lagnese: "Please do not wave to a bartender. If he or she is qualified they will acknowledge you in some way—eye contact, 'be with you in a moment.' Don't worry, they are not ignoring you (most of the time)."

Setting Up Your Home Bar

Sally Ann Berk, amateur bartender: "When I moved to New York, I lived in a studio apartment not much larger than a good-sized walk-in closet. In the kitchen area there was barely enough room for food and dishes, let alone a well-stocked bar. I still wanted to entertain, and found improvisation to be the answer to the space problem. Underneath the one window in the apartment was a large hole in the wall that had been cut out for a wall-unit air conditioner. I used that hole for a liquor cabinet/wine cellar. It was perfect."

The Basics for a Small Bar

Here are the "bar essentials" for a complete small bar. Nothing is too fancy. Improvise and tailor your bar to the tastes of your friends and guests.

BEER, WINE, AND SPIRITS

Beer, Lager (refrigerate)

Bourbon

Brandy

Crème de Cassis

Gin

Red wine, Cabernet Sauvignon and/or dry French

Rum, light

Scotch

Tequila, silver

Triple Sec

Vermouth, dry and sweet

Vodka, plain and at least two flavored (keep in freezer)

White wine, dry French or California (refrigerate)

Red Wine, Bordeaux or dry California

MIXERS

(Keep refrigerated, use fresh fruit juices when possible)

Cola

Cranberry juice

Diet soda

Ginger ale

Grapefruit juice

Lemon juice

Lemon-lime soda

Lime juice

Orange juice

Sparkling water

Tomato juice

Tonic water

GARNISHES AND CONDIMENTS

Angostura bitters

Bar sugar

Black pepper

Spanish olives

Grenadine

Lemons

Limes

Oranges

Tabasco® sauce

Worcestershire sauce

GLASSWARE

Brandy snifter

Champagne flute

Cocktail glass

Highball glass

Pilsner glass

Wine goblet

BARTENDING TOOLS

Bar spoon

Blender

Bottle opener

Citrus reamer

Corkscrew

Jigger

Measuring cup

Measuring spoons

Mixing glass

Paring knife

Standard shaker

Strainer

The Basics for a Full Home Bar

If you have enough room for a full bar, add the following components to those mentioned on p. 13. For mixers and ice, you may want to purchase a small refrigerator and keep it next to your liquor cabinet or bar. It is extremely convenient and saves time and space when you are entertaining.

BEER, WINE, AND SPIRITS

Ale, Pale and Amber
  (keep in refrigerator)

Amaretto

Armangnac

Benedictine

Brut Champagne

Bourbon, blended and
  single barrel

Calvados

Campari

Canadian whiskey

Cognac

Cointreau

Crème de Bananes

Crème de Cacao, light and dark

Crème de Cassis

Crème de Menthe, white

Crème de Noyaux

Curaçao, blue and white

Drambuie

Dubonnet, blanc and rouge

Eau de Framboise and another
  eau de vie

Flavored vodkas (citrus, vanilla,
  chocolate, pepper, berry; keep
  in the freezer)

Grand Marnier

Grappa

Irish Cream liqueur

Irish whiskey

Jagermeister

Kirshwasser

Madeira

Maraschino liqueur

Peppermint Schnapps

Pernod

Poire William

Port (ruby, tawny, and vintage)

Porter

Punt e Mes

Rum, Anejo, dark, Demerara,
  and gold

Sake

Sherry, amontillado, fino and
  cream

Scotch, single malt and blended

Slivovitz

Strega

Stout

Tequila, gold, silver, aged finest
  agave

White Sambuca

MIXERS

(Keep refrigerated)

Apple cider

Bitter lemon soda

Clamato juice

Coconut cream

Coffee

Ginger beer

Guava nectar

Half-and-Half

Milk

Peach nectar

Pineapple juice

Spring water,
 bottled

GARNISHES AND CONDIMENTS

Allspice

Apples

Bananas

Celery

Cinnamon, ground

Cinnamon sticks

Cocktail onions

Coriander

Cucumber

Eggs*

Honey

Horseradish

Margarita salt

Mint, fresh

Cuba Libre

Nutmeg, ground

Orange bitters

Orgeat (Almond) syrup

Passion fruit syrup

Peaches

Peychaud's Bitters

Pickled jalapeño peppers

Pineapple

Raspberry syrup

Raspberries

Rose's Lime Juice

Semi-sweet chocolate

Strawberries

Sugar cubes

Sugar syrup

Tamarind syrup

White pepper

Whole cloves

* Please use caution
when using raw eggs
in any of the recipes
included in this book.
Raw eggs have been
known to cause
salmonella poisoning

GLASSWARE

Balloon wine glass

Beer mug

Brandy snifter

Champagne glass

Cocktail glass

Collins glass

Double Old-Fashioned glass

Highball glass

Irish Coffee glass

Margarita

Parfait glass

Pilsner glass

Pony

Pousse Café

Punch cup

Red wine glass

Sherry glass

Shot glass

Sour glass

White wine glass

BARTENDING TOOLS

Champagne stopper

Glass pitcher

Ice bucket

Ice tongs

Muddler, or mortar and pestle

Punch bowl

A Note on Ingredients

Making a great cocktail is not just a question of technique. You must use quality ingredients. It may be tempting to save a few dollars on a cheaper brand of gin, but your Martini will suffer for it. Using reconstituted lemon juice may be easier than squeezing fresh, but the taste of fresh juice is far superior. When bartending for guests, offer them the best.

Many of the recipes in this book call for fresh juice. A small electric citrus reamer makes squeezing citrus fruits a cinch and can be purchased for under $30. If you use bottled juices, make sure you buy 100 percent juice, which should be free of added sugars or syrups. Read the labels. Even cranberry juice is available in most supermarkets sweetened with grape juice, rather than sugar or high-fructose corn syrup. Be sure to buy juices in glass bottles whenever possible. When you buy citrus juices, go for the ones in the dairy case marked "not from concentrate."

When a recipe calls for spices, use freshly ground ones. Keep whole nutmeg and cinnamon sticks in your kitchen. You can use a nutmeg grater for both. Freshly ground pepper makes a Bloody Mary perfect, and a Margarita tastes much better when the glass is rimmed with the proper coarse salt.

Finding some of the more exotic ingredients may prove a challenge, but it is worth the effort. If you live in an urban area, you can find ingredients such as tamarind syrup and guava nectar at many Caribbean or Mexican grocery stores. Many natural food and specialty food stores carry hard-to-find components, too. Use mail-order gourmet catalogues, the Internet, or call friends who have access to more variety and ask them to have the exotica mailed to you. If you don't find what you're looking for, your grocer or liquor store manager often will be happy to special order something for you.

Glossary of Drink Terms

Apéritif Traditionally, a drink served before a meal to stimulate the appetite, such as a fortified or aromatized wine in a vermouth style. These include Byrrh, Dubonnet, Lillet, Campari, Pernod, Amer Picon, and St. Raphael. The term apéritif now refers more to the time the drink is served than its ingredients.

Aromatized Wine This includes vermouth (Italian and French types) and the quinined or other apéritif wines of various countries. Alcohol content is 15 to 20 percent.

Blended Whiskey Straight whiskey combined with neutral grain spirits.

Bitters A flavor enhancer made from berries, roots, and herbs, usually used to provide smoothness to a biting whiskey. (See also section on A Guide to Beer.)

Brandy A spirit aged in wood, obtained from a fermented mash of fruit or the distillation of wine.

Cobbler A tall drink served in a collins or highball glass, filled with crushed ice, wine or liquor, and garnished with fresh fruit and mint sprigs. The traditional cobbler is made with sherry, pineapple syrup and fresh fruit garnishes.

Cocktail A beverage that combines an alcohol (usually brandy, whiskey, vodka, or gin) with a mixer (fruit juice, soft drink, or another liquor) and usually served chilled.

Collins A tall glass filled with ice, sugar, a spirit, citrus juice, and club soda or seltzer.

Cooler Usually served in a tall glass, such as a collins or highball, and consisting of a carbonated beverage, such as ginger ale or club soda, a wine or spirit, and a lime or orange rind cut in a continuous spiral, hooking over the rim of the glass.

Daisy An oversize cocktail such as a Margarita, made with proportionally more alcohol, sweetened with fruit-syrup, and served over crushed ice.

Distillation The process of separating the components in a liquid by heating it to the point of vaporization, then cooling it so it condenses in a purified form, thereby increasing the alcohol content.

Dry A term used for wine, liquor, or a cocktail to indicate a lack of sweetness. For example, a dry Martini is one with very little vermouth, the fortified wine that adds sweetness to the spirit.

Falernum A syrup from the Caribbean made of mixed fruits, sugar cane, and spices, used to sweeten mixed drinks, or an alcoholic liqueur.

Fix A drink mixed in the serving glass, may be another name for a highball—always served over ice.

Fizz A drink named for the siphon bottle that added "fizz" to a recipe of sugar, citrus juice, and, traditionally, gin.

Flip A cold, creamy drink made with eggs, sugar, citrus juice, and a spirit. It got its name in Colonial times, when a hot flip iron was used to mull the ingredients in the drink. There are few flips in this new edition due to the risks of using raw eggs.

Fortified Wine It includes Sherry, Port, Madeira, Marsala, etc. The alcohol content is between 14 and 24 percent.

Grog A rum-based drink originally served to sailors. The contemporary version consists of rum, fruit, and sugar.

Jigger A small drinking glass-shaped container used to measure liquor. Also called a shot.

Julep Made with crushed ice, usually Kentucky bourbon, sugar, and mint leaves.

Liqueur A beverage, usually sweet, naturally processed or manufactured by adding a flavoring to a distilled spirit. The flavor accents include, but are not limited to, almond, strawberry, orange, coffee, hazelnut, mint, and chocolate.

Mist Spirits added to a full glass of crushed ice.

Muddle To mash or crush ingredients with a spoon or muddler (a rod with a flattened end).

Mull Drinks where the ingredients are heated for thorough blending.

Neat Term for serving a spirit straight, in a glass without any ice or mixers.

Negus A hot, sweet wine drink traditionally made with Sherry or Port.

On the Rocks Term denoting wine or spirits poured over ice cubes.

Pousse-Café Made from several liqueurs and cordials, each having a different weight and color so that when poured one on top of another, they layer and "float."

Proof The measure of strength of alcohol. One (degree) proof equals one-half of one percent total alcohol. For example, 100 proof liquor is 50 percent alcohol.

Rickey A drink consisting of lime or lemon juice, mixed with gin or some other spirit and club soda, usually with no added sweetener.

Shooter A mixed drink or shot of some kind of spirit, swallowed in one gulp.

Sling A tall drink usually served cold, made with spirits, lemon juice, and sugar, and topped off with club soda.

Sour A short drink made with lime or lemon juice, sugar, and spirits.

Spirit A beverage made from the distillation of a liquid containing alcohol. The alcohol content of the original liquid matters very little, as the distillation process separates all the alcohol out from the liquid. Congeners—flavor compounds—may also be separated from the original liquid along with the alcohol. The congeners provide the spirit with its distinct characteristics.

Straight Up Term used to describe cocktails that are served without ice.

Swizzle Originally, this was a tall rum beverage filled with cracked ice and stirred with a long spoon, twig, or stirring instrument until the glass was frosty. Now, any tall drink made with spirits and crushed ice and stirred with a rod until frosty is called a "swizzle."

Toddy Originally, this was a hot mixture of spirits, sugar, and spices, such as cloves and cinnamon, lemon peel, and water, served in a tall glass. Today it may be served cold, with any combination of spirits, spices, and ice.

Varietal A term used to classify a type of grape used in the production of wine. Varietal is the term for types of grapes whose juice or wine is blended together. The term varietal wine means a wine made with at least 51 percent of one grape variety.

Whiskey A spirit aged in wood, produced from the distillation of a fermented mash of grain. Examples are Bourbon whiskey, Canadian whiskey, Irish whiskey, Rye whiskey, and Scotch whiskey.

A Note on the Recipes

Many of these cocktails are served "straight up" in a cocktail glass. You may prepare them "on the rocks" if you prefer. Simply follow the recipe, then strain or pour the mixture over ice cubes into an old-fashioned glass.

These recipes make generous cocktails. If you want a short cocktail, halve the recipe, split the drink with a friend, or save the rest in the refrigerator (sans the ice).

Many new shooter recipes have been included in this edition. A shooter is something between a shot and a mixed cocktail. Like a shot, it is served in a small glass, often—though not always—a shot glass, and may sometimes complement another drink as a chaser or as something to be chased. Unlike a shot, it has more than a single ingredient. A shooter recipe may include a mixer, or it may be a blend of alcoholic parts. Because it is a mix, it is often served in glasses larger than a shot glass. Cordial and pony glasses are commonly used for shooters.

In the past decade, the "shooter" has seen an enormous increase in popularity. In bars across this country and in the U.K., the shooter trend has led to the creation of hundreds of new recipes. The shooter recipes in this book include a selection of traditional shooters, as well as a sampling of more recent popular concoctions, which have been chosen with the aim of imparting a flavor of this popular trend.

Like the shooter phenomenon, flavored vodkas have come into vogue in the past ten years; hence many new recipes in this edition include flavored vodkas. Vodka has long been a popular base for mixed drinks because its neutral taste allows the flavors of mixers to stand in the foreground. Vodka's inert flavor lends itself—for the same reason—to flavoring. Through flavoring, the spirit is infused with the character of any of a large variety of herbs, spices, and fruits. The result often makes for a more complex and satisfying drink.

Although infusing vodka is a centuries-old tradition among Slavic distillers and long popular in Nordic regions, the trend has taken hold in this country only recently. While the first flavored vodkas were introduced here in the late 1970s, only in the past decade or so have they become a popular trend.

Many people adore gin, but many do not. The gin drinks in this book are varied and interesting, but you may substitute vodka for gin in any of the gin recipes. The cocktail will be different, but delicious, although the special gin flavor will be lost.

If you crave a Mint Julep but are out of bourbon, try substituting another whiskey in its place. You may try this with other whiskey recipes. Rye is a decent substitute for bourbon; Canadian whiskey is also a good substitute for blended or American whiskey. Experiment, but keep in mind that the whiskey called for in the recipe is the preferred and recommended one. There is no acceptable replacement for Scotch.

Tequila is in a class by itself, although some of the tequila drinks will work as rum drinks, and vice-versa. Again, experiment and invent your own specialties. Bartending is an evolving art form.

Measurements

SPIRITS

Old Bottle Size	Old U.S. Measure	New U.S. Measure	Metric Measure
Miniature	1.6 oz.	1.7 oz.	50 ml.
Half pint	8.0 oz.	6.8 oz.	200 ml.
Pint	16.0 oz.	16.9 oz.	500 ml.
Fifth	25.6 oz.	25.4 oz.	750 ml.
Quart	32.0 oz.	33.8 oz.	1 liter
Half gallon	64.0 oz.	59.2 oz.	1.75 liter

WINE

Name	U.S. Measure	Metric Measure
Split	6.3 oz.	187 ml.
Tenth	12.7 oz.	373 ml.
Fifth	25.4 oz.	750 ml.
Quart	33.8 oz.	1 liter
Magnum	50.7 oz.	1.5 liters
Double Magnum	101.4 oz.	3 liters

BAR MEASUREMENTS

1 dash	$\frac{1}{32}$ ounce
1 teaspoon	$\frac{1}{8}$ ounce
1 tablespoon	$\frac{3}{8}$ ounce
1 pony	1 ounce
1 jigger	$1\frac{1}{2}$ ounces
1 wine glass	4 ounces
1 split	6 ounces
1 cup	8 ounces

Calorie Count (Approximate Amounts)

Alcoholic Beverage	Amount	Calories (KCAL)
Beer		
Regular	12 fl. oz./355 ml.	146
Light	12 fl. oz./355 ml.	100
Cider, fermented	1 fl. oz./30 ml.	12

Distilled Spirit	Amount	Calories (KCAL)
Gin, Rum, Vodka, Whiskey		
(80 proof/40% vol. alcohol)	1 ½ fl. oz./45 ml.	96
(86 proof/43% vol. alcohol)	1 ½ fl. oz./45 ml.	104
(90 proof/45% vol. alcohol)	1 ½ fl. oz./45 ml.	109
(94 proof/47% vol. alcohol)	1 ½ fl. oz./45 ml.	115
(100 proof/50% vol. alcohol)	1 ½ fl. oz./45 ml.	123

Liqueur and Brandies	Amount	Calories (KCAL)
Brandy, Cognac	1 ½ fl. oz./45 ml.	75
Coffee liqueur (Kahlua)	1 ½ fl. oz./45 ml.	176
Crème de menthe	1 ½ fl. oz./45 ml.	186
Curaçao	½ fl. oz./15 ml.	60

Wine	Amount	Calories (KCAL)
Champagne (Sparkling wine)	4 fl. oz./120 ml.	90
Sherry, dry	2 fl. oz./60 ml.	84
Table, red	3 ½ fl. oz./105 ml.	74
Table, blush	3 ½ fl. oz./105 ml.	73
Table, white	3 ½ fl. oz./105 ml.	70
Vermouth, dry	1 fl. oz./30 ml.	33
Vermouth, sweet	1 fl. oz./30 ml.	44

Mixers	Amount	Calories (KCAL)
Club soda	12 fl. oz./355 ml.	0
Cola	12 fl. oz./355 ml.	144
Cranberry juice	3 fl. oz./90 ml.	54
Diet cola	12 fl oz./355 ml.	0
Fresh lemon juice	1 fl. oz./30 ml.	8
Fresh lime juice	1 fl. oz./30 ml.	8
Fresh orange juice	2 fl. oz./60 ml.	28
Ginger ale	12 fl./355 ml.	124
Heavy cream	1 tbs./15 ml.	53
Pineapple juice, unsweetened	2 fl. oz./60 ml.	34
Tomato juice	2 fl. oz./60 ml.	12
Tonic water	12 fl. oz./355 ml.	113

Glass Icon Key

Almost every drink recipe has an icon next to it denoting the proper glassware to use. The following is a key to the glassware specified by the icons.

Balloon wine glass

Parfait glass

Beer mug

Pilsner glass

Brandy snifter

Pitcher

Champagne flute

Pony

Cocktail glass

Pousse Café

Coffee mug

Punch cup

Collins glass

Red wine glass

Double Old-Fashioned glass

Sherry glass

Highball glass

Shot glass

Old-Fashioned glass

Sour glass

A Guide to Wine

Wine has become popular in many drinking establishments and at home. Since the first edition of *The New York Bartender's Guide*, the health benefits of drinking wine in moderation have become widely accepted, and many people have switched from an after work cocktail to a glass of California Zinfandel or a nice Pinot. People have moved away from jug wines and white wine spritzers, and are experimenting with a full variety of reds, whites, blushes, and

Red Wine (from Judson Grill)

sparkling wines from various countries. The world's most popular wines are produced in France, Italy, Spain, Portugal, Germany, the United States (especially in California), Argentina, Chile, Australia, and New Zealand. Since the fall of apartheid, many wine drinkers have discovered some wonderful South African wines. New Zealand's Sauvignon Blancs are widely recognized as world-class whites. Many Oregon vintners have stopped trying to replicate California and French wines, and are beginning to take advantage of the unique soils and climates in the Willamette River and Columbia River Valleys. Oregon's cabernet franc and Viognier grapes make up some of the best wine in the United States.

Wine is not as confusing as it may appear. The old rule that white must be drunk with fish and red with meat has been largely abandoned. If you come across a spicy red wine that complements a salmon dish, go ahead and drink it. Try a Beaujolais with roast turkey at your next Thanksgiving meal. Focus on the characteristics of a particular region and variety of grape and get creative. A simple rule to follow is this: light wines go best with subtler, more delicate foods; full-bodied wines go best with spicier, more robust foods. Learn how your palate responds to a dry or a sweet wine.

White wine should be served at about 55°F/12°C; blush wines and Beaujolais red wines at about 60°F/15°C. The key is to avoid chilling a wine to the point where its flavors become masked. Red wines should be served at room temperature. Their flavors are enhanced when the cork is removed so the wine can be decanted, or let to stand in the bottle or in glasses before drinking. This permits it to "breathe." When wine is aerated, its tannic or astringent flavors will soften and mellow. Generally, the older and better the wine, the more important "breathing" becomes. Most reds should breathe for about thirty minutes. The better reds should always be decanted.

The following is an explanation of how various countries categorize their wines. The most common classifications are by region and by grape variety, though wine classifications differ from country to country.

French Wines

The French wines here are grouped according to appellation, which refers to the town name or place of origin. The main regions are: Bordeaux, Loire, Rhône, Burgundy, Alsace, and Champagne. The best wines are classified by *Appellations d'Origine Contrôllées*, which is a term used by the French government to guarantee the origin and quality of the wine.

BORDEAUX

Red Bordeaux Bordeaux is a 260,000-acre wine producing area that yields millions of bottles each year.

The Bordeaux wine-maker blends Cabernet Sauvignon, Merlot, Cabernet Franc, Malbec, and Petit Verdot grapes into combinations that will yield the best vintage blend.

Selected Popular Regions:

Médoc/ Haut Médoc	St. Emilion
Pomerol	Graves
Margaux	

White Bordeaux Made primarily from the Sauvignon Blanc grape.

Selected Popular Regions:

Graves	Sauternes/Barsac
Entre-Deux-Mers	

LOIRE

The majority of these wines made from the Chenin Blanc and Sauvignon Blanc grape are white, though some are rosé, red, or sparkling.

Selected Popular Regions:

Sancerre	Pouilly-Fumé
Vouvray	Coteaux Du Layon
Muscadet	Chinon

RHÔNE VALLEY

Famous for full-flavored reds, typically bigger and heavier. These wines contain up to thirteen different types of grapes, the Syrah grape being the most common.

Selected Popular Regions:

Côte Rotie	Hermitage
Cornas	Châteauneuf-du-Pape
Condrieu	St. Joseph
Côtes du Rhône	

BURGUNDY

Red Burgundy The main grapes used to produce these wines are Pinot Noir and Gamay.

Selected Popular Regions:

Côte de Nuits	Beaujolais
Gevrey-Chambertin	Volnay
Chambolle Musigny	Mâconnais
Côte de Beaune	

White Burgundy Made mostly from Chardonnay and Aligoté grapes.

Selected Popular Regions:

Chablis	Meursault
Montrachet	Aloxe Corton
Côte de Nuits	Mâconnais

ALSACE

These wines are made primarily from the Riesling grape and the Gewürztraminer grape. They are similar to German-style wines, but drier.

CHAMPAGNE

Wine makers of this region blends three grapes, Chardonnay, Pinot Noir, and Pinot Meunier. Champagne ages in the bottle along with yeast cells to help develop its complex, toasty character and carbonation. Its yeasty body and relative dryness vary from producer to producer. When the wine is properly chilled, the Champagne bubbles should be very active and tiny. "Brut" Champagne is very, very dry; "Extra dry" is a bit sweeter; "Dry" or "Sec" is medium-sweet; and "Demi-sec" is sweet.

Non-Vintage Brut This is a blend of wines made in two or more years.

Vintage Brut Aged five or more years, this made in an occasional outstanding vintage.

Rosé Champagne The pink tint comes from a small portion of red juice added at the time of fermentation. Rosés are usually richer and more flavorful than other Champagnes.

Italian Wines

Italian wines are named either for the grape variety used or for the towns near where the grapes are grown. The categorizations given here are first by region; then, within each region, are town and varietal.

PIEDMONT

The most widely planted grapes in this region are the Nebbiolo and the Barbera. The wines are labeled by varietal and then by place, as in as Barbera d'Alba, Barbera d'Asti, Nebbiolo d'Alba, etc.

Barolo This red wine is made mostly from the Nebbiolo variety. All Barolos must spend at least two years in barrels of chestnut or oak.

Barbaresco Produced from the Nebbiolo vines, but variations in the soil of this area create different wines.

TUSCANY

Chianti The region is subdivided into seven districts, and the wine is made from several grape varieties. The principle grape is the Sangiovese; then comes the Canaiolo Nero; the white Trebbiano Tuscano; and Malvasia del Chianti.

Types of Chianti include a wine light in body and in color, made for early consumption (Chianti); a wine of better quality whose tannins soften after about a year of aging (Chianti Vecchio); a high-quality wine with a higher alcohol content, which takes longer to mellow (Chianti Classico); and Chianti Riserva, released after an additional two years in the barrel.

Brunello di Montalcino This red varietal wine is made exclusively from a clone of the Sangiovese grape, locally called Brunello.

Vino Nobile de Montepulciano This wine uses the same grapes as Chianti but requires a two-year minimum oak aging. If the wine is labeled Riserva, there is a three- to four-year aging minimum.

VENETO

Valpolicella

Soave

ITALIAN WHITE WINES (VARIOUS REGIONS)

Trentino

Alto Adige

Friuli

German Wines

The Riesling grape accounts for 20 percent of total plantings. The Müeller-Thurgau grape is the biggest producer, and constitutes 27 percent of Germany's grapes. This particular grape ripens earlier than others, producing light-bodied, highly aromatic wines. The Silvaner grape makes up 11 percent of total plantings. The Gewürztraminer makes a very spicy wine. The Ruländer, or Pinot of Burgundy, produces wines with intense flavor and full aroma.

German wines range from very dry to very sweet and are rated on their bottles along a six-level "ripeness" scale. Kabinett wines are the driest, and Eiswein, whose grapes are harvested after a deep frost and frozen, are the sweetest.

Spanish Wines

The most important wine-producing regions of Spain are Rioja and Valdepeñas.

RIOJA

This region has three wine-growing districts. The Rioja Alta produces wines with high acidity. The Rioja Alavesa produces fruity wines. The Rioja Baja is the hottest district and produces wines high in alcohol. Traditionally, wines from Rioja are of the harvest of all three districts.

The red grapes of Rioja are the Tempranillo, Garnacha Tinta (Grenache), Graciano, and Mazuelo. The main white wine grape is the Viura, which is blended with Garnacha Blanca and Malvasia.

VALDEPEÑAS

This central region produces wines less delicate than the wines of the north; they are popular as carafe wines in Madrid. The popular red grape is the Cencibel, and the white is the Airen.

SHERRY

Spain is known for its Sherries, which are fortified wines. Jerez has been famous for its Sherry for centuries, producing excellent wines for a range of palates, from the driest to the sweetest.

Portuguese Wines

Portugal produces mainly Port and table wines.

PORT

Vintage Port This fortified wine has a deep ruby color.

Ruby and Tawny Ports These are blended wines. Ruby Port has a bright ruby color. Tawny Port is paler and usually drier.

Late Bottled Vintage (LBV) LBV is a Tawny Port from a single good year that remains in a cask and is not blended.

TABLE WINES

Colares This is a dry white wine.

Bucelas This is a dry red wine.

Vinho Verde This wine is white, red, or rosé, but always light.

MADEIRA

A Portuguese island in the Atlantic off the North African coast gives Madeira its name. Madeira wines range from very dry to very sweet.

United States Wines

The most popular wine-producing regions in America are California and the Northwest. There are, however, some lesser well-known wine-makers in Texas, Idaho, New Mexico, New York, and Virginia. The basic identifier of American wines is the type of grape, although California vintners are moving towards an appellation system. Grape types are and will always be very important in the classification of American wines. Californians and other maverick winemakers in the United States have no fear when it comes to trying an old country grape. Witness the acreage devoted to the Pinot Gris, the Sangiovese, and other varietals and you will see that fine winemaking has a long future in the United States.

RED WINES

Pinot Noir The finest Pinot Noirs are light in color. Oregon is highly regarded for its Pinot Noirs. This grape is the American version of a Red Burgundy.

Merlot This wine has an oaky richness because of its oak-barrel fermentation process.

Cabernet Sauvignon These wines have the same basic characteristics as Red Bordeaux from France, because they are made from the same primary grape.

Zinfandel While similar to the French Rhône wines, the Zinfandel grape is considered a "native American" grape. It is a versatile food wine.

WHITE WINES

Sauvignon Blanc This wine is made from the same grapes as White Bordeaux from France.

Chardonnay This wine may be made in a medium-bodied style, or a buttery, oak-enhanced style. The difference in characteristic is due to fermentation techniques. It is made from the same grape as the French White Burgundy.

Gewürztraminer This is a slightly sweet and spicy wine.

Blush wines Wines containing any red coloring are classified as red wines. The coloring comes from the grape skins during fermentation. Wines only come in white and red—and red wines vary from pink to deep inky reds.

Viognier Having made a remarkable comeback from near extinction only two generations past, this varietal is best represented by its plantings in California and Oregon. Often used as a blender, this wine also stands well alone, with a rich complexity that will appeal to those who appreciate a good Chardonnay.

SPARKLING WINES

These wines are made like French Champagne, but cannot legally be called Champagne. California sparkling wines have more of a fruit accent than French Champagnes, although California winemakers have made great strides in developing lovely, oaky, dry sparklers.

Argentinean Wines

The three principle wine regions of Argentina are Mendoza, San Juan, and Río Negro. The varietals used for red table wines are the Criolla, Malbec, Cabernet Sauvignon, Barbera, Petite Sirah, Pinot Noir, Tempranilla, Merlot, Sangiovese, and Lambrusco. White table wines use the Criolla, Sémillon, Sauvignon Blanc, Pinot Blanc, Riesling, Chardonnay, and Trebbiano. Fortified and dessert wines are made from Malvasia, Muscat of Alexandria, and Pedro Ximenez. The most widely produced wines of the region are made from a blend of Criolla, Malbec, and Barbera grapes.

Chilean Wines

The three principle wine-producing regions are divided among the Chilean provinces as follows:

Atacama and Coquimbo The wines from this northern area are mainly sweet, fortified types with a high alcohol content.

Aconcagua to Talca These central provinces produce the best table wines of Chile.

Maule to Bío Bío These southern provinces produce the bulk of the country's wine.

The red wine producers use mostly the Cabernet Sauvignon, Malbec, Cabernet Franc, Merlot, Pinot Noir, and Petit Verdot grapes. The white varieties most used are the Sauvignon Blanc, Sémillon, Pinot Blanc, Chardonnay, Trebbiano, Riesling, and a specifically Chilean variety, Loca Blanca.

Bellini (from Cipriani)

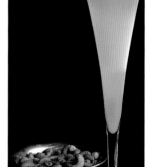

Australian Wines

Australian wines are produced in South Australia, New South Wales Victoria, Western Australia, and Tasmania. Many varieties of grapes are grown, but if a wine is labeled by varietal, there must be a minimum of 80 percent of the named grape in the wine.

Shiraz is the most widely planted grape for the production of red table and fortified wines. Cabernet Sauvignon, Merlot, and Pinot Noirs are also used for red wine production. The white wine varieties include: Sémillon, Chardonnay, Rhine Riesling, Sultana and Muscat Gordo Blanco, Traminer, Doradillo, Palomino, and Pedro Ximenez.

New Zealand Wines

New Zealand is composed of two large islands, North Island and South Island. The biggest wine-growing areas are Marlborough on South Island, and Poverty and Hawkes Bays on North Island. White grape varieties account for more than 80 percent of the total grape plantings in New Zealand. In addition, there are Riesling-Sylvaner, Chardonnay, Gewürztraminer, Savignon Blanc, and Rhine Riesling. Red varietals include Pinot Noir, Cabernet Sauvignon, Pinotage (a hybrid of Pinot Noir and Cinsaut), and Shiraz.

New Zealand's Sauvignon Blanc is widely regarded as among the very best produced in the world. Two distinct incarnations of this varietal come from the Hawkes Bays (North) and from Marlborough (South). The northern grape produces a richer, fruitier wine while the southern grape is drier and crisper.

New Zealand is also notable for successfully having tamed the difficult Pinot Noir grape. It is now the most widely planted red, and several good New Zealand Pinot Noirs are well worth having. Many of the Cabernet Sauvignons and the Merlots that are grown in the North are also top-flight and worth trying.

South African Wines

Although it has a long vinicultural history with heritage grapes, the South African wine industry has made a concerted effort to move toward noble varieties in order to expand its presence on the world market. That effort has paid off in many regards, and the results include some world-class wines. Although it was traditionally a heavily white grape region, the majority of new plantings in South Africa have been reds, including Shiraz, Cabernet, and Merlot, and even Pinot Noir. All of these—even the fickle Pinot Noir—have done well in South African soil.

South African Shiraz can be first-rate, and Merlots bottled as a varietal can be excellent. As with Pinot Noirs, generally the South African incarnations of this variety can be hit-or-miss. White varieties with a potential for excellence include Chardonnay, Chenin Blanc, and Sauvignon Blanc.

A Guide to Beer

Beer comes in many flavors and styles, but until relatively recently, most American beer drinkers had just a handful of products to choose from, which were supplied by the larger domestic brewers and savvy importers. However, in the past ten years, a true beer revival has occurred, sparked by the explosive growth of micro-breweries in every state of the Union. Now you can travel anywhere in the United States and you will likely find at least one micro-brewery. These small batch beers—ales, stout, lagers, marzens, por-ters, and more—each have their own distinct character. Many craft beer makers have developed signature ales and lagers that were unheard of only twenty years ago. Other beer crafters have revived old style beers with venerable heritages, such as India Pale Ale, a crisp, dry ale.

Beer is a fermented beverage made from malted barleys and other starchy cereals, which gets its bitter flavor from hops. During fer-mentation the yeast sinks to the bottom; therefore, beer is known as a bottom-fermentation brew. Beer is a generic term for all malt beverages. The various types of beer are as follows:

Ale Sharp and strong with a fruity characteristic, it is more bitter than beer. Ale is a top-fermentation brew because it is fermented at a higher temperature, causing the yeast to rise to the top.

Amber Ale This is any ale that is amber to red in color, and has a toasted malt flavor.

Bitter Usually more acidic and bronze-colored than the ales, it is a well-hopped style of ale with a bitter taste. Its alcohol content is slightly lower than the ales. This style is popular in the British Isles, and has gained a small but loyal following in the United States.

Blonde Ale Colored a pale yellow, this is usually an all malt bever-age. It may have a slightly fruity character.

Bock Beer or Bockbier This is a robust brew of heavy beer, sweeter and darker than ales or other lagers. It is a bottom fermenting lager with a strong malt presence. It is said to have originated in medieval times, when monks brewed it for sustenance during Lent. Today it is made by many microbreweries, and in the venerable old Ger-man breweries as well. Doppelbock is its stronger, darker, heavier sibling. It has a higher alcohol content than bock, and may be closer to what those monks were brewing many centuries ago.

Brown Ale An English beer with a nutty flavor, it is dark brown, malty, and slightly sweet.

Beer (from Pete's Tavern)

Cream Ale This American original is smooth in character, and very light. It is usually a pale, straw color.

Dry Beer This beer is cold-filtered, leaving no aftertaste. This is not surprising since the beer itself tastes like little more than weak, beer-flavored alcohol and water. Some Japanese breweries bottle good dry beers that go well with a light meal. Seek out these Japanese versions, and avoid American dry beers at all cost.

Fruit Ales Many microbreweries in both the United States and abroad have created fruit ales. Some tasty examples are SLO (California) Brewery's Blueberry Ale, New Glarus (Wisconsin) Brewery's Apple Ale, and Bar Harbor (Maine) Brewing Company's Peach Ale.

India Pale Ale Also known as IPA, this is a beer with a long history. It was created by the British in the eighteenth century in India. It is an excellent hot weather beer, and many American microbreweries report that IPA is their most popular offering. It is crisp, and hoppy, and slightly bitter. The English version is lighter. American craft beer makers have elevated this beer to an art.

Lager This is a light-bodied, bright, clear, sparkling beer brewed from malt, hops, and water—and in some cases made from cereals such as cracked rice or corn grits. The brew is fermented and lagered (stored or layed down) for aging. It is then carbonated before bottling. Popular brands of American beer, like Budweiser and Michelob, are lagers. Amber and Red Lagers are slightly sweeter and maltier than their mass-produced kin.

Marzen Its name refers to the month of March when this Bavarian beer originally was brewed. Brewing before refrigeration required that beer only be brewed in the fall and winter, with much brewing done in March. The barrels would be stored or lagered in alpine caves during the warm months. By October, the supply of earlier brews would be almost gone, except for the Marzen. Even though beer is brewed year-round now, Marzen is the traditional beverage served in October in Germany. Many American brewers have tried their hand at this malty, strong beer and have achieved delicious results.

Pale Ale Not to be confused with blonde ale or cream ale, pale ale is brewed with hops and malt. It may be slightly bitter.

Pilsner A term used for light-colored beers. They are all bright, light, and lagered. The world's first pilsner was brewed in Pilsen, in what is now the Czech Republic. It was notable then for its golden color; before pilsner, beers were dark. It is a hoppy beer with a creamy head. Like other beers from the continent, American micro-breweries like the Brooklyn (New York) Brewery have achieved greatness with their interpretation of this classic.

Porter This dark colored, almost black brew, has enjoyed popularity since the 1700s. Porter is made primarily of brown malt, with some brewers adding toasted light malt to their mix. Its alcohol content is slightly higher than most beers.

Pumpkin Ale In the Fall, brewers add pumpkin to the mash of hops and malt. Some add pumpkin pie spices, too. This ale, mild, tasty, and a little bitter, is perfect for those chilly autumn nights.

Stout Very dark, almost black, stout has a slightly bitter and malty taste and little to no head. Roasted barley added to the malt gives stout a caramel flavor and its dark color. Many stouts have a slight chocolate or coffee taste; some brewers both in the United States and Britain are making chocolate stout by including roasted dark chocolate in their brew. Stout has been around in one form or another since the 1600s, and for many years it was considered to have medicinal properties; some brewers added milk to their stouts to shore up the nutritional claims. Oatmeal stout, a vestige of stout's past life, is still being made today. Its key ingredient, in addition to the malt, is oatmeal, which gives it a smoother, slightly sweet taste. It is more filling than most "regular" stouts. The most famous stout is Ireland's Guinness beer. It is a perfect example of an Irish stout.

A Note About the Drink Chapters

The drink recipes are organized into sections by alcohol and then alphabetically within each section. There is a separate section for non-alcoholic drinks. All recipes are cross-referenced by recipe name and ingredient in the index. Amounts are listed in parts and then parenthetically in ounces, for easy proportion adjustments (1 part is equal to $\frac{1}{2}$ oz./ 15 ml.). Icons appear next to each recipe designating the proper glassware to use for each drink.

BOURBON

Bourbon, the only spirit with a true American pedigree, was created in the late 1880s in Bourbon County, Kentucky. By law, this whiskey can be called bourbon only if it is made with a fermented "mash" of at least 51 percent corn (the rest is barley and another grain); aged for at least two years in charred white oak barrels; and entirely produced—from grain to bottle—in Kentucky. If a distiller in Virginia were to make whiskey following the time-honored bourbon distillation process to the last detail, legally, it would have to be sold as Corn Whiskey, Sour Mash, or American Whiskey.

The finest bourbons are called "single barrel" bourbons, bottled from one single barrel of bourbon. Small batch bourbons are blended from a very small group of barrels—no more than twenty-five, and usually much less. These rare bourbons are best tasted alone. There are many very good "regular" bourbons that work well both alone and in mixed drinks. Each distillery has a different character—consider hosting a bourbon-tasting party and share the enjoyable journey from county to county. You can almost smell the blue grass....

Allegheny   Y

3 parts bourbon (1½ oz./45 ml.)
2 parts dry vermouth (1 oz./30 ml.)
Blackberry brandy (1 tbsp.)
Lemon juice (2 tsp.)
Lemon twist

Shake all liquid ingredients with
ice in cocktail shaker. Strain into
chilled cocktail glass. Garnish with
lemon twist.

Anchors Aweigh

3 parts bourbon (1½ oz./45 ml.)
Triple Sec (2 tsp.)
Peach brandy (2 tsp.)
Cherry liqueur (2 tsp.)
Half-and-half (2 tbsp.)

Mix all ingredients with cracked ice
in cocktail shaker or blender. Pour
into a chilled old-fashioned glass.

Black Dog

6 parts bourbon (3 oz./90 ml.)
2 parts dry vermouth (1 oz./30 ml.)
1 part blackberry brandy
  (½ oz./15 ml.)

Combine all ingredients in mixing
glass with cracked ice. Stir well and
strain into an old-fashioned glass
over ice cubes.

Black Dog

Blended Comfort

4 parts bourbon (2 oz./60 ml.)

2 parts Southern Comfort
  (1 oz./30 ml.)
1 part dry vermouth (½ oz./15 ml.)
2 parts fresh lemon juice
  (1 oz./30 ml.)
Bar sugar (½ tsp.)
Fresh peach slices

Combine all ingredients, except
peach slices, in a blender with
cracked ice. Blend at low speed
until smooth. Pour into a chilled
collins glass over ice cubes. Garnish
with peach slices.

Blizzard

6 parts bourbon (3 oz./90 ml.)
2 parts cranberry juice
  (1 oz./30 ml.)
Fresh lemon juice (1 tbsp.)
Bar sugar (1 tbsp.)

Shake all ingredients with cracked
ice in a cocktail shaker. Pour into
chilled highball glass.

Allegheny

Blue Grass Cocktail

4 parts bourbon (2 oz./60 ml.)
2 parts pineapple juice
 (1 oz./30 ml.)
2 parts fresh lemon juice
 (1 oz./30 ml.)
Maraschino liqueur (1 tsp.)

Combine all ingredients with crushed ice in a cocktail shaker. Shake well. Strain into chilled cocktail glass.

Bourbon à la Crème

4 parts bourbon (2 oz./60 ml.)
1 part dark crème de cacao
 (½ oz./15 ml.)
3 vanilla beans

Combine all ingredients in a cocktail shaker with cracked ice. Chill in the refrigerator for at least one hour. When ready, shake well and strain into chilled cocktail glass.

Bourbon and Branch

6 parts single barrel bourbon
 (3 oz./90 ml.)
4 parts bottled water
 (2 oz./60 ml.)

Pour the bourbon and water over ice cubes in a highball glass. Do not chill the glass. This drink may also be served "straight up" at room temperature.

Bourbon Cobbler

4 parts bourbon (2 oz./60 ml.)
2 parts Southern Comfort
 (1 oz./30 ml.)
Peach brandy (1 tsp.)
Fresh lemon juice (2 tsp.)
Bar sugar (½ tsp.)
Sparkling water
Peach slice

Combine all ingredients, except sparkling water and peach slice, with cracked ice in a cocktail shaker. Shake well. Strain into a chilled highball glass over ice cubes and top off with sparkling water. Stir and garnish with peach slice.

Bourbon Collins

4 parts bourbon (2 oz./60 ml.)
1 part fresh lime juice
 (½ oz./15 ml.)
Bar sugar (½ tsp.)
Sparkling water
Lime twist

Combine all ingredients, except sparkling water and lime twist, in a cocktail shaker and shake well. Strain over ice cubes into chilled collins glass. Fill with sparkling water and garnish with lime twist.

Bourbon Cooler

6 parts bourbon (3 oz./90 ml.)
1 part grenadine (½ oz./15 ml.)
Bar sugar (½ tsp.)
3 – 5 dashes peppermint schnapps
3 – 5 dashes orange bitters
Sparkling water
Pineapple spear

Combine all ingredients, except sparkling water and pineapple spear, in a cocktail shaker with cracked ice. Shake well. Pour into chilled collins glass and fill with sparkling water. Stir and garnish with pineapple spear.

Bourbon Milk Punch

4 parts bourbon (2 oz./60 ml.)
6 parts milk (3 oz./90 ml.)
Honey (1 tsp.)
Dash vanilla extract
Freshly grated nutmeg

Combine all ingredients, except the nutmeg, in a cocktail shaker with cracked ice. Shake well. Strain into chilled old-fashioned glass and sprinkle with nutmeg.

Bourbon Satin

3 parts bourbon (1½ oz./45 ml.)
2 parts white crème de cacao
(1 oz./30 ml.)
2 parts half-and-half (1 oz./30 ml.)

Combine all ingredients with cracked ice in a cocktail shaker and shake well. Strain into chilled cocktail glass.

Bourbon Sidecar

4 parts bourbon (2 oz./60 ml.)
2 parts Triple Sec (1 oz./30 ml.)
1 part fresh lemon juice
(½ oz./15 ml.)

Combine all ingredients with cracked ice in a cocktail shaker and shake well. Strain into chilled cocktail glass.

Bourbon Sloe Gin Fizz

4 parts bourbon (2 oz./60 ml.)
2 parts sloe gin (1 oz./30 ml.)
Fresh lemon juice (1 tsp.)
Sugar syrup (1 tsp.)
Sparkling water
Lemon slice
Maraschino cherry

Pour all ingredients, except water and fruit, into a chilled collins glass. Add some cracked ice and stir. Add three ice cubes, fill with sparkling water and garnish with fruit.

Bourbon Sour

4 parts bourbon (2 oz./60 ml.)
2 parts fresh lemon juice
(1 oz./30 ml.)
Bar sugar (½ tsp.)
Orange slice

Combine all ingredients, except orange slice, in a cocktail shaker with cracked ice. Shake well. Strain into chilled sour glass and garnish with orange slice.

Brooklyn Eagle

4 parts bourbon (2 oz./60 ml.)
2 parts Triple Sec (1 oz./30 ml.)
1 part sweet vermouth
(½ oz./15 ml.)
2 parts fresh lime juice
(1 oz./30 ml.)

Combine all ingredients with cracked ice in a cocktail shaker. Shake well and strain into chilled cocktail glass.

Bourbon Cobbler

Chapel Hill 🍸

4 parts bourbon (2 oz./60 ml.)
1 part white Curaçao (½ oz./15 ml.)
1 part fresh lemon juice
  (½ oz./15 ml.)
Orange slice

Combine all ingredients, except
orange slice, with cracked ice in
a cocktail shaker. Shake well and
strain into chilled cocktail glass.
Garnish with orange slice.

Chelsea Piers Cocktail 🍸

4 parts bourbon (2 oz./60 ml.)
Cointreau (½ tsp.)
White crème de menthe (½ tsp.)
Bar sugar (½ tsp.)
Dash Angostura bitters

Shake all ingredients with cracked
ice in a cocktail shaker. Strain into
chilled cocktail glass.

Commodore Cocktail 🍸

4 parts bourbon (2 oz./60 ml.)
2 parts white crème de cacao
  (1 oz./30 ml.)
1 part fresh lemon juice
  (½ oz./15 ml.)

Combine ingredients with cracked
ice in a cocktail shaker and shake
well. Strain into chilled cocktail
glass.

Daring Clementine 🍸

4 parts bourbon (2 oz./60 ml.)
2 parts cherry liqueur (1 oz./30 ml.)
2 parts whole milk (1 oz./30 ml.)
Dash Cointreau
Orange peel

Combine all ingredients in a
cocktail shaker with cracked ice
and shake well. Strain into chilled
cocktail glass and garnish with
orange peel.

D.U.M.B.O. Drop

4 parts bourbon (2 oz./60 ml.)
2 parts Triple Sec (1 oz./30 ml.)
3 – 5 dashes Angostura bitters
Sparkling water

Combine all ingredients, except
sparkling water, with cracked ice
in a cocktail shaker. Shake well
and pour into chilled old-fashioned
glass. Top off with sparkling water.

Ebbets Field Millionaire 🍸

4 parts bourbon (2 oz./60 ml.)
2 parts Pernod (1 oz./30 ml.)
Triple Sec (¼ tsp.)
Grenadine (¼ tsp.)
1 tbsp. egg white substitute

Combine all ingredients with
cracked ice in a cocktail shaker and
shake vigorously. Strain into chilled
cocktail glass.

Forester

4 parts bourbon (2 oz./60 ml.)
1 part cherry liqueur (½ oz./15 ml.)
Fresh lemon juice (1 tsp.)
Maraschino cherry

Combine all ingredients, except
cherry, with cracked ice in a
cocktail shaker. Shake well. Pour
into a chilled old-fashioned glass
and garnish with cherry.

French Kiss 🍸

4 parts bourbon (2 oz./60 ml.)
2 parts apricot liqueur (1 oz./30 ml.)
Fresh lemon juice (1 tsp.)
Grenadine (2 tsp.)

Combine all ingredients with
cracked ice in a cocktail shaker
and shake well. Strain into chilled
cocktail glass.

Frozen Mint Julep

4 parts bourbon (2 oz./60 ml.)
2 parts fresh lemon juice
 (1 oz./30 ml.)
2 parts sugar syrup (1 oz./30 ml.)
6 fresh mint leaves
Fresh mint sprig

Muddle all ingredients, except
mint sprig, in a glass. Pour into a
blender with ½ cup of cracked ice
and blend at low speed until slushy.
Pour into chilled highball glass and
garnish with mint sprig.

Golden Glow

4 parts bourbon (2 oz./60 ml.)
2 parts dark rum (1 oz./30 ml.)
4 parts fresh orange juice
 (2 oz./60 ml.)
Fresh lemon juice (1 tbsp.)
Sugar syrup (½ tsp.)
Dash grenadine

Combine all ingredients, except
grenadine, with cracked ice in a
cocktail shaker. Shake well and
strain into a chilled cocktail glass.
Float grenadine on top.

Hawaiian Eye

4 parts bourbon (2 oz./60 ml.)
2 parts vodka (1 oz./30 ml.)
2 parts coffee liqueur
 (1 oz./30 ml.)
1 part Pernod (½ oz./15 ml.)
2 parts half-and-half
 (1 oz./30 ml.)
4 parts maraschino cherry juice
 (2 oz./60 ml.)
1 egg white
Pineapple spear
Maraschino cherry

Combine all ingredients, except
fruit, in a blender with cracked ice.
Blend until smooth, then pour into
chilled old-fashioned glass. Garnish
with fruit.

Jamaica Shake

4 parts bourbon (2 oz./60 ml.)
3 parts dark rum (1½ oz./45 ml.)
3 parts half-and-half
 (1½ oz./45 ml.)

Combine all ingredients with
cracked ice in a cocktail shaker
and shake well. Strain into chilled
cocktail glass.

Kentucky Cocktail

6 parts bourbon (3 oz./90 ml.)
2 parts pineapple juice
 (1 oz./30 ml.)

Combine ingredients with cracked
ice in a cocktail shaker. Shake
well and strain into chilled cocktail
glass.

Kentucky Colonel Cocktail

6 parts bourbon (3 oz./90 ml.)
2 parts Benedictine (1 oz./30 ml.)
Lemon twist

Stir liquid ingredients with ice cubes
in a mixing glass. Strain into chilled
cocktail glass and garnish with
lemon twist.

Lafayette

4 parts bourbon (2 oz./60 ml.)
1 part dry vermouth (½ oz./15 ml.)
1 part Dubonnet rouge
 (½ oz./15 ml.)
Bar sugar (½ tsp.)
½ egg white or 1 tsp. egg white
 substitute

Combine all ingredients with
cracked ice in a cocktail shaker.
Shake vigorously and pour into
chilled old-fashioned glass.

Little Italy

4 parts bourbon (2 oz./60 ml.)
2 parts Campari (1 oz./30 ml.)
1 part sweet vermouth
Dash Angostura bitters
Lemon twist

Combine all ingredients, except lemon, in a mixing glass with ice cubes and stir well. Strain into chilled cocktail glass and garnish with lemon twist.

Manhattan Beach Julep

6 parts bourbon (3 oz./90 ml.)
2 parts green crème de menthe
 (1 oz./30 ml.)
3 parts fresh lime juice
 (1½ oz./45 ml.)
Bar sugar (1 tsp.)
5 fresh mint leaves
Sparkling water
Sprig of fresh mint

Combine all ingredients, except sparkling water and mint sprig, in a blender with cracked ice. Blend until smooth and pour into chilled collins glass over ice cubes. Fill with sparkling water and garnish with mint sprig. Stir gently.

Midnight Cowboy

4 parts bourbon (2 oz./60 ml.)
2 parts fresh lemon juice
 (1 oz./30 ml.)
Grenadine (2 tsp.)
Southern Comfort (2 tsp.)
Sparkling water
Orange slice

Combine bourbon, lemon juice and grenadine with cracked ice in a cocktail shaker. Shake well. Pour into a chilled highball glass and fill with sparkling water. Float Southern Comfort on top and garnish with orange slice.

Mint Julep

6 parts bourbon (3 oz./90 ml.)
Sugar syrup (1 tbsp.)
10 – 15 large fresh mint leaves
Mint sprig

Muddle mint leaves with sugar syrup in the bottom of a chilled highball glass. Fill glass with shaved or crushed ice and add bourbon. Garnish with mint sprig.

Narragansett

4 parts bourbon (2 oz./60 ml.)
2 parts sweet vermouth
 (1 oz./30 ml.)
Dash Pernod
Lemon twist

Stir liquid ingredients in a chilled old-fashioned glass with ice cubes. Top with lemon twist.

Nevins

4 parts bourbon (2 oz./60 ml.)
1 parts apricot brandy
 (½ oz./15 ml.)
2 parts grapefruit juice (1 oz./30 ml.)
1 part fresh lemon juice
 (½ oz./15 ml.)
Dash Angostura bitters

Combine all ingredients with cracked ice in a cocktail shaker. Shake well and strain into chilled cocktail glass.

New Orleans Cocktail

4 parts bourbon (2 oz./60 ml.)
1 part Pernod (½ oz./15 ml.)
Dash Angostura bitters
Dash anisette
Dash orange bitters
Sugar syrup (½ tsp.)
Lemon twist

Combine all ingredients, except lemon twist, in a cocktail shaker with cracked ice. Shake well and pour into chilled old-fashioned glass. Garnish with lemon twist.

Nolita Night Owl Punch

Bourbon (1 qt. or 32 oz./960 ml.)
Red wine (1 qt. or 32 oz./960 ml.)
Dark rum (1 pint or 16 oz./480 ml.)
Apricot brandy
  (1 cup or 8 oz./240 ml.)
Gin (1 cup or 8 oz./240 ml.)
Strong white tea
  (1 qt. or 32 oz./960 ml.)
Fresh orange juice
  (1 pint or 16 oz./480 ml.)
8 parts fresh lemon juice
  (4 oz./120 ml.)
8 parts fresh lime juice
  (4 oz./120 ml.)
Bar sugar (¼ cup)
1 lemon, sliced thinly
1 lime, sliced thinly

Mix all ingredients, except for fruit slices, and chill in refrigerator for at least one hour. When ready to serve, pour over block of ice in large punch bowl. Garnish with lemon and lime slices. Serves 30 to 35.

Orange Blossom Special

4 parts bourbon (2 oz./60 ml.)
1 part Cointreau (½ oz./15 ml.)
2 parts fresh orange juice
  (1 oz./30 ml.)
Lemon twist

Combine all ingredients, except lemon twist, with cracked ice in a cocktail shaker. Shake well and pour into chilled old-fashioned glass. Garnish with lemon twist.

Oscar Party

6 parts bourbon (3 oz./90 ml.)
1 part cherry liqueur (½ oz./15 ml.)
Lemon lime soda
Maraschino cherry

Shake bourbon and liqueur together with cracked ice in a cocktail shaker. Strain into collins glass over ice cubes. Fill glass with soda, stir, and garnish with cherry and straw.

Polo Fields

4 parts bourbon (2 oz./60 ml.)
2 parts fresh orange juice
  (1 oz./30 ml.)
1 part Orgeat (almond) syrup
  (½ oz./15 ml.)

Combine ingredients with cracked ice in a cocktail shaker. Shake well and strain into chilled cocktail glass.

Presbyterian

6 parts bourbon (3 oz./90 ml.)
Ginger ale
Sparkling water

Pour bourbon over ice cubes into a chilled highball glass. Add equal parts ginger ale and sparkling water. Stir gently.

Royal Roost

4 parts bourbon (2 oz./60 ml.)
2 part Dubonnet rouge (1 oz./30 ml.)
White Curaçao (¼ tsp.)
Pernod (¼ tsp.)
Dash Angostura bitters
Lemon twist
Orange slice
Pineapple spear

Combine all ingredients, except fruit, with cracked ice in a mixing glass. Stir and strain into chilled old-fashioned glass over ice cubes. Garnish with fruit.

Sazerac Classic

6 parts bourbon or rye (3 oz./90 ml.)
Pernod (½ tsp.)
Bar sugar (½ tsp.)
2 dashes Angostura bitters
Water (1 tsp.)
Lemon twist

Pour the Pernod into chilled old-fashioned glass and swirl around until inside of the glass is coated. Add the sugar, water and bitters. Muddle until the sugar is dissolved. Fill with ice cubes and add bourbon. Stir well and garnish with lemon twist.

Sexy Sadie Smash

6 parts bourbon (3 oz./90 ml.)
2 parts sparkling water
  (1 oz./30 ml.)
Bar sugar (1 tsp.)
4 fresh mint sprigs
Orange slice
Maraschino cherry

Muddle the mint sprigs with sugar and sparkling water in the bottom of a chilled old-fashioned glass. Fill the glass with ice cubes and add bourbon. Stir and garnish with fruits.

Soho Kiss

4 parts bourbon (2 oz./60 ml.)
2 parts dry vermouth (1 oz./30 ml.)
1 part Dubonnet rouge
  (½ oz./15 ml.)
1 part fresh orange juice
  (½ oz./15 ml.)

Combine ingredients with cracked ice in a cocktail shaker. Shake well and strain into chilled cocktail glass.

Soho Kiss

Southern Ginger

4 parts 100-proof bourbon
  (2 oz./60 ml.)
1 part ginger brandy (½ oz./15 ml.)
1 part fresh lemon juice
  (½ oz./15 ml.)
Ginger ale
Lemon twist

Combine all ingredients, except ginger ale and lemon twist, with cracked ice in a cocktail shaker and pour into chilled highball glass. Fill with ginger ale and stir gently. Garnish with lemon twist.

Stiletto

4 parts bourbon (2 oz./60 ml.)
1 parts amaretto (½ oz./15 ml.)
2 parts fresh lemon juice
  (1 oz./30 ml.)

Combine ingredients with cracked ice in a cocktail shaker. Shake well and strain into a chilled old-fashioned glass over ice cubes.

Subway Breeze

6 parts bourbon (3 oz./90 ml.)
Cranberry juice
Grapefruit juice

Pour bourbon into a chilled collins glass filled with ice cubes. Add equal parts of each juice. Stir well.

Sweet and Sour

4 parts bourbon (2 oz./60 ml.)
3 parts fresh lemon juice
 (1 oz./30 ml.)
6 parts fresh orange juice
 (3 oz./90 ml.)
Dash salt
Bar sugar (¼ tsp.)
Maraschino cherry
Lemon peel

Combine all ingredients, except cherry, with cracked ice in a cocktail shaker. Shake well and strain into chilled sour glass. Garnish with cherry and lemon peel.

Take The "A" Train

4 parts bourbon (2 oz./60 ml.)
3 parts Madeira (1½ oz./45 ml.)
Grenadine (1 tsp.)
Red maraschino cherry
Green maraschino cherry

Stir liquid ingredients with ice in a mixing glass. Strain into chilled cocktail glass and garnish with cherries.

Trilby Cocktail

6 parts bourbon (3 oz./90 ml.)
2 parts sweet vermouth
 (1 oz./30 ml.)
3 dashes Angostura bitters

Combine all ingredients with cracked ice in a cocktail shaker. Shake well and strain into chilled cocktail glass.

Waldorf Cocktail

4 parts bourbon (2 oz./60 ml.)
2 parts Pernod (1 oz./30 ml.)
1 part sweet vermouth
 (½ oz./15 ml.)
Dash Angostura bitters

Combine all ingredients with cracked ice in a cocktail shaker. Shake well and strain into chilled cocktail glass.

Wavy Hill

4 parts bourbon (2 oz./60 ml.)
1 part Benedictine (½ oz./15 ml.)
1 parts fresh lemon juice
 (½ oz./15 ml.)
1 part fresh lime juice
 (½ oz./15 ml.)
Sugar syrup (1 tsp.)
Lemon slice
Lime slice

Combine all ingredients, except fruit, with cracked ice in a cocktail shaker. Strain into chilled sour glass and garnish with fruit.

BRANDY

Brandy's origins go as far back as the early Middle Ages, when Middle Eastern physicians visiting Spain and southern France tried to make medicines by experimenting with grape and other fruit distillations. Dutch traders later introduced a drink they called brandewijn, or "burnt wine," to Northern Europe, where it caught on in a very big way. Brandy is made from fermented grape juice aged in wooden casks. The best-known brandies are from France: Cognac, which is made in the Cognac region, and Armagnac, the very finest and oldest brandy, which is made in the Armagnac region. The designations for all brandies—VS, VSP, VSOP, and XO—are not determined by any legal code, but most distillers use these terms to let the buyer know the approximate aging time in the cask. VSOP (very superior old pale) is at least ten years old, and XO, at least twenty. Nothing younger than VSOP is recommended for snifter use, but a decent VSP is fine for cocktails. VS should be used for cooking only.

Pomace brandy is made from fermented grapes, skins, seeds, pulp, and even stems. It is better known as grappa in Italy, marc in France, and pisco in Brazil. Fruit brandy is made from fermenting any fruit other than grapes. Don't confuse fruit brandies with fruit-flavored brandies, which are merely cheap grape brandies flavored with fruit or artificial fruit flavoring. Two excellent fruit brandies are Poire William and Calvados, an apple brandy.

A.J.

3 parts apple brandy (1½ oz./45 ml.)
2 parts grapefruit juice (1 oz./30 ml.)

Mix ingredients in cocktail shaker
and strain into chilled cocktail glass.

After Dinner Cocktail

2 parts apricot brandy (1 oz./30 ml.)
2 parts Triple Sec or Cointreau
  (1 oz./30 ml.)
Juice of one lime
Slice of lime

Pour brandy, Triple Sec and lime
juice into a cocktail shaker. Strain
into cocktail glass and garnish with
lime slice.

Ambrosia

3 parts brandy (1½ oz./45 ml.)
3 parts apple brandy
  (1½ oz./45 ml.)
Raspberry syrup (½ tsp.)
Chilled champagne or sparkling wine
Fresh raspberries

Pour both brandies and syrup into
a cocktail shaker with cracked ice.
Shake well. Strain into chilled white
wine glass. Top off with champagne.
Drop in a few raspberries.

American Beauty

3 parts brandy (1½ oz./45 ml.)
2 parts dry vermouth (1 oz./30 ml.)
2 parts fresh orange juice (1 oz./30 ml.)
2 – 3 dashes grenadine
2 – 3 dashes white crème de
  menthe
1 part port (½ oz./15 ml.)

Shake all ingredients, except the
port, in a cocktail shaker with
cracked ice. Strain into chilled
cocktail glass. Float the port on top.

American Rose

3 parts brandy (1½ oz./45 ml.)
Grenadine (1 tsp.)
½ fresh peach, peeled and mashed
Pernod (½ tsp.)
Champagne or sparkling wine
Small wedge of fresh peach

Mix all ingredients, except the
champagne and peach slice, in a
cocktail shaker. Pour the mixture
into a chilled white wine glass. Top
off with champagne and stir gently.
Garnish with peach wedge.

Apple

6 parts apple brandy or applejack
  (3 oz./90 ml.)
Sugar syrup (1 tsp.)
Fresh lemon juice (½ tsp.)
1 egg white
Sparkling water

Combine all ingredients, except
sparkling water, in cocktail shaker
with cracked ice. Shake well. Strain
into chilled highball glass over ice
cubes. Fill with sparkling water.

Apple Annie Fruit Punch

Apple brandy (1 qt./1 l.)
6 parts raspberry liqueur
  (3 oz./90 ml.)
20 parts fresh orange juice
  (10 oz./300 ml.)
16 parts fresh grapefruit juice
  (8 oz./240 ml.)
4 parts fresh lemon juice
  (2 oz./60 ml.)
Ginger ale (1 qt./1 l.)
Sparkling water or lemon-lime soda
  (1 qt./1 l.)
1 orange, sliced thin
1 apple, sliced thin
1 lemon, sliced thin
12 –15 fresh raspberries

Combine applejack, raspberry
liqueur and fruit juices in a large
punch bowl. Stir well. Add one large
block of ice. Garnish with fresh fruit.
Add the sodas just before serving
and stir again. Serves 20.

Apple Blossom

4 parts brandy (2 oz./60 ml.)
3 parts apple juice (1½ oz./45 ml.)
Fresh lemon juice (1 tsp.)
Lemon slice

Combine all ingredients in mixing glass except for lemon slice. Stir well. Pour into chilled old-fashioned glass over ice cubes. Garnish with lemon slice.

Apple Brandy Cooler

4 parts brandy (2 oz./60 ml.)
2 parts light rum (1 oz./30 ml.)
2 parts dark rum (1 oz./30 ml.)
8 parts apple juice (4 oz./120 ml.)
Sugar syrup (1 tsp.)
1 part fresh lime juice
  (½ oz./45 ml.)
Slice of lime

Mix all ingredients, except dark rum and lime slice, with cracked ice in a cocktail shaker and shake well. Pour into chilled collins glass. Float dark rum on top and garnish with lime slice.

Apple Cart

2 parts apple brandy (1 oz./30 ml.)
1½ parts Cointreau (¾ oz./22.5 ml.)
1 part fresh lemon juice
  (½ oz./15 ml.)

Pour all ingredients into mixing glass and stir well. Pour into chilled old-fashioned glass over ice cubes.

Apple Fizz

4 parts apple brandy (2 oz./60 ml.)
8 parts apple juice (4 oz./120 ml.)
Fresh lime juice (½ tsp.)
Sparkling water
Lime slice

Pour all liquid ingredients into chilled highball glass filled with ice cubes. Stir gently and garnish with lime.

Apple Rum Rickey

2 parts apple brandy (1 oz./30 ml.)
1 part light rum (½ oz./15 ml.)
Sparkling water
Twist of lime

In a cocktail shaker, combine the rum and brandy with cracked ice. Shake well. Strain over ice cubes into a chilled highball glass. Top off with sparkling water and lime twist.

Apple Swizzle

4 parts apple brandy (2 oz./60 ml.)
3 parts light rum (1½ oz./45 ml.)
1 part fresh lime juice (1 oz./30 ml.)
Sugar syrup (1 tsp.)
2 – 3 dashes Angostura bitters

Mix all ingredients with cracked ice in mixing glass. Pour into chilled old-fashioned glass.

Applejack Manhattan

4 parts applejack (2 oz./60 ml.)
1 part sweet vermouth
  (½ oz./15 ml.)
Dash orange bitters
Maraschino cherry

Mix liquid ingredients with cracked ice in a mixing glass. Strain into a chilled cocktail glass. Garnish with bitters and cherry.

Apricot Cocktail

2 parts apricot brandy (1 oz./30 ml.
Vodka (1 tbsp.)
Fresh lemon juice (1 tbsp.)
Fresh orange juice (1 tbsp.)

Combine all ingredients with cracked ice in a cocktail shaker. Shake well. Strain into chilled cocktail glass.

Apricot Fizz

4 parts apricot brandy (2 oz./60 ml.)
2 parts fresh lemon juice
  (1 oz./30 ml.)
Sugar syrup (1 tsp.)
Sparkling water
Lemon peel

Combine all ingredients, except
sparkling water and lemon peel,
with cracked ice in a mixing glass.
Stir well. Strain over ice cubes into
a chilled highball glass. Top off with
sparkling water and stir again. Twist
lemon peel over glass and drop in.

Apricot Sour

4 parts apricot brandy (2 oz./60 ml.)
2 parts fresh lemon juice
  (1 oz./30 ml.)
Bar sugar (½ tsp.)
Lemon slice

Combine all ingredients, except
lemon slice, in a cocktail shaker
with cracked ice. Shake well. Strain
into chilled cocktail glass. Garnish
with lemon slice.

Autumn in New York

4 parts apple brandy (2 oz./60 ml.)
Hot apple cider
Ground cinnamon
Cinnamon stick

Rim a sour glass with cinnamon
by wetting the rim and dipping
in cinnamon. Add brandy and
hot cider. Stir and garnish with
cinnamon stick.

Babbie's Special Cocktail

4 parts apricot brandy (2 oz./60 ml.)
2 parts whole milk (1 oz./30 ml.)
Gin (1 tsp.)

Combine ingredients with cracked
ice in a cocktail shaker. Shake well.
Strain into chilled cocktail glass.

Barton Special

4 parts apple brandy or Calvados
  (2 oz./60 ml.)
2 parts gin (1 oz./30 ml.)
2 parts scotch (1 oz./30 ml.)
Lemon peel

Combine all ingredients, except for
lemon peel, in a cocktail shaker
with cracked ice. Shake well. Strain
over ice cubes into chilled old-
fashioned glass. Twist lemon peel
over drink and drop in.

Bentley Cocktail

4 parts apple brandy or Calvados
  (2 oz./60 ml.)
2 parts Dubonnet rouge (1 oz./30 ml.)
Lemon twist

Stir liquid ingredients with cracked
ice in a mixing glass. Strain into
chilled cocktail glass and garnish
with lemon twist.

Betsy Ross

3 parts brandy (1½ oz./45 ml.)
3 parts port (1½ oz./45 ml.)
Bar sugar (½ tsp.)
1 egg yolk or 1 tbsp. egg substitute
3 – 5 dashes Triple Sec
3 – 5 dashes Angostura bitters
Freshly ground nutmeg

Combine all ingredients, except
nutmeg, in a cocktail shaker with
cracked ice. Shake vigorously.
Strain into chilled cocktail glass.
Sprinkle with nutmeg.

Between the Sheets

1 part brandy (½ oz./15 ml.)
1 part triple sec (½ oz./15 ml.)
1 part rum (½ oz./15ml.)
1 splash lemon juice

Mix ingredients over ice in a shaker and strain into a shot glass.

Between the Streets

4 parts brandy or cognac
  (2 oz./60 ml.)
3 parts light rum (1½ oz./45 ml.)
1 part white Curaçao (½ oz./15 ml.)
1 part fresh lemon juice (½ oz./15 ml.)

Combine all ingredients in shaker with cracked ice and shake well. Strain into chilled cocktail glass.

Big Apple

Big Apple

4 parts apple brandy (2 oz./60 ml.)
1 part amaretto (½ oz./15 ml.)
6 parts apple juice (3 oz./90 ml.)
Apple sauce (1 tbsp.)
Ground cinnamon

Combine all ingredients, except cinnamon, in a blender with ice. Blend at medium speed until smooth. Pour into a chilled parfait glass and sprinkle with cinnamon.

Black Jack

4 parts brandy (2 oz./60 ml.)
1 part cherry brandy (½ oz./15 ml.)
3 parts cold black coffee
  (1½ oz./45 ml.)
Lemon twist

Stir liquid ingredients with cracked ice in mixing glass. Strain over ice cubes into chilled old-fashioned glass. Garnish with lemon twist.

Blue Angel

2 parts brandy (1 oz./30 ml.)
1 part blue Curaçao (½ oz./15 ml.)
1 part vanilla liqueur (½ oz./15 ml.)
1 part whole milk (½ oz./15 ml.)
Dash lemon juice

Combine all ingredients with cracked ice and shake well in a cocktail shaker. Strain into chilled cocktail glass.

Bombay Cocktail

4 parts brandy (2 oz./60 ml.)
1 part dry vermouth (½ oz./15 ml.)
1 part sweet vermouth (½ oz./15 ml.)
Triple Sec (½ tsp.)
Dash of Pernod

Stir ingredients with cracked ice in a mixing glass. Strain into chilled cocktail glass.

Black Jack

Bombay Punch

Brandy (1 l.)
Dry sherry (1 l.)
8 parts Triple Sec (½ cup or
 4 oz./120 ml.)
8 parts maraschino liqueur (½ cup
 or 4 oz./120 ml.)
4 parts cherry brandy (2 oz./60 ml.)
4 bottles chilled champagne or
 sparkling wine (750 ml.)
Bar sugar (½ cup/100 g.)
Juice of 12 lemons
Juice of 6 limes
Sparkling water (2 l.)
Fresh fruit in season

Stir the fruit juices and sugar
together in a large punch bowl until
sugar is dissolved. Add remaining
liquid ingredients and stir well. Add
one large block of ice. Garnish with
sliced seasonal fruit. Serves 25.

Bosom Caresser

4 parts brandy (2 oz./60 ml.)
2 parts Madeira (1 oz./30 ml.)
2 parts Triple Sec (1 oz./30 ml.)
Grenadine (1 tsp.)
1 egg yolk or 1 tbsp. egg substitute

Shake all ingredients vigorously in
a cocktail shaker. Strain into chilled
red wine glass.

Brandied Apricot

4 parts brandy (2 oz./60 ml.)
1 part apricot brandy (½ oz./15 ml.)
1 part fresh lemon juice
 (½ oz./15 ml.)
Slice fresh apricot

Combine all ingredients, except
apricot, in a cocktail shaker with
cracked ice. Shake well and strain
into chilled cocktail glass. Garnish
with apricot.

Brandied Madeira

3 parts brandy (1½ oz./45 ml.)
3 parts Madeira (1½ oz./45 ml.)
1 part dry vermouth (½ oz./15 ml.)
Lemon twist

Stir all liquid ingredients in a mixing
glass. Pour into a cocktail glass and
garnish with lemon twist.

Brandied Port

2 parts brandy (1 oz./30 ml.)
2 parts tawny port (1 oz./30 ml.)
1 part maraschino liqueur
 (½ oz./15 ml.)
2 parts fresh lemon juice
 (1 oz./30 ml.)
Orange slice

Combine all ingredients, except
orange slice, with cracked ice in a
cocktail shaker. Shake well. Strain
into chilled cocktail glass and
garnish with orange slice.

Brandy Alexander

3 parts brandy (1½ oz./45 ml.)
3 parts dark crème de cacao
(1½ oz./45 ml.)
3 parts half-and-half
(1½ oz./45 ml.)

Shake all ingredients with cracked
ice in a cocktail shaker. Strain into
chilled cocktail glass.

Brandy Buck

4 parts brandy (2 oz./60 ml.)
1 part white crème de menthe
(½ oz./15 ml.)
1 part fresh lemon juice
(½ oz./15 ml.)
Sparkling water
Seedless grapes

Combine all ingredients, except
water and grapes, in a cocktail
shaker with cracked ice. Shake well.
Pour into chilled highball glass.
Fill with sparkling water and stir.
Garnish with grapes.

Brandy Cassis

4 parts brandy (2 oz./60 ml.)
1 part crème de cassis (½ oz./15 ml.)
1 part fresh lemon juice (½ oz./15 ml.)
Lemon twist

Combine all ingredients, except
lemon twist, in a mixing glass with
cracked ice. Stir well. Strain into
chilled cocktail glass and garnish
with lemon twist.

Brandy Cobbler

4 parts brandy (2 oz./60 ml.)
Bar sugar (1 tsp.)
6 parts sparkling water
(3 oz./90 ml.)
Maraschino cherry
Lemon slice

Dissolve the sugar in the sparkling
water in a chilled old-fashioned
glass. Add cracked ice until the
glass is almost full. Add the brandy
and stir well. Garnish with cherry
and orange.

Brandy Cocktail

4 parts brandy (2 oz./60 ml.)
Bar sugar (½ tsp.)
2 dashes Angostura bitters
Lemon twist

Combine liquid ingredients in a
mixing glass and stir until sugar is
dissolved. Pour into cocktail shaker
with cracked ice and shake well.
Strain into chilled cocktail glass
and garnish with lemon twist.

Brandy Crusta

4 parts brandy (2 oz./60 ml.)
1½ parts Cointreau (¾ oz./22.5 ml.)
Maraschino liqueur (2 tsp.)
1 part fresh lemon juice (½ oz./15 ml.)
Bar sugar (1 tbsp.)
Lemon wedge

Rim the edge of a chilled cocktail
glass with sugar by rubbing it with
the lemon wedge and dipping it
in the sugar. Combine all liquid
ingredients in a cocktail shaker with
cracked ice. Shake well and strain
into sugar-rimmed glass.

Brandy Alexander

Brandy Fix

6 parts brandy (3 oz./90 ml.)
2 parts fresh lemon juice
  (1 oz./30 ml.)
Bar sugar (½ tsp.)
Splash of mineral water

Stir lemon juice, sugar and water in
a chilled highball glass. Fill glass
with cracked ice and brandy. Stir.

Brandy Fizz

4 parts brandy (2 oz./60 ml.)
Bar sugar (½ tsp.)
1 part fresh lemon juice
  (½ oz./15 ml.)
Sparkling water

Combine all ingredients, except
sparkling water, in cocktail shaker
with cracked ice and shake well.
Strain into chilled highball glass
over ice cubes and fill with sparkling
water.

Brandy Flip

4 parts brandy (2 oz./60 ml.)
Half-and-half (1 tbsp.)
Bar sugar (½ tsp.)
1 egg or 1 tbsp. egg substitute
Freshly ground nutmeg

Combine all ingredients, except
nutmeg, in a cocktail shaker with
cracked ice. Shake vigorously.
Strain into chilled sour glass and
sprinkle with nutmeg.

Brandy Manhattan

4 parts brandy (2 oz./60 ml.)
1 part sweet vermouth (½ oz./15 ml.)
Dash Angostura bitters
Maraschino cherry

Combine all ingredients, except
cherry, in a mixing glass with
cracked ice. Stir and strain into
chilled cocktail glass. Garnish with
cherry.

Brandy Melba

4 parts brandy (2 oz./60 ml.)
1 part peach brandy (½ oz./15 ml.)
1 part raspberry liqueur (½ oz./15 ml.)
1 part fresh lemon juice
  (½ oz./15 ml.)
3 – 5 dashes orange bitters
Peach slice

Combine all ingredients, except
peach slice, with cracked ice in a
cocktail shaker. Shake well and
strain into chilled cocktail glass.
Garnish with peach.

Brandy Milk Punch

4 parts brandy (2 oz./60 ml.)
12 parts whole milk (6 oz./180 ml.)
Bar sugar (1 tsp.)
Freshly ground nutmeg

Combine all ingredients, except
nutmeg, in a cocktail shaker with
cracked ice. Shake well. Pour into
chilled double old-fashioned glass
and sprinkle nutmeg on top.

Brandy Old Fashioned

6 parts brandy (3 oz./90 ml.)
3 – 5 dashes Angostura bitters
Sugar cube
Dash of water
Lemon twist

Muddle sugar cube with bitters
and a dash of water in the bottom
of a chilled old-fashioned glass.
Add brandy and ice cubes. Stir and
garnish with lemon peel.

Brandy Sangaree

5 parts brandy (2½ oz./75 ml.)
Bar sugar (½ tsp.)
Dash water
Freshly ground nutmeg

Dissolve sugar with a dash of water
in a chilled double old-fashioned
glass. Add ice cubes and brandy
and stir well. Sprinkle with ground
nutmeg.

Brandy Sour

5 parts brandy (2½ oz./75 ml.)
2 parts fresh lemon juice (1 oz./30 ml.)
Bar sugar (½ tsp.)
Orange slice
Maraschino cherry

Combine all ingredients, except
the fruit, in a cocktail shaker with
cracked ice. Shake well and strain
into chilled sour glass. Garnish with
cherry and orange.

Brandy Swizzle

4 parts brandy (2 oz./60 ml.)
3 parts fresh lime juice (1½ oz./45 ml.)
Bar sugar (1 tsp.)
Dash Angostura bitters
Sparkling water

Combine all ingredients, except
sparkling water, in a cocktail shaker
with cracked ice. Shake well. Strain
into collins glass filled with cracked
ice. Add sparkling water. Stir gently
and serve with a swizzle stick.

Brandy Vermouth Cocktail

6 parts brandy (3 oz./90 ml.)
1 part sweet vermouth (½ oz./15 ml.)
Dash Angostura bitters

Shake all ingredients together with
cracked ice in a cocktail shaker.
Strain into chilled cocktail glass.

Bronx Cheer

4 parts apricot brandy (2 oz./60 ml.)
Raspberry soda
Orange peel
Fresh raspberries

Pour brandy into a chilled collins
glass almost filled with ice cubes.
Fill with raspberry soda. Stir gently
and garnish with orange peel and a
few fresh raspberries.

Bronx Cheer

Bull's Milk

5 parts brandy (2½ oz./75 ml.)
2 parts dark rum (1 oz./30 ml.)
10 parts milk (5 oz./150 ml.)
Bar sugar (½ tsp.)
Freshly grated nutmeg

Combine all ingredients, except
nutmeg, with cracked ice in a
mixing glass. Stir well. Pour into
chilled highball glass and sprinkle
with nutmeg.

Button Hook

2 parts brandy (1 oz./30 ml.)
2 parts apricot brandy (1 oz./30 ml.)
2 parts white crème de menthe
  (1 oz./30 ml.)
2 parts Pernod (1 oz./30 ml.)

Combine all ingredients with
cracked ice in a cocktail shaker
and shake well. Strain into chilled
cocktail glass.

Café Royale

4 parts brandy or cognac (2 oz./60 ml.)
1 sugar cube
Hot black coffee (1 cup/250 ml.)
Half-and-half to taste

Pour hot coffee into mug. Rest a tablespoon on top of the cup and put the sugar cube in it. Soak the sugar with the brandy. After the spoon heats up, ignite the sugar. Hold until flame burns out and pour the sugar/brandy mixture into the coffee. Float half-and-half on top.

Carroll Gardens Cocktail

4 parts brandy (2 oz./60 ml.)
1 part dry vermouth (½ oz./15 ml.)
Maraschino cherry

Stir liquid ingredients with cracked ice in a mixing glass. Strain into chilled cocktail glass.

Champagne Cooler

3 parts brandy (1½ oz./45 ml.)
2 parts Triple Sec (1 oz./30 ml.)
Champagne or sparkling wine
Fresh mint

Pour brandy and Triple Sec into a chilled red wine glass, fill with champagne, and stir. Garnish with sprig of fresh mint.

Champagne Cup

1 part cognac (½ oz./15 ml.)
1 part white Curaçao (½ oz./15 ml.)
Champagne or sparkling wine
Orange slice
Fresh mint sprig

Pour cognac and Curaçao into chilled wine glass, add one ice cube and fill with champagne. Garnish with orange slice and mint sprig.

Champagne Punch

16 parts cognac (1 cup or 8 oz./240 ml.)
16 parts cherry liqueur (1 cup or 8 oz./240 ml.)
16 parts Triple Sec (1 cup or 8 oz./240 ml.)
8 parts sugar syrup (½ cup or 4 oz./120 ml.)
8 parts fresh lemon juice (½ cup or 4 oz./120 ml.)
Champagne or sparkling wine (2 bottles or 750 ml.)

Pre-chill ingredients. Pour all ingredients except champagne into a large punch bowl with a block of ice and stir well. Before serving, add champagne and stir gently. Serves 15 – 20.

Café Royale

Champs Elysées

4 parts cognac (2 oz./60 ml.)
1 part yellow Chartreuse (½ oz./15 ml.)
1 part fresh lemon juice (½ oz./15 ml.)
Bar sugar (½ tsp.)
Dash Angostura bitters

Combine all ingredients with cracked ice in a cocktail shaker and shake well. Pour into chilled cocktail glass.

Charles Street Cocktail

4 parts brandy (2 oz./60 ml.)
1 part sweet vermouth (½ oz./15 ml.)
2 – 3 dashes Angostura bitters

Combine all ingredients in a mixing glass with cracked ice and stir. Strain into chilled cocktail glass.

Cherry Blossom

4 parts brandy (2 oz./60 ml.)
2 parts kirshwasser (1 oz./30 ml.)
1 part Triple Sec (½ oz./15 ml.)
1 part fresh lemon juice (½ oz./15 ml.)
Grenadine (1 tbsp.)
Bar sugar (½ tsp.)

Combine all ingredients with cracked ice in a cocktail shaker and shake well. Strain into chilled cocktail glass.

Chicago

4 parts brandy (2 oz./60 ml.)
Dash Triple Sec
Dash Angostura bitters
Champagne or sparkling wine
Lemon wedge
Bar sugar

Rim a chilled balloon wine glass with sugar by moistening the rim of the glass with the lemon wedge and rolling it in sugar. Mix brandy, Triple Sec and bitters with cracked ice in a mixing glass and strain into wine glass. Fill with champagne.

Chocolatier Cake

2 parts brandy (1 oz./30 ml.)
2 parts crème de cacao (1 oz./30 ml.)
2 parts heavy cream (1 oz./30 ml.)

Pre-chill all ingredients. Using a bar spoon, carefully pour each ingredient into a chilled pony glass in the order listed.

Cider Cup

8 parts brandy (4 oz./120 ml.)
4 parts Cointreau (2 oz./60 ml.)
32 parts apple cider (16 oz./480 ml.)
16 parts sparkling water
 (8 oz./240 ml.)
Bar sugar (4 tsp.)
Apple slices
Fresh mint sprigs

Stir all ingredients, except apples and mint, with ice cubes in a large pitcher. Garnish with apple slices and mint. Serve in red wine glasses. Serves 3 – 4.

Chocolatier Cake

Classic Cocktail

4 parts brandy (2 oz./60 ml.)
1 part white Curaçao (½ oz./15 ml.)
1 part cherry liqueur (½ oz./15 ml.)
1 part fresh lemon juice (½ oz./15 ml.)
Lemon twist
Lemon wedge
Bar sugar

Rim a chilled cocktail glass with sugar by moistening the edge with the lemon wedge and dipping in sugar. Combine remaining ingredients, except lemon twist, in a cocktail shaker with cracked ice. Shake well. Strain into sugar-rimmed cocktail glass and garnish with lemon twist.

Coffee Flip

4 parts cognac (2 oz./60 ml.)
2 parts ruby port (1 oz./30 ml.)
10 parts cold coffee (5 oz./150 ml.)
Bar sugar (½ tsp.)
1 egg or 1 tbsp. egg substitute
Freshly ground nutmeg

Combine all ingredients, except nutmeg, in a blender with cracked ice. Blend until smooth. Pour into chilled red wine glass and sprinkle with nutmeg.

Cognac Coupling

4 parts cognac (2 oz./60 ml.)
2 parts tawny port (1 oz./30 ml.)
1 part Pernod (½ oz./15 ml.)
2 – 3 dashes Angostura bitters
Fresh lemon juice (1 tsp.)

Shake all ingredients with cracked ice in a cocktail shaker. Strain over ice into a chilled old-fashioned glass.

Cold Deck

4 parts brandy (2 oz./60 ml.)
1 part sweet vermouth (½ oz./15 ml.)
1 part white crème de menthe
 (½ oz./15 ml.)

Combine all ingredients with cracked ice in a cocktail shaker and shake well. Strain into chilled cocktail glass.

Columbia

4 parts brandy (2 oz./60 ml.)
1 part sweet vermouth (½ oz./15 ml.)
Fresh lemon juice (1 tbsp.)
Grenadine (1 tsp.)
Dash Angostura bitters

Combine all ingredients with cracked ice in a cocktail shaker. Shake well and strain into chilled cocktail glass.

Corpse Reviver

4 parts apple brandy (2 oz./60 ml.)
2 parts brandy (1 oz./30 ml.)
1 part sweet vermouth
 (½ oz./15 ml.)

Combine all ingredients in a cocktail shaker with cracked ice. Shake well. Strain into chilled cocktail glass.

Cuban Cocktail

4 parts brandy (2 oz./60 ml.)
2 parts apricot brandy (1 oz./30 ml.)
Light rum (1 tsp.)
2 parts fresh lime juice
 (1 oz./30 ml.)

Combine ingredients in a cocktail shaker with cracked ice and shake well. Strain into chilled cocktail glass.

Deauville

3 parts brandy (1½ oz./45 ml.)
2 parts apple brandy (1 oz./30 ml.)
1 part Cointreau (½ oz./15 ml.)
1 part fresh lemon juice
 (½ oz./15 ml.)

Combine ingredients with cracked ice in a cocktail shaker and shake well. Strain into chilled cocktail glass.

Egg Nog

Egg Nog

Brandy (1 bottle/750 ml.)
Milk (1½ qt./1½ l.)
Whipped heavy cream (1 pint/480 ml.)
Bar sugar (1 cup or 8 oz./200 g.)
Dozen eggs
Freshly grated nutmeg

Separate the eggs and beat the yolks with the sugar in a large punch bowl. Reserve the whites. Stir in the milk and whipped cream. Add the brandy and refrigerate for at least one hour. Before serving, whip the egg whites stiff and fold into the egg nog. Sprinkle with freshly grated nutmeg. Serves 25.

Fancy Brandy

4 parts brandy (2 oz./60 ml.)
Cointreau (½ tsp.)
Bar sugar (½ tsp.)
3 dashes Angostura bitters
Lemon twist

Combine all ingredients, except lemon, in a cocktail shaker with cracked ice. Shake well and strain into chilled cocktail glass. Garnish with lemon twist.

Depth Bomb

4 parts brandy (2 oz./60 ml.)
2 parts apple brandy (1 oz./30 ml.)
Fresh lemon juice (½ tsp.)
Grenadine (½ tsp.)

Combine all ingredients in a cocktail shaker with cracked ice and shake well. Strain over ice cubes into chilled old-fashioned glass.

Dream Cocktail

4 parts brandy (2 oz./60 ml.)
2 parts Triple Sec (1 oz./30 ml.)
Pernod (½ tsp.)

Combine ingredients with cracked ice in a cocktail shaker and shake well. Strain into chilled cocktail glass.

East India

4 parts brandy (2 oz./60 ml.)
1½ parts Triple Sec (¾ oz./22.5 ml.)
1½ parts pineapple juice
 (¾ oz./22.5 ml.)
2 dashes Angostura bitters

Combine ingredients in a mixing glass with cracked ice. Stir well and strain into chilled cocktail glass.

Fantasio

4 parts brandy (2 oz./60 ml.)
2 parts dry vermouth (1 oz./30 ml.)
Maraschino liqueur (2 tsp.)
White crème de menthe (2 tsp.)

Combine all ingredients with cracked ice in a mixing glass and stir well. Strain into chilled cocktail glass.

Fjord

4 parts brandy (2 oz./60 ml.)
2 parts aquavit (1 oz./30 ml.)
4 parts fresh orange juice
 (2 oz./60 ml.)
2 parts fresh lime juice (1 oz./30 ml.)
Grenadine (2 tsp.)

Combine all ingredients with cracked ice in a cocktail shaker and shake well. Strain into chilled cocktail glass.

French Connection

4 parts cognac (2 oz./60 ml.)
2 parts amaretto (1 oz./30 ml.)

Pour ingredients into a chilled old-fashioned glass over ice cubes. Stir well.

French '75'

4 parts cognac (2 oz./60 ml.)
Sugar syrup (1 tbsp.)
2 parts fresh lemon juice
  (1 oz./30 ml.)
Champagne
Lemon twist

Combine all ingredients, except champagne and lemon twist, with cracked ice in a cocktail shaker. Shake well and pour into chilled highball glass. Fill with cold champagne and garnish with lemon twist.

Froupe

4 parts brandy (2 oz./60 ml.)
3 parts sweet vermouth
  (1½ oz./45 ml.)
Benedictine (1 tsp.)

Combine all ingredients in a mixing glass with ice cubes. Stir well and strain into chilled old-fashioned glass.

Frozen Apple

4 parts apple brandy (2 oz./60 ml.)
1 part fresh lime juice (½ oz./15 ml.)
Bar sugar (1 tsp.)
½ egg white
1 apple slice

Combine all ingredients, except apple slice, with a cup of crushed ice in a blender. Blend at low speed until slushy and pour into chilled old-fashioned glass.

Frozen Brandy and Rum

4 parts brandy (2 oz./60 ml.)
3 parts light rum (1½ oz./45 ml.)
Fresh lemon juice (1 tbsp.)
1 egg yolk or 1 tbsp. egg substitute
Bar sugar (1 tsp.)

Combine all ingredients with 1 cup of crushed ice in a blender. Blend at low speed until slushy and pour into chilled old-fashioned glass.

Gazette

4 parts brandy (2 oz./60 ml.)
1 part sweet vermouth (½ oz./15 ml.)
Fresh lemon juice (1 tsp.)
Bar sugar (½ tsp.)

Combine all ingredients with cracked ice in a cocktail shaker. Shake well and strain into chilled cocktail glass.

Georgia Peach Fizz

4 parts brandy (2 oz./60 ml.)
2 parts peach brandy (1 oz./30 ml.)
2 parts fresh lemon juice (1 oz./30 ml.)
Crème de bananes (1 tbsp.)
Sugar syrup (1 tsp.)
Sparkling water
Fresh peach slice

Combine all ingredients in a mixing glass, except sparkling water and peach slice, with cracked ice. Stir well and pour into chilled collins glass. Fill with club soda and stir gently. Garnish with peach slice.

Georgia Peach Fizz

Ginger Beer

4 parts ginger brandy (2 oz./60 ml.)
Dark beer

Fill a frosted beer mug with dark beer and add ginger brandy. Do not stir.

Golden Dragon

4 parts brandy (2 oz./60 ml.)
4 parts yellow Chartreuse
 (2 oz./60 ml.)
Lemon twist

Stir liquid ingredients with cracked ice in a mixing glass and strain into chilled cocktail glass. Garnish with lemon twist.

Grenada

3 parts brandy (1½ oz./45 ml.)
2 parts dry sherry (1 oz./30 ml.)
1 part white Curaçao (½ oz./15 ml.)
Tonic water
Orange slice

Combine all ingredients, except tonic and orange, with cracked ice in a cocktail shaker and shake well. Pour into chilled highball glass and fill with tonic water. Stir gently and garnish with orange slice.

Harvard Club Cocktail

4 parts brandy (2 oz./60 ml.)
1 part sweet vermouth
 (½ oz./15 ml.)
Fresh lemon juice (2 tsp.)
Grenadine (1 tsp.)
1 dash Angostura bitters

Combine all ingredients with cracked ice in a cocktail shaker and shake well. Strain into chilled cocktail glass.

Harvard Cooler

4 parts apple brandy (2 oz./60 ml.)
Bar sugar (1 tsp.)
Sparkling water
Lemon twist

Dissolve sugar in brandy in a chilled collins glass. Add ice cubes and fill with sparking water. Garnish with lemon twist and stir gently.

Honeymoon

4 parts apple brandy (2 oz./60 ml.)
2 parts Benedictine (1 oz./30 ml.)
2 parts fresh lemon juice
 (1 oz./30 ml.)
Triple Sec (1 tsp.)

Combine all ingredients with cracked ice and shake well. Strain into chilled cocktail glass.

Hoopla

2 parts brandy (1 oz./30 ml.)
2 parts Cointreau (1 oz./30 ml.)
2 parts Lillet blanc (1 oz./30 ml.)
2 parts fresh lemon juice (1 oz./30 ml.)

Combine all ingredients with cracked ice in a cocktail shaker. Shake well and strain into chilled cocktail glass.

International Cocktail

4 parts cognac (2 oz./60 ml.)
1 part Pernod (½ oz./15 ml.)
1 part Triple Sec (½ oz./15 ml.)
Vodka (2 tsp.)

Combine all ingredients with cracked ice in a cocktail shaker. Shake well and strain into chilled cocktail glass.

Jack-in-the-Box

4 parts apple jack or apple brandy
(2 oz./60 ml.)
2 parts fresh lemon juice
(1 oz./30 ml.)
2 parts pineapple juice (1 oz./30 ml.)
3 – 5 dashes Angostura bitters

Combine all ingredients with
cracked ice in a cocktail shaker.
Shake well and strain into chilled
cocktail glass.

Jack Straw

4 parts applejack or Calvados
(2 oz./60 ml.)
1 part fresh lime juice
(½ oz./15 ml.)
Grenadine (1 tsp.)

Combine all ingredients with
cracked ice in a cocktail shaker.
Shake well and strain into chilled
cocktail glass.

Jersey Lightning

4 parts apple brandy (2 oz./60 ml.)
2 parts sweet vermouth
(1 oz./30 ml.)
4 parts fresh lime juice
(2 oz./60 ml.)

Combine ingredients with cracked
ice in a cocktail shaker and shake
well. Strain into chilled cocktail
glass.

Kahlua Toreador

4 parts brandy (2 oz./60 ml.)
2 parts Kahlua or coffee liqueur
(1 oz./30 ml.)
½ egg white

Combine all ingredients with
cracked ice in a blender. Blend
until smooth and pour into chilled
cocktail glass.

Kiss the Boys Good-Bye

4 parts brandy (2 oz./60 ml.)
2 parts sloe gin (1 oz./30 ml.)
3 parts fresh lemon juice
(1½ oz./45 ml.)

Combine all ingredients in a
cocktail shaker with cracked ice and
shake vigorously. Strain into chilled
cocktail glass.

Lady Be Good

4 parts brandy (2 oz./60 ml.)
1 part white crème de menthe
(½ oz./15 ml.)
1 part sweet vermouth
(½ oz./15 ml.)

Combine ingredients with cracked
ice in a cocktail shaker. Shake
well and strain into chilled cocktail
glass.

Liberty Cocktail

4 parts apple brandy (2 oz./60 ml.)
2 parts light rum (1 oz./30 ml.)
Bar sugar (¼ tsp.)

Combine ingredients with cracked
ice in a mixing glass. Stir well and
strain into chilled cocktail glass.

Loudspeaker

4 parts brandy (2 oz./60 ml.)
3 parts gin (1½ oz./45 ml.)
1 part Triple Sec (½ oz./15 ml.)
2 parts fresh lemon juice
(1 oz./30 ml.)

Combine all ingredients with
cracked ice in a cocktail shaker.
Shake well and strain into chilled
cocktail glass.

Liberty Cocktail

Lugger

4 parts brandy (2 oz./60 ml.)
3 parts Calvados (1½ oz./45 ml.)
Apricot brandy (¼ tsp.)

Combine all ingredients in a
cocktail shaker with cracked ice.
Shake well and strain into chilled
cocktail glass.

Marconi Wireless

6 parts apple brandy (3 oz./90 ml.)
1 part sweet vermouth (½ oz./15 ml.)
3 – 5 dashes orange bitters

Combine ingredients with cracked
ice in a cocktail shaker. Shake well
and strain into cocktail glass.

Metropolitan

4 parts brandy (2 oz./60 ml.)
2 parts sweet vermouth
 (1 oz./30 ml.)
Bar sugar (½ tsp.)
Dash Angostura bitters

Combine all ingredients with
cracked ice in a cocktail shake
and shaker well. Strain into chilled
cocktail glass.

Midnight Cocktail

4 parts apricot brandy (2 oz./60 ml.)
Triple Sec (1 tbsp.)
Fresh lemon juice (1 tbsp.)

Combine ingredients with cracked
ice in a cocktail shaker. Shake
well and strain into chilled cocktail
glass.

Montana

4 parts brandy (2 oz./60 ml.)
2 parts ruby port (1 oz./30 ml.)
2 parts dry vermouth (1 oz./30 ml.)
Dash Angostura bitters

Combine ingredients with cracked
ice in a mixing glass. Stir well and
strain into chilled old-fashioned
glass over ice cubes.

Moonlight

4 parts apple brandy (2 oz./60 ml.)
4 parts fresh lemon juice
 (2 oz./60 ml.)
Bar sugar (½ tsp.)

Combine ingredients with cracked
ice in a cocktail shaker and shake
well. Strain into chilled old-
fashioned glass over ice cubes.

Morning Cocktail

4 parts brandy (2 oz./60 ml.)
2 parts dry vermouth (1 oz./30 ml.)
White Curaçao (1 tsp.)
Cherry liqueur (1 tsp.)
Pernod (1 tsp.)
3 – 5 dashes orange bitters
Maraschino cherry

Combine all ingredients, except
cherry, with cracked ice in a
cocktail shaker. Shake well and
strain into a cocktail glass. Garnish
with cherry.

MTA Special

4 parts brandy (2 oz./60 ml.)
2 parts crème de cassis (1 oz./30 ml.)
Fresh lemon juice (1 tbsp.)
Fresh orange juice (1 tsp.)

Combine ingredients with cracked
ice in a cocktail shaker. Shake
well and strain into chilled cocktail
glass.

Mule's Hind Leg

4 parts apple brandy (2 oz./60 ml.)
2 parts gin (1 oz./30 ml.)
Apricot brandy (1 tbsp.)
Benedictine (1 tbsp.)
Maple syrup (1 tbsp.)

Combine all ingredients with
cracked ice in a cocktail shaker.
Shake well and strain over ice cubes
into chilled old-fashioned glass.

NOTE: Mulled and hot-buttered
drinks can be made in the
microwave. Instead of a saucepan,
put ingredients into the mug and
microwave on high for 45 – 60
seconds.

Metropolitan

Netherlands

4 parts brandy (2 oz./60 ml.)
2 parts white Curaçao (1 oz./30 ml.)
Dash orange bitters

Combine ingredients with cracked
ice in a cocktail shaker. Shake well
and strain into chilled old-fashioned
glass over ice cubes.

Olympic City Cocktail

4 parts brandy (2 oz./60 ml.)
3 parts white Curaçao (1½ oz./45 ml.)
3 parts fresh orange juice
  (1½ oz./45 ml.)
Orange twist

Combine all ingredients with
cracked ice in a cocktail shaker
and shake well. Strain into chilled
cocktail glass and garnish with
orange twist.

Panama Cocktail

4 parts brandy (2 oz./60 ml.)
3 parts white crème de cacao
  (1½ oz./45 ml.)
3 parts whole milk (1½ oz./45 ml.)

Combine ingredients with cracked
ice in a cocktail shaker. Shake
well and strain into chilled cocktail
glass.

Panda

2 parts apple brandy (1 oz./30 ml.)
2 parts slivovitz (1 oz./30 ml.)
2 parts gin (1 oz./30 ml.)
2 parts fresh orange juice
  (1 oz./30 ml.)
Dash sugar syrup

Combine all ingredients with
cracked ice in a cocktail shaker.
Shake well and strain into chilled
cocktail glass.

Paradise Cocktail ▼

4 parts apricot brandy (2 oz./60 ml.)
1 part gin (½ oz./15 ml.)
3 parts fresh orange juice
 (1½ oz./45 ml.)
Grenadine (½ tsp.)

Combine ingredients with cracked
ice in a cocktail shaker. Shake
well and strain into chilled cocktail
glass.

Pisco Sour ▼

4 parts Pisco (2 oz./60 ml.)
3 parts lemon or lime juice
 (1½ oz./45 ml.)
½ tbsp. bar sugar
Lemon twist

Combine all ingredients with
crushed ice in a cocktail shaker.
Shake vigorously until ice is nearly
dissolved and pour into cocktail
glass. Garnish with lemon twist.

Plum Fizz ▮

4 parts slivovitz (plum brandy)
 (2 oz./60 ml.)
1 part lime juice (½ oz./15 ml.)
Sugar syrup (1 tsp.)
Club soda
Plum slice

Mix all ingredients, except for club
soda and plum slice, in a cocktail
shaker. Shake well. Pour into chilled
highball glass. Add more ice if
necessary and fill with cold club
soda. Garnish with plum slice.

Polonaise ▮

4 parts brandy (2 oz./60 ml.)
1 part blackberry brandy
 (½ oz./15 ml.)
1 part dry sherry (½ oz./15 ml.)
3 dashes fresh lemon juice
Dash orange bitters

Combine ingredients with cracked
ice in a cocktail shaker. Shake
well and strain into a chilled old-
fashioned glass over ice cubes.

Poop Deck Cocktail ▼

4 parts brandy (2 oz./60 ml.)
2 parts ruby port (1 oz./30 ml.)
1 part blackberry brandy
 (½ oz./15 ml.)

Combine ingredients with cracked
ice in a cocktail shaker. Shake
well and strain into chilled cocktail
glass.

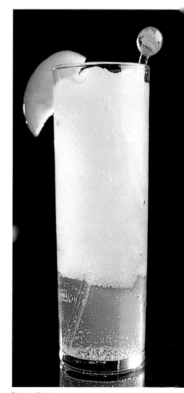

Plum Fizz

Prairie Oyster

4 parts brandy (2 oz./60 ml.)
1 part red wine vinegar
 (½ oz./15 ml.)
1 part Worcestershire sauce
 (½ oz./15 ml.)
Tomato catsup (1 tsp.)
Dash Tabasco® sauce
Cayenne pepper to taste
1 egg yolk

Combine all ingredients, except
egg yolk and cayenne, with cracked
ice in a cocktail shaker. Strain into
chilled old-fashioned glass. Float
unbroken egg yolk on top and
sprinkle with cayenne. Swallow in
one swig without breaking the yolk.

Presto Cocktail

4 parts brandy (2 oz./60 ml.)
2 parts sweet vermouth
 (1 oz./30 ml.)
Pernod (1 tsp.)
1 part fresh orange juice (1 oz./30 ml.)

Combine all ingredients with
cracked ice in a cocktail shaker.
Shake well and strain into chilled
cocktail glass.

Prince of Wales

2 parts brandy (1 oz./30 ml.)
2 parts Madeira (1 oz./30 ml.)
1 part white Curaçao (½ oz./15 ml.)
3 – 5 dashes Angostura bitters
Champagne or sparkling wine
Orange slice

Combine all ingredients, except
champagne and orange slice, with
cracked ice in a cocktail shaker.
Shake well and strain into chilled
red wine glass. Fill with champagne
and stir gently. Garnish with orange
slice.

Princess Mary's Pride

4 parts apple brandy (2 oz./60 ml.)
2 parts Dubonnet rouge
 (1 oz./30 ml.)
1 part dry vermouth (½ oz./15 ml.)

Combine ingredients with cracked
ice in a cocktail shaker. Shake
well and strain into chilled cocktail
glass.

Puerto Apple

4 parts apple brandy (2 oz./60 ml.)
2 parts light rum (1 oz./30 ml.)
1 part fresh lime juice
 (½ oz./15 ml.)
1 part Orgeat (almond) syrup
 (½ oz./15 ml.)
Lime slice

Combine all ingredients, except lime
slice, with cracked ice in a cocktail
shaker. Shake well and strain into a
chilled old-fashioned glass over ice
cubes. Garnish with lime slice.

Quaker Cocktail

5 parts brandy (2½ oz./75 ml.)
3 parts light rum (1½ oz./45 ml.)
1 part fresh lemon juice (½ oz./15 ml.)
1 part raspberry syrup
 (½ oz./15 ml.)
Lemon twist

Combine all ingredients, except
lemon twist, with cracked ice in
a cocktail shaker. Shake well and
strain into chilled cocktail glass.
Garnish with lemon twist.

Red Apple

4 parts apple brandy (2 oz./60 ml.)
4 parts grapefruit juice
 (2 oz./60 ml.)
3 – 5 dashes grenadine

Combine all ingredients with
cracked ice in a cocktail shaker.
Shake well and strain into chilled
cocktail glass.

Rose Hall Nightcap

4 parts cognac (2 oz./60 ml.)
2 parts Pernod (1 oz./30 ml.)
Dark crème de cacao (1 tbsp.)
4 parts half-and-half (2 oz./60 ml.)

Combine all ingredients, except crème de cacao, in a cocktail shaker with cracked ice. Shake well and strain into chilled cocktail glass.

Royal Smile Cocktail

4 parts apple brandy (2 oz./60 ml.)
2 parts gin (1 oz./30 ml.)
2 parts fresh lemon juice (1 oz./30 ml.)
Grenadine (1 tsp.)

Combine ingredients with ice cubes in a mixing glass and stir. Strain into chilled cocktail glass.

Saratoga Cocktail

6 parts brandy (3 oz./90 ml.)
Maraschino liqueur (½ tsp.)
Fresh lemon juice (1 tsp.)
Pineapple juice (1 tbsp.)

Combine all ingredients with cracked ice in a cocktail shaker. Shake well and strain into chilled cocktail glass.

Saucy Susanna

4 parts apple brandy (2 oz./60 ml.)
2 parts apricot brandy (1 oz./30 ml.)
Crème de Cassis (¼ tsp.)
Orange twist

Combine all ingredients, except orange twist, with cracked ice in a cocktail shaker. Shake well and strain into chilled cocktail glass. Garnish with orange twist.

Shriner Cocktail

4 parts brandy (2 oz./60 ml.)
2 parts sloe gin (1 oz./30 ml.)
3 dashes Angostura bitters
Bar sugar (¼ tsp.)
Lemon twist

Combine all ingredients, except lemon twist, with cracked ice in a cocktail shaker. Shake well and strain into chilled cocktail glass. Garnish with lemon twist.

Sidecar

4 parts brandy (2 oz./60 ml.)
2 parts Triple Sec (1 oz./30 ml.)
2 parts fresh lemon juice (1 oz./30 ml.)

Combine all ingredients with cracked ice in a cocktail shaker. Shake well and strain into chilled cocktail glass.

Saratoga Cocktail

Sink or Swim

4 parts brandy (2 oz./60 ml.)
1 part sweet vermouth (½ oz./15 ml.)
3 – 5 dashes Angostura bitters

Combine ingredients with cracked ice in a cocktail shaker. Shake well and strain into chilled cocktail glass.

Sledgehammer

2 parts apple brandy (1 oz./30 ml.)
2 parts brandy (1 oz./30 ml.)
2 parts gold rum (1 oz./30 ml.)
Pernod (¼ tsp.)

Combine ingredients with cracked ice in a cocktail shaker. Shake well and strain into chilled cocktail glass.

Sleepy Head

6 parts brandy (3 oz./90 ml.)
5 mint leaves
Ginger ale
Orange twist

Lightly muddle mint leaves with brandy in the bottom of a chilled highball glass. Fill with ice cubes and ginger ale. Stir gently and garnish with orange twist.

Sloppy Seconds

4 parts brandy (2 oz./60 ml.)
3 parts ruby port (1½ oz./45 ml.)
Grenadine (½ tsp.)
Triple Sec (½ tsp.)
3 parts pineapple juice
  (1½ oz./45 ml.)

Combine all ingredients with cracked ice in a cocktail shaker. Shake well and strain into chilled cocktail glass.

Snarky Punch

4 parts Calvados (2 oz./60 ml.)
2 parts Canadian whiskey
  (1 oz./30 ml.)
Bar sugar (½ tsp.)
Sparkling water

Combine all ingredients, except sparkling water, with cracked ice in a cocktail shaker. Shake well and pour into chilled old-fashioned glass. Fill with sparkling water and stir gently.

South Pacific

4 parts brandy (2 oz./60 ml.)
2 parts vodka (1 oz./30 ml.)
6 parts pineapple juice (3 oz./90 ml.)
2 parts fresh lemon juice
  (1 oz./30 ml.)
Grenadine (¼ tsp.)

Combine ingredients with cracked ice in a cocktail shaker. Shake well and strain into chilled sour glass.

Special Rough

4 parts apple brandy (2 oz./60 ml.)
3 parts brandy (1½ oz./45 ml.)
Pernod (1 tsp.)

Combine ingredients with ice cubes in a mixing glass. Stir well and strain into chilled cocktail glass.

Star Cocktail

4 parts apple brandy (2 oz./60 ml.)
2 parts sweet vermouth (1 oz./30 ml.)
Dash Angostura bitters
Lemon twist

Combine all ingredients, except for lemon twist, with cracked ice in a cocktail shaker. Shake well and strain into chilled cocktail glass. Garnish with lemon twist.

Stinger

Stinger

4 parts brandy (2 oz./60 ml.)
2 parts white crème de menthe
  (1 oz./30 ml.)

Combine ingredients with cracked
ice in a cocktail shaker. Shake well
and pour into chilled old-fashioned
glass.

Stirrup Cup

4 parts brandy (2 oz./60 ml.)
3 parts cherry brandy (1½ oz./45 ml.)
3 parts fresh lemon juice
  (1½ oz./45 ml.)
Bar sugar (1 tsp.)

Combine ingredients with cracked
ice in a cocktail shaker. Shake well
and strain into chilled old-fashioned
glass over ice cubes.

Third Rail Cocktail

4 parts apple brandy (2 oz./60 ml.)
4 parts brandy (2 oz./60 ml.)
1 part light rum (½ oz./15 ml.)
Crème de Cassis (¼ tsp.)

Combine ingredients with cracked
ice in a cocktail shaker. Shake
well and strain into chilled cocktail
glass.

Thunder Cocktail

4 parts brandy (2 oz./60 ml.)
Bar sugar (1 tsp.)
Cayenne pepper (¼ tsp.)
1 egg yolk or 1 tbsp. egg substitute

Combine ingredients with cracked
ice in a cocktail shaker. Shake
vigorously and pour into chilled
cocktail glass.

Torpedo

4 parts apple brandy (2 oz./60 ml.)
2 parts brandy (1 oz./30 ml.)
Gin (¼ tsp.)

Combine ingredients with cracked
ice in a cocktail shaker. Shake
well and strain into chilled cocktail
glass.

Tulip Cocktail

4 parts apple brandy (2 oz./60 ml.)
3 parts sweet vermouth
  (1½ oz./45 ml.)
1 part apricot brandy (½ oz./15 ml.)
1 parts fresh lemon juice
  (½ oz./15 ml.)

Combine ingredients with cracked
ice in a cocktail shaker. Shake
well and strain into chilled cocktail
glass.

Vanderbilt Cocktail 🍸

4 parts brandy (2 oz./60 ml.)
2 parts cherry brandy (1 oz./30 ml.)
Bar sugar (½ tsp.)
3 dashes Angostura bitters

Combine ingredients with cracked ice in a cocktail shaker. Shake well and strain into chilled cocktail glass.

Vanity Fair 🍸

4 parts apple brandy (2 oz./60 ml.)
2 parts kirshwasser (1 oz./30 ml.)
1 part maraschino liqueur
 (½ oz./15 ml.)
Amaretto (1 tbsp.)

Combine all ingredients, except amaretto, with cracked ice in a cocktail shaker. Strain into chilled cocktail glass and float amaretto on top.

Via Veneto ▪

4 parts brandy (2 oz./60 ml.)
2 parts white Sambuca (1 oz./30 ml.)
2 parts fresh lemon juice
 (1 oz./30 ml.)
Bar sugar (½ tsp.)
1 egg white

Combine all ingredients with cracked ice in a cocktail shaker. Shake vigorously and pour into chilled old-fashioned glass.

Waterbury Cocktail 🍸

4 parts brandy (2 oz./60 ml.)
2 parts fresh lime juice
 (1 oz./30 ml.)
Grenadine (1 tsp.)
Sugar syrup (1 tsp.)
1 egg white

Combine ingredients with cracked ice in a cocktail shaker. Shake vigorously and strain into chilled cocktail glass.

Third Rail Cocktail

Yellow Parrot 🍸

4 parts brandy (2 oz./60 ml.)
4 parts Pernod (2 oz./60 ml.)
4 parts yellow Chartreuse
 (2 oz./60 ml.)

Combine ingredients with cracked ice in a cocktail shaker. Strain into chilled cocktail glass.

GIN

The precise origins of gin are hard to pin down but it has certainly been around since at least the early 1600s. First distilled in the Netherlands, gin was sold as a medicine and, during the Thirty Years War, British soldiers drank it for endurance and what they called "Dutch courage." Imported to England, gin became widely popular. In fact, the British embraced gin and in many ways made it their own. To this day, the finest and best gins come from England. English literature, art, and history are filled with gin and gin-related events, from the Gin Act of 1736 to Daniel Defoe's essays to William Hogarth's drawings—one can trace the zeitgeist of the United Kingdom by examining how its citizens viewed gin.

Gin is made by combining neutral spirits with botanical ingredients. Juniper berries, by law, must be one of the botanicals. Different distillers have different formulas for their gin. Some of the plants used are coriander, orange peel, cardamom, cinnamon, and nutmeg. The best gins have at least six botanical ingredients. Cheaper gins may employ essential oils instead of plants, but they may not be called "London" gins or distilled gins if they do so.

Abbey　　　　　　　　🍸

3 parts gin (1½ oz./45 ml.)
3 parts Lillet (1½ oz./45 ml.)
2 parts orange juice (1 oz./30 ml.)
2 dashes orange bitters
Maraschino cherry or orange peel

Pour all ingredients, except cherry
or peel, into cocktail shaker. Strain
over cracked ice into cocktail glass.
Garnish with cherry or orange peel.

Alaska　　　　　　　　🍸

4 parts gin (2 oz./60 ml.)
1 part green Chartreuse (½ oz./15 ml.)
3 dashes orange bitters
Lemon twist

Stir all of the ingredients, except the
lemon twist, in a mixing glass with
ice. Strain into chilled cocktail glass
and garnish with lemon twist.

Albemarle Fizz　　　▐

4 parts gin (2 oz./60 ml.)
1 part fresh lemon juice (½ oz./15 ml.)
Raspberry syrup (1 tsp.)
Dash of Framboise
Sparkling water

Mix all ingredients, except the
sparkling water, with cracked ice
in a cocktail shaker. Strain into a
highball glass over ice cubes and fill
the glass with sparkling water.

Alexander　　　　　　🍸

2 parts gin (1 oz./30 ml.)
2 parts crème de cacao (1 oz./30 ml.)
2 parts half-and-half (1 oz./30 ml.)
Nutmeg to taste (freshly ground)

Combine all ingredients, except
the nutmeg, with crushed ice in a
cocktail shaker and mix well. Strain
into a chilled cocktail glass and
sprinkle with freshly ground nutmeg.

Alexander's Sister　🍸

3 parts gin (1½ oz./45 ml.)
2 parts crème de menthe (white or
　green) (1 oz./30 ml.)
2 parts half-and-half (1 oz./30 ml.)
Nutmeg to taste (freshly ground)

Combine all ingredients, except
the nutmeg, with crushed ice in a
cocktail shaker and mix well. Strain
into a chilled cocktail glass and
sprinkle with freshly ground nutmeg.

Allen Cocktail　　　🍸

3 parts gin (1½ oz./45 ml.)
1 part maraschino cherry liqueur
　(½ oz./15 ml.)
Lemon juice (1½ tsp.)

Combine ingredients in cocktail
shaker and shake well with ice.
Strain into cocktail glass.

Allies　　　　　　　　▐

2 parts gin (1 oz./30 ml.)
2 parts dry vermouth (1 oz./30 ml.)
Jagermeister (¾ tsp.)

Stir all ingredients with cracked
ice in a cocktail shaker. Pour into
chilled old-fashioned glass.

Almond Cocktail　　▐

4 parts gin (2 oz./60 ml.)
2 parts dry vermouth (1 oz./30 ml.)
1 part peach brandy (½ oz./15 ml.)
Kirsch (1 tsp.)
1 part sugar syrup (½ oz./15 ml.)
6 almond slivers

Warm gin in a mixing glass. Add
peach brandy, sugar syrup and
almond slivers. Chill mixture. Pour
into chilled old-fashioned glass
filled with ice cubes. Add remaining
ingredients and stir well.

Angel Face

3 parts gin (1½ oz./45 ml.)
1 part apricot brandy (½ oz./15 ml.)
1 parts apple brandy (½ oz./15 ml.)

Combine all ingredients and shake well in cocktail shaker with cracked ice. Strain into chilled cocktail glass.

Angler's Cocktail

4 parts gin (2 oz./60 ml.)
3 dashes Angostura bitters
3 dashes orange bitters
3 dashes grenadine

Shake all ingredients in cocktail shaker with cracked ice. Strain over ice cubes into chilled old-fashioned glass.

Antibes

4 parts gin (2 oz./60 ml.)
1½ parts Benedictine
  (¾ oz./22.5 ml.)
5 parts grapefruit juice
  (2½ oz./75 ml.)
Orange slice

Pour all ingredients, except orange slice, in a mixing glass with cracked ice. Stir well. Pour into chilled old-fashioned glass and garnish with orange slice.

Apertivo

4 parts gin (2 oz./60 ml.)
3 parts white Sambuca
  (1½ oz./45 ml.)
3 – 5 dashes orange bitters

Pour all ingredients in a mixing glass with cracked ice and stir well. Strain into a chilled cocktail glass.

Artillery Cocktail

4 parts gin (2 oz./60 ml.)
1 part sweet vermouth (½ oz./15 ml.)

Combine gin and vermouth in cocktail shaker with cracked ice. Mix well. Strain into chilled cocktail glass.

Aruba

4 parts gin (2 oz./60 ml.)
1 part white Curaçao (½ oz./15 ml.)
2 parts fresh lemon juice
  (1 oz./30 ml.)
Orgeat (almond) syrup (1 tsp.)

Combine all ingredients with cracked ice in a cocktail shaker. Shake well. Strain into chilled cocktail glass.

Aviation

4 parts gin (2 oz./60 ml.)
1 part fresh lemon juice
  (½ oz./15 ml.)
Maraschino liqueur (½ tsp.)
Apricot brandy (½ tsp.)

Combine all ingredients with cracked ice in a cocktail shaker. Shake well. Strain into chilled cocktail glass.

Bachelor's Bait

4 parts gin (2 oz./60 ml.)
3 dashes orange bitters
Grenadine (¾ tsp.)

Combine all ingredients in a cocktail shaker with cracked ice. Shake well. Strain into chilled cocktail glass.

GIN

Bayard Fizz

4 parts gin (2 oz./60 ml.)
Maraschino liqueur (1 tbsp.)
Fresh lime juice (1 tbsp.)
Raspberry syrup (1 tsp.)
Sparkling water
Fresh raspberries

Combine all ingredients, except the water and raspberries, in a cocktail shaker with ice cubes. Shake well. Strain over ice cubes into chilled highball glass. Top off with sparkling water and drop in a few fresh raspberries.

Beauty Spot

4 parts gin (2 oz./60 ml.)
1 part dry vermouth (½ oz./15 ml.)
1 part sweet vermouth (½ oz./15 ml.)
Fresh orange juice (2 tsp.)
2 dashes of grenadine

Drizzle grenadine in bottom of chilled cocktail glass. Combine other ingredients in a cocktail shaker with cracked ice and shake well. Strain into glass.

Belmont

4 parts gin (2 oz./60 ml.)
1 part raspberry syrup
  (½ oz./15 ml.)
1½ parts half-and-half
  (¾ oz./22.5 ml.)

Stir all ingredients with cracked ice in a mixing glass. Strain into chilled cocktail glass.

Bennett

4 parts gin (2 oz./60 ml.)
1 part fresh lime juice
  (½ oz./15 ml.)
Bar sugar (½ tsp.)
3 dashes Angostura bitters

Combine all ingredients in a cocktail shaker with cracked ice. Shake well. Strain into chilled cocktail glass.

Bermuda Bouquet

4 parts gin (2 oz./60 ml.)
2 parts apricot brandy (1 oz./30 ml.)
1 part fresh lemon juice
  (½ oz./15 ml.)
1 part fresh orange juice
  (½ oz./15 ml.)
Bar sugar (1 tsp.)
Grenadine (1 tsp.)
Cointreau (1 tsp.)
Orange twist

Combine all ingredients in cocktail shaker, except orange twist, with ice cubes and shake well. Pour into chilled highball glass. Add more ice if necessary. Garnish with orange twist.

Bermuda Highball

3 parts gin (1½ oz./45 ml.)
2 parts brandy (1 oz./30 ml.)
2 parts dry vermouth (1 oz./30 ml.)
Sparkling water
Lemon peel

Pour liquors into chilled highball glass over ice cubes. Stir well. Fill with sparkling water. Add twist of lemon peel and stir again gently.

Bermuda Rose

4 parts gin (2 oz./60 ml.)
Fresh lime juice (1 tbsp.)
Apricot brandy (2 tsp.)
Grenadine (2 tsp.)

Shake all ingredients with cracked ice in cocktail shaker. Strain over ice cubes in chilled old-fashioned glass.

Bijou Cocktail

3 parts gin (1½ oz./45 ml.)
2 parts green Chartreuse
 (1 oz./30 ml.)
2 parts sweet vermouth (1 oz./30 ml.)
Dash orange bitters
Lemon peel (optional)
Maraschino cherry (optional)

Stir liquid ingredients in mixing glass with cracked ice. Strain into chilled cocktail glass. Garnish with lemon peel and/or cherry.

Billy Taylor

4 parts gin (2 oz./60 ml.)
3 parts fresh lime juice
 (1½ oz./45 ml.)
Bar sugar (½ tsp.)
Sparkling water

Combine all ingredients, except water, in cocktail shaker with cracked ice. Shake well. Strain over ice cubes into chilled collins glass. Fill with sparkling water and gently stir.

Bird of Paradise Cooler

4 parts gin (2 oz./60 ml.)
2 parts fresh lemon juice
 (1 oz./30 ml.)
Bar sugar (1 tsp.)
Grenadine (1 tsp.)
Sparkling water

Combine all ingredients, except sparkling water, in a cocktail shaker with cracked ice. Shake vigorously. Strain over ice cubes into chilled highball glass. Fill with sparkling water and stir gently.

Biscayne Bay Cocktail

4 parts gin (2 oz./60 ml.)
2 parts light rum (1 oz./30 ml.)
2 parts crème de cassis
 (1 oz./30 ml.)
2 parts fresh lime juice
 (1 oz./30 ml.)
Lime slice

Combine all liquid ingredients with cracked ice in a cocktail shaker. Shake well. Strain into chilled cocktail glass and garnish with lime slice.

Bloodhound

4 parts gin (2 oz./60 ml.)
2 parts dry vermouth (1 oz./30 ml.)
2 parts sweet vermouth (1 oz./30 ml.)
3 fresh strawberries, halved and
 stems removed

Combine all ingredients in a blender with cracked ice. Mix at low speed until smooth but not watery. Pour into chilled cocktail glass.

Blue Devil

4 parts gin (2 oz./60 ml.)
1 part fresh lime juice
 (½ oz./15 ml.)
Maraschino liqueur (1 tbsp.)
Blue Curaçao (1 tsp.)

Combine all ingredients with cracked ice in a cocktail shaker and shake well. Strain into chilled cocktail glass.

Blue Moon

4 parts gin (2 oz./60 ml.)
1 part blue Curaçao (½ oz./15 ml.)
Lemon twist

Stir liquid ingredients with ice in a mixing glass. Strain into chilled cocktail glass and garnish with lemon twist.

Bonnie Prince

4 parts gin (2 oz./60 ml.)
1 part white wine (½ oz./15 ml.)
½ part Drambuie (¼ oz./7.5 ml.)
Orange peel

Combine all ingredients, except
orange peel, in a cocktail shaker
and shake well. Strain into chilled
cocktail glass and garnish with
orange peel.

Boomerang

4 parts gin (2 oz./60 ml.)
1 part dry vermouth (½ oz./15 ml.)
Dash Angostura bitters
Dash maraschino liqueur
Lemon twist

Stir all liquid ingredients with ice
cubes in a mixing glass. Strain into
cocktail glass and add lemon twist.

Boston Cocktail

3 parts gin (1½ oz./45 ml.)
2 parts apricot brandy (1 oz./30 ml.)
Fresh lemon juice (1 tsp.)
Grenadine (1 tsp.)

Combine all ingredients with
cracked ice in a cocktail shaker.
Shake well and strain into chilled
cocktail glass.

Brittany

4 parts gin (2 oz./60 ml.)
1 part Amer Picon (½ oz./15 ml.)
1 part fresh lemon juice
  (½ oz./15 ml.)
1 part fresh orange juice
  (½ oz./15 ml.)
Bar sugar (½ tsp.)
Orange twist

Combine all ingredients, except
orange twist, with cracked ice in
a cocktail shaker. Shake well and
strain into chilled cocktail glass.
Garnish with orange twist.

Bronx Cocktail

4 parts gin (2 oz./60 ml.)
1 part dry vermouth (½ oz./15 ml.)
1 part sweet vermouth
  (½ oz./15 ml.)
2 parts fresh orange juice
  (1 oz./30 ml.)

Combine all ingredients in a mixing
glass with cracked ice. Stir and
strain into chilled cocktail glass.

Bronx Silver Cocktail

4 parts gin (2 oz./60 ml.)
1 part dry vermouth (½ oz./15 ml.)
2 parts fresh orange juice
  (1 oz./30 ml.)

Combine all ingredients with
cracked ice in a cocktail shaker.
Shake vigorously. Strain into chilled
cocktail glass.

Bronx Terrace Cocktail

4 parts gin (2 oz./60 ml.)
1 part dry vermouth (½ oz./15 ml.)
2 parts fresh lime juice
  (1 oz./30 ml.)
Maraschino cherry

Combine liquid ingredients with
cracked ice in a cocktail shaker
and shake well. Strain into chilled
cocktail glass and garnish with
cherry.

Brown Cocktail

3 parts gin (1½ oz./45 ml.)
2 parts light rum (1 oz./30 ml.)
1 part dry vermouth (½ oz./15 ml.)

Stir all ingredients with cracked ice
in a mixing glass and strain into
chilled cocktail glass.

Buckeye Martini

6 parts gin (3 oz./90 ml.)
1 part dry vermouth (½ oz./15 ml.)
Black olive

Combine liquid ingredients in a
cocktail shaker with cracked ice
and shake well. Strain into a chilled
cocktail glass and garnish with
black olive.

Cabaret

4 parts gin (2 oz./60 ml.)
3 parts Dubonnet rouge
 (1½ oz./45 ml.)
3 – 5 dashes Angostura bitters
3 – 5 dashes Pernod
Maraschino cherry

Combine all ingredients, except
cherry, in a cocktail shaker and shake
well. Strain into chilled cocktail glass
and garnish with cherry.

Café de Paris
Cocktail

4 parts gin (2 oz./60 ml.)
Pernod (1 tsp.)
Half-and half (1 tsp.)

Combine all ingredients with
cracked ice in a cocktail shaker.
Shake vigorously. Strain into chilled
cocktail glass.

Cape Cod Cooler

4 parts sloe gin (2 oz./60 ml.)
2 parts gin (1 oz./30 ml.)
1 part fresh lime juice
 (½ oz./15 ml.)
1 part Orgeat (almond) syrup
 (½ oz./15 ml.)
10 parts cranberry juice (5 oz./150 ml.)
Lime slice

Combine all ingredients, except
lime slice, in a cocktail shaker with
cracked ice. Shake well. Pour into
chilled collins glass and garnish
with lime.

Caruso

4 parts gin (2 oz./60 ml.)
1 part dry vermouth (½ oz./15 ml.)
1 part green crème de menthe
 (½ oz./15 ml.)

Combine ingredients in mixing glass
with cracked ice and stir. Strain into
chilled cocktail glass.

Casino

5 parts gin (2½ oz./75 ml.)
1 part fresh lemon juice (½ oz./15 ml.)
Cherry liqueur (1 tsp.)
2 dashes orange bitters

Combine all ingredients with
cracked ice in a cocktail shaker
and shake well. Strain into chilled
cocktail glass.

Chanticleer

4 parts gin (2 oz./60 ml.)
2 parts fresh lemon juice
(1 oz./30 ml.)
Raspberry syrup (1 tbsp.)

Combine all ingredients with
cracked ice in a cocktail shaker
and shake vigorously. Strain into a
chilled old-fashioned glass.

Charlie Chaplin

4 parts sloe gin (2 oz./60 ml.)
4 parts apricot brandy (2 oz./60 ml.)
3 parts fresh lemon juice
 (1½ oz./45 ml.)

Combine all ingredients with
cracked ice in a cocktail shaker and
shake well. Strain over ice cubes
into a chilled old-fashioned glass.

Chatham Cocktail ▼

4 parts gin (2 oz./60 ml.)
1 part ginger brandy (½ oz./15 ml.)
1 part fresh lemon juice
  (½ oz./15 ml.)
Bar sugar (½ tsp.)
Small piece of candied ginger

Combine all ingredients, except
ginger, in a cocktail shaker with
cracked ice. Shake well. Strain into
chilled cocktail glass and garnish
with ginger.

Chelsea Sidecar ▼

4 parts gin (2 oz./60 ml.)
1 part Triple Sec (½ oz./15 ml.)
1 part fresh lemon juice
  (½ oz./15 ml.)

Combine all ingredients with
cracked ice in a cocktail shaker
and shake well. Strain into chilled
cocktail glass.

Cherry Cobbler ▪

4 parts gin (2 oz./60 ml.)
1 part cherry Heering (½ oz./15 ml.)
1 part crème de cassis (½ oz./15 ml.)
1 part fresh lemon juice
  (½ oz./15 ml.)
Sugar syrup (1 tbsp.)
Maraschino cherry
Lemon slice

Combine all ingredients, except
lemon slice and cherry, in a cocktail
shaker with cracked ice. Shake well
and strain into chilled old-fashioned
glass. Garnish with cherry and
lemon slice.

Claridge's Cocktail ▼

4 parts gin (2 oz./60 ml.)
1 part dry vermouth (½ oz./15 ml.)
1 part apricot brandy (½ oz./15 ml.)
1 part Triple Sec (½ oz./15 ml.)

Combine all ingredients in a
cocktail shaker with cracked ice.
Shake well and strain into chilled
cocktail glass.

Cloister ▼

4 parts gin (2 oz./60 ml.)
1 part yellow Chartreuse
  (½ oz./15 ml.)
1 part fresh grapefruit juice
  (½ oz./15 ml.)
Fresh lemon juice (1 tsp.)
Bar sugar (½ tsp.)

Combine all ingredients with
cracked ice in a cocktail shaker.
Shake well and strain into chilled
cocktail glass.

Coco Chanel ▼

3 parts gin (1½ oz./45 ml.)
3 parts coffee liqueur
  (1½ oz./45 ml.)
3 parts half-and-half
  (1½ oz./45 ml.)

Combine all ingredients with
cracked ice in a cocktail shaker.
Shake well and strain into chilled
cocktail glass.

Chatham Cocktail

Colonial Cocktail

4 parts gin (2 oz./60 ml.)
Maraschino liqueur (1 tsp.)
1 part grapefruit juice (½ oz./15 ml.)
1 Spanish olive

Shake all ingredients, except olive, in a cocktail shaker with cracked ice. Strain into chilled cocktail glass and garnish with olive.

Colony Club

4 parts gin (2 oz./60 ml.)
Pernod (1 tsp.)
3 – 5 dashes orange bitters

Combine all ingredients in a cocktail shaker with cracked ice and shake well. Strain into chilled cocktail glass.

Cooperstown Cocktail

4 parts gin (2 oz./60 ml.)
1 part dry vermouth (½ oz./15 ml.)
1 part sweet vermouth (½ oz./15 ml.)
Fresh mint sprig

Combine all ingredients, except mint, with cracked ice in a cocktail shaker and shake well. Strain into chilled cocktail glass and garnish with mint.

Cornell Cocktail

4 parts gin (2 oz./60 ml.)
1 part cherry liqueur (½ oz./15 ml.)

Combine ingredients with cracked ice in a cocktail shaker. Shake vigorously. Strain into chilled cocktail glass.

Coronado

4 parts gin (2 oz./60 ml.)
1 part white Curaçao (½ oz./15 ml.)
4 parts pineapple juice
  (2 oz./60 ml.)
3 – 5 dashes kirshwasser
Maraschino cherry

Combine all ingredients, except cherry, with cracked ice in a cocktail shaker. Shake well and strain into chilled old-fashioned glass. Garnish with cherry.

Costa del Hudson

4 parts gin (2 oz./60 ml.)
2 parts pear brandy (1 oz./30 ml.)
2 parts Cointreau (1 oz./30 ml.)

Combine all ingredients with cracked ice in a cocktail shaker. Shake well and pour into chilled old-fashioned glass.

Damn the Weather

4 parts gin (2 oz./60 ml.)
Sweet vermouth (1 tbsp.)
Triple Sec (2 tsp.)
1 part fresh orange juice
  (½ oz./15 ml.)

Combine all ingredients with cracked ice in a cocktail shaker and shake well. Strain into chilled cocktail glass.

Dance a Little Closer

3 parts gin (1½ oz./45 ml.)
2 parts dry vermouth (1 oz./30 ml.)
2 parts raspberry brandy
  (1 oz./30 ml.)
1 part fresh lemon juice (½ oz./15 ml.)

Combine all ingredients with cracked ice in a cocktail shaker and shake well. Strain into chilled cocktail glass

Danish Gin Fizz

4 parts gin (2 oz./60 ml.)
1 part cherry Heering (½ oz./15 ml.)
Kirshwasser (1 tsp.)
1 part fresh lime juice
 (½ oz./15 ml.)
Bar sugar (½ tsp.)
Sparkling water
Lime slice
Maraschino cherry

Combine all ingredients, except
sparkling water and fruit, in a
cocktail shaker with cracked ice.
Shake well and strain over ice
cubes into a chilled highball glass.
Fill with sparkling water and stir
gently. Garnish with lime slice and
cherry.

Deep Sea

4 parts gin (2 oz./60 ml.)
2 parts dry vermouth(1 oz./30 ml.)
Pernod (½ tsp.)
Dash orange bitters

Stir ingredients with cracked ice in
a mixing glass. Strain into chilled
cocktail glass.

Delmonico Martini

6 parts gin (3 oz./90 ml.)
1½ parts dry vermouth
 (¾ oz./22.5 ml.)
1½ parts sweet vermouth
 (¾ oz./22.5 ml.)
1½ parts brandy (¾ oz./22.5 ml.)
Orange twist

Shake liquid ingredients in a
cocktail shaker with ice. Strain into
chilled cocktail glass and garnish
with orange twist.

Dempsey

4 parts gin (2 oz./60 ml.)
2 parts apple brandy (1 oz./30 ml.)
Pernod (1 tsp.)
Grenadine (1 tsp.)

Combine ingredients with cracked
ice in a mixing glass and stir. Strain
into chilled cocktail glass.

Diamond Fizz

4 parts gin (2 oz./60 ml.)
1 part fresh lemon juice (½ oz./15 ml.)
Bar sugar (1 tsp.)
Champagne or sparkling wine

Shake all ingredients, except
champagne, with cracked ice in
a cocktail shaker. Strain over ice
cubes in a chilled highball glass
and fill with champagne. Stir gently.

Diamond Head

4 parts gin (2 oz./60 ml.)
1 part apricot brandy (½ oz./15 ml.)
2 parts fresh lemon juice
 (1 oz./30 ml.)
Bar sugar (½ tsp.)
½ egg white

Combine all ingredients in cocktail
shaker with cracked ice. Shake
vigorously and strain into chilled
cocktail glass.

Dirty Martini

6 parts gin (3 oz./90 ml.)
2 parts dry vermouth (1 oz./30 ml.)
1 part olive brine (½ oz./15 ml.)
Spanish olives

Combine liquid ingredients with
cracked ice in a cocktail shaker
and shake well. Strain into a chilled
cocktail glass and garnish with one
or two olives.

GIN

Dubarry Cocktail

4 parts gin (2 oz./60 ml.)
1 part dry vermouth (½ oz./15 ml.)
Pernod (½ tsp.)
Dash orange bitters
Orange slice

Stir all ingredients, except orange slice, in a mixing glass with cracked ice. Strain into chilled cocktail glass and garnish with orange.

Dubonnet Cocktail

4 parts gin (2 oz./60 ml.)
3 parts Dubonnet rouge
 (1½ oz./45 ml.)
Dash of Angostura bitters
Lemon twist

Stir liquid ingredients with cracked ice in a mixing glass. Strain into chilled cocktail glass and garnish with lemon twist.

Emerald Isle Cocktail

5 parts gin (2½ oz./75 ml.)
Green crème de menthe (2 tsp.)
3 dashes Angostura bitters
Green maraschino cherry

Stir liquid ingredients in a mixing glass with cracked ice. Strain into chilled cocktail glass and garnish with cherry.

Emerson

4 parts gin (2 oz./60 ml.)
2 parts sweet vermouth
 (1 oz./30 ml.)
1 part fresh lime juice
 (½ oz./15 ml.)
Cherry liqueur (1 tsp.)

Combine all ingredients with cracked ice in a cocktail shaker. Shake well. Strain into chilled cocktail glass.

Fairy Belle Cocktail

4 parts gin (2 oz./60 ml.)
2 parts apricot brandy (1 oz./30 ml.)
Crème de Cassis (1 tsp.)

Combine all ingredients with cracked ice in a cocktail shaker and shake vigorously. Strain into chilled cocktail glass.

Fallen Angel

4 parts gin (2 oz./60 ml.)
White crème de menthe (1 tsp.)
2 parts fresh lime juice
 (1 oz./30 ml.)
Dash Angostura bitters
Maraschino cherry

Combine all ingredients, except cherry, with cracked ice in a cocktail shaker. Shake well and strain into chilled cocktail glass. Garnish with cherry.

Fare Thee Well

4 parts gin (2 oz./60 ml.)
1 part dry vermouth (½ oz./15 ml.)
Dash sweet vermouth
Dash Cointreau

Combine all ingredients with cracked ice and shake well. Strain into chilled old-fashioned glass.

Farmer's Cocktail

4 parts gin (2 oz./60 ml.)
1 part dry vermouth (½ oz./15 ml.)
1 part sweet vermouth
 (½ oz./15 ml.)
3 dashes Angostura bitters

Combine all ingredients with cracked ice in a cocktail shaker and shake well. Strain into chilled cocktail glass.

Favorite ♷

3 parts gin (1½ oz./45 ml.)
2 parts apricot brandy (1 oz./30 ml.)
2 parts dry vermouth (1 oz./30 ml.)
Lemon juice (½ tsp.)

Combine all ingredients with cracked ice in a cocktail shaker and shake well. Strain into a chilled cocktail glass.

Fifty-Fifty ♷

4 parts gin (2 oz./60 ml.)
4 parts dry vermouth (2 oz./60 ml.)
Spanish olive

Stir liquid ingredients in mixing glass with cracked ice. Strain into chilled cocktail glass and garnish with olive.

Fine and Dandy ♷

4 parts gin (2 oz./60 ml.)
2 parts Triple Sec (1 oz./30 ml.)
2 parts fresh lemon juice
   (1 oz./30 ml.)
Dash orange bitters

Combine all ingredients with cracked ice in a cocktail shaker and shake well. Strain into chilled cocktail glass.

Fino Martini ♷

6 parts gin or vodka (3 oz./90 ml.)
Fino sherry (1 tsp.)
Lemon twist

Stir gin (or vodka) and sherry in a mixing glass with ice cubes. Strain into chilled cocktail glass and garnish with lemon twist.

Flamingo ♷

4 parts gin (2 oz./60 ml.)
1 part apricot brandy (½ oz./15 ml.)
1 part fresh lime juice
   (½ oz./15 ml.)
Grenadine (1 tsp.)

Combine all ingredients with ice in a cocktail shaker and shake well. Strain into chilled cocktail glass.

Floradora ▮

4 parts gin (2 oz./60 ml.)
4 parts fresh lime juice
   (2 oz./60 ml.)
Grenadine (1 tbsp.)
Bar sugar (½ tsp.)
Sparkling water

Combine all ingredients, except sparkling water, with cracked ice in a cocktail shaker. Shake well and strain over ice cubes into a chilled highball glass. Fill with sparkling water and stir gently.

Florida ▮

4 parts gin (2 oz./60 ml.)
1 part kirshwasser (½ oz./15 ml.)
1 part Cointreau (½ oz./15 ml.)
Fresh lemon juice (1 tbsp.)
Fresh orange juice

Combine all ingredients, except orange juice, in a cocktail shaker with cracked ice. Shake well and strain over ice cubes into a chilled highball glass. Fill with orange juice and stir again.

Flying Dutchman ▮

4 parts gin (2 oz./60 ml.)
Pernod (1 tsp.)

Stir ingredients with ice cubes in a chilled old-fashioned glass.

Foghorn

4 parts gin (2 oz./60 ml.)
Chilled ginger beer
Lemon slice

Fill a chilled pilsner glass almost to the top with ginger beer. Pour in gin and stir gently. Garnish with lemon slice.

Fraise Fizz

4 parts gin (2 oz./60 ml.)
2 parts strawberry liqueur
  (1 oz./30 ml.)
1 part fresh lemon juice
  (½ oz./15 ml.)
Bar sugar (½ tsp.)
Sparkling water
Lemon twist
1 fresh strawberry

Combine gin, liqueur, lemon juice, and sugar with cracked ice in a cocktail shaker. Shake well and strain into chilled highball glass over ice cubes. Fill with sparkling water and stir gently. Garnish with lemon twist and strawberry.

Gibson

Frankenjack

4 parts gin (2 oz./60 ml.)
2 parts dry vermouth (1 oz./30 ml.)
2 parts apricot brandy (1 oz./30 ml.)
2 parts Triple Sec (1 oz./30 ml.)
Maraschino cherry

Combine all ingredients, except cherry, with cracked ice in a cocktail shaker. Shake well and pour into chilled old-fashioned glass. Garnish with cherry.

Free Silver

4 parts gin (2 oz./60 ml.)
2 parts dark rum (1 oz./30 ml.)
2 parts fresh lemon juice
  (1 oz./30 ml.)
Bar sugar (½ tsp.)
Milk (1 tbsp.)
Sparkling water

Combine all ingredients, except sparkling water, with cracked ice in a cocktail shaker and shake well. Strain over ice cubes into chilled collins glass. Fill with sparkling water and stir gently.

Froth Blower

4 parts gin (2 oz./60 ml.)
Grenadine (1 tsp.)
1 egg white

Combine all ingredients with cracked ice in a blender. Blend until smooth and pour into a chilled old-fashioned glass.

Genoa

4 parts gin (2 oz./60 ml.)
3 parts grappa (1½ oz./45 ml.)
1 part white Sambuca
  (½ oz./15 ml.)
Dry vermouth (2 tsp.)
Spanish olive

Stir liquid ingredients with cracked ice in a mixing glass. Strain into chilled cocktail glass and garnish with the olive.

GIN

Gibson

6 parts gin or vodka (3 oz./90 ml.)
3 – 5 dashes dry vermouth (to taste)
Cocktail onions

Pour gin or vodka in a mixing glass
with ice cubes and stir well. Pour
into chilled cocktail glass and
garnish with 2 or 3 cocktail onions.

Gilroy

4 parts gin (2 oz./60 ml.)
2 parts cherry brandy (1 oz./30 ml.)
1 part dry vermouth (½ oz./15 ml.)
1 part fresh lemon juice (½ oz./15 ml.)
3 – 5 dashes orange bitters

Combine all ingredients with
cracked ice in a cocktail shaker and
shake well. Pour into chilled old-
fashioned glass.

Gimlet

6 parts gin (3 oz./90 ml.)
2 parts Rose's lime juice
   (1 oz./30 ml.)

Combine ingredients with cracked
ice in a cocktail shaker and shake
well. Strain into chilled cocktail
glass.

Gin Aloha

4 parts gin (2 oz./60 ml.)
3 parts Triple Sec (1½ oz./45 ml.)
1 part unsweetened pineapple juice
   (½ oz./15 ml.)
Dash orange bitters

Combine all ingredients with
cracked ice in a cocktail shaker.
Shake well and strain into chilled
cocktail glass.

Gin and Bitters (Pink Gin)

1 tsp. Angostura bitters
Gin

Pour bitters into cocktail glass
and swirl around until it is entirely
coated with bitters. Fill with gin.
This drink should be served at room
temperature

Gimlet

Gin and Ginger

4 parts gin (2 oz./60 ml.)
Ginger ale
Lemon twist

Pour gin into chilled highball glass
filled with ice cubes. Twist lemon
over glass and drop in. Fill with
ginger ale and stir gently.

Gin and It

6 parts gin (3 oz./90 ml.)
2 parts sweet vermouth
   (1 oz./30 ml.)

Stir ingredients without ice in a
mixing glass. Pour into cocktail
glass.

Gin and Sin

4 parts gin (2 oz./60 ml.)
4 parts fresh lemon juice
  (2 oz./60 ml.)
4 parts fresh orange juice
  (2 oz./60 ml.)
2 dashes grenadine

Combine all ingredients with
cracked ice in a cocktail shaker.
Strain into chilled cocktail glass.

Gin and Tonic

4 parts gin (2 oz./60 ml.)
Tonic water
Lime wedge

Pour gin and tonic water into a
chilled collins glass. Add ice cubes
and stir. Squeeze lime wedge over
drink and drop in.

Gin Buck

4 parts gin (2 oz./60 ml.)
2 parts fresh lemon juice
  (1 oz./30 ml.)
Ginger ale

Pour all ingredients into chilled
old-fashioned glass over ice cubes.
Stir well.

Gin Rickey

Gin Cassis

4 parts gin (2 oz./60 ml.)
1 part crème de cassis
  (½ oz./15 ml.)
1 part fresh lemon juice
  (½ oz./15 ml.)

Combine all ingredients with
cracked ice in a cocktail shaker and
shake well. Pour into chilled old-
fashioned glass.

Gin Cooler

4 parts gin (2 oz./60 ml.)
Bar sugar (½ tsp.)
Sparkling water
Lemon peel

Mix gin with sugar in the bottom
of a chilled collins glass. Add ice
cubes and fill with sparkling water.
Stir gently and garnish with lemon
peel.

Gin Daisy

6 parts gin (3 oz./90 ml.)
2 parts fresh lemon juice
  (1 oz./30 ml.)
Grenadine (1 tbsp.)
Sugar syrup (1 tsp.)
Sparkling water
Orange slice

Combine all ingredients, except
orange slice and sparkling water,
in a cocktail shaker with cracked
ice. Shake well. Pour into chilled
highball glass. Top off with sparkling
water, stir gently, and garnish with
orange slice.

GIN

Gin Fix

6 parts gin (3 oz./90 ml.)
2 parts fresh lemon juice
 (1 oz./30 ml.)
Water (1 tsp.)
Bar sugar (1 tsp.)
Lemon slice

Dissolve sugar in lemon juice and water in the bottom of a chilled highball glass. Add gin and stir. Fill glass with ice cubes and garnish with lemon slice.

Gin Fizz

4 parts gin (2 oz./60 ml.)
2 parts fresh lemon juice
 (1 oz./30 ml.)
Bar sugar (1 tsp.)
Sparkling water

Combine all ingredients, except sparkling water, in a cocktail shaker with cracked ice. Shake well and strain over ice cubes into chilled highball. Fill with sparkling water and stir gently.

Gin Milk Punch

4 parts gin (2 oz./60 ml.)
12 parts milk (6 oz./180 ml.)
Bar sugar (½ tsp.)
Freshly ground nutmeg

Combine all ingredients, except nutmeg, in a cocktail shaker with cracked ice. Shake well and pour into chilled highball glass. Sprinkle with nutmeg.

Gin Rickey

4 parts gin (2 oz./60 ml.)
2 parts fresh lime juice
 (1 oz./30 ml.)
Sparkling water

Pour gin and lime juice over ice cubes into chilled highball glass. Fill with sparkling water and stir gently.

Gin Sangaree

4 parts gin (2 oz./60 ml.)
Ruby port (1 tbsp.)
Water (1 tsp.)
Bar sugar (½ tsp.)
Sparkling water

Dissolve sugar in water in the bottom of a chilled highball glass. Add gin and stir. Add ice cubes and fill glass with sparkling water. Stir gently and float port on top.

Gin Sidecar

4 parts gin (2 oz./60 ml.)
2 parts Triple Sec (1 oz./30 ml.)
2 parts fresh lemon juice
 (1 oz./30 ml.)

Combine all ingredients with cracked ice in a cocktail shaker and shake well. Pour into chilled old-fashioned glass.

Gin Sling

4 parts gin (2 oz./60 ml.)
1 part fresh lemon juice
 (½ oz./15 ml.)
Water (1 tsp.)
Bar sugar (1 tsp.)
Orange twist

In the bottom of a mixing glass, dissolve sugar in water and lemon juice. Add gin and stir. Pour over ice cubes into a chilled old-fashioned glass and garnish with orange twist.

GIN

Gin Smash

6 parts gin (3 oz./90 ml.)
2 parts sparkling water
 (1 oz./30 ml.)
Bar sugar (1 tsp.)
4 fresh mint sprigs
Lemon twist

In the bottom of a chilled old-
fashioned glass, muddle the mint
sprigs with the sugar and sparkling
water. Fill the glass with ice cubes
and add gin. Stir well and garnish
with lemon twist.

Golden Dawn

4 parts gin (2 oz./60 ml.)
2 parts apricot liqueur (1 oz./30 ml.)
2 parts fresh lime juice
 (1 oz./30 ml.)
4 parts fresh orange juice
 (2 oz./60 ml.)
Dash grenadine

Combine all ingredients with
cracked ice in a cocktail shaker
and shake well. Strain into chilled
cocktail glass.

Golden Daze

4 parts gin (2 oz./60 ml.)
2 parts peach brandy (1 oz./30 ml.)
2 parts fresh orange juice
 (1 oz./30 ml.)

Combine all ingredients with
cracked ice in a cocktail shaker.
Shake well and strain into chilled
cocktail glass.

Golden Fizz

5 parts gin (2½ oz./75 ml.)
2 parts fresh lime juice
 (1 oz./30 ml.)
Bar sugar (½ tsp.)
1 egg yolk or 1 tbsp. egg yolk
 substitute
Sparkling water
Lemon slice

Combine all ingredients, except
sparkling water and lemon, in
a cocktail shaker with cracked
ice. Shake vigorously and pour
into chilled collins glass. Fill with
sparkling water and stir gently.
Garnish with lemon slice.

Golden Hornet

4 parts gin (2 oz./60 ml.)
1 part scotch (½ oz./15 ml.)
1 part amontillado sherry
 (½ oz./15 ml.)
Lemon twist

Stir gin and sherry in a mixing glass
with ice cubes. Pour into chilled
old-fashioned glass. Float scotch on
top and garnish with lemon twist.

Golden Rooster

4 parts gin (2 oz./60 ml.)
1 part dry vermouth (½ oz./15 ml.)
1 part Cointreau (½ oz./15 ml.)
1 part apricot brandy (½ oz./15 ml.)
Maraschino cherry

Combine all ingredients, except
cherry, with cracked ice in a
cocktail shaker. Shake well and
pour into a chilled old-fashioned
glass. Garnish with cherry.

Golf Cocktail

6 parts gin (3 oz./90 ml.)
2 parts dry vermouth (1 oz./30 ml.)
3 dashes Angostura bitters

Stir ingredients with cracked ice
in a mixing glass and strain into
chilled cocktail glass.

Gradeal Special

4 parts gin (2 oz./60 ml.)
2 parts light rum (1 oz./30 ml.)
2 parts apricot brandy (1 oz./30 ml.)

Combine all ingredients with cracked ice in a cocktail shaker and shake well. Strain into chilled cocktail glass.

Grand Passion

4 parts gin (2 oz./60 ml.)
2 parts dry vermouth (1 oz./30 ml.)
2 parts passion fruit syrup (1 oz./30 ml.)
1 part fresh lemon juice (½ oz./15 ml.)
Orange peel

Combine all liquid ingredients with cracked ice in a cocktail shaker and shake well. Strain into chilled cocktail glass and garnish with orange twist.

Grand Royal Fizz

4 parts gin (2 oz./60 ml.)
Maraschino liqueur (1 tsp.)
3 parts fresh orange juice (1½ oz./45 ml.)
2 parts fresh lemon juice (1 oz./30 ml.)
Bar sugar (½ tsp.)
Half-and-half (2 tsp.)
Sparkling water

Combine all ingredients, except sparkling water, with cracked ice in a cocktail shaker and shake well. Strain into a chilled highball glass over ice cubes. Fill with sparkling water and stir gently.

Granville

4 parts gin (2 oz./60 ml.)
Grand Marnier (1 tsp.)
Calvados (1 tsp.)
Fresh lemon juice (1 tsp.)

Combine all ingredients with cracked ice in a cocktail shaker and shake well. Strain into chilled cocktail glass.

Grapefruit Cocktail

4 parts gin (2 oz./60 ml.)
4 parts grapefruit juice (2 oz./60 ml.)
Maraschino liqueur (2 tsp.)
Maraschino cherry

Combine liquid ingredients with cracked ice in a cocktail shaker and shake well. Strain into chilled cocktail glass and garnish with cherry.

Grapevine

4 parts gin (2 oz./60 ml.)
4 parts red grape juice (2 oz./60 ml.)
2 parts fresh lemon juice (1 oz./30 ml.)
Sugar syrup (½ tsp.)
Dash grenadine

Pour all ingredients over ice cubes into a chilled old-fashioned glass and stir well.

Great Dane

4 parts gin (2 oz./60 ml.)
2 parts cherry Heering (1 oz./30 ml.)
1 part dry vermouth (½ oz./15 ml.)
Kirshwasser (1 tsp.)
Lemon twist

Combine all ingredients, except lemon twist, with cracked ice in a cocktail shaker and shake well. Strain into chilled cocktail glass and garnish with lemon twist.

Great Secret

4 parts gin (2 oz./60 ml.)
2 parts Lillet blanc (1 oz./30 ml.)
3 – 5 dashes Angostura bitters
Orange twist

Combine all ingredients, except orange twist, with cracked ice in a cocktail shaker and shake well. Strain into chilled cocktail glass and garnish with orange twist.

Green Devil

4 parts gin (2 oz./60 ml.)
4 parts green crème de menthe
 (2 oz./60 ml.)
1 part fresh lime juice
 (½ oz./15 ml.)

Combine all ingredients with cracked ice in a cocktail shaker and shake well. Strain over ice cubes into chilled old-fashioned glass.

Green Dragon

Green Dragon

4 parts gin (2 oz./60 ml.)
2 parts green crème de menthe
 (1 oz./30 ml.)
1 part Jagermeister (½ oz./15 ml.)
1 part fresh lime juice
 (½ oz./15 ml.)
3 – 5 dashes orange bitters

Combine all ingredients with cracked ice in a cocktail shaker and shake well. Strain into chilled cocktail glass.

Greenback

4 parts gin (2 oz./60 ml.)
2 parts green crème de menthe
 (1 oz./30 ml.)
2 parts fresh lemon juice
 (1 oz./30 ml.)

Combine ingredients with cracked ice in a cocktail shaker and shake well. Strain into chilled old-fashioned glass over ice cubes.

Harlem Cocktail

4 parts gin (2 oz./60 ml.)
3 parts pineapple juice
 (1½ oz./45 ml.)
Maraschino liqueur (1 tsp.)
Diced fresh pineapple (1 tbsp.)

Combine all ingredients with cracked ice in a cocktail shaker. Shake well. Strain into chilled old-fashioned glass.

Hasty Cocktail

4 parts gin (2 oz./60 ml.)
1 part dry vermouth (½ oz./15 ml.)
3 – 5 dashes Pernod
Grenadine (1 tsp.)

Combine all ingredients with cracked ice in a mixing glass. Stir well and strain into chilled cocktail glass.

GIN

Hawaiian Cocktail   🍸

4 parts gin (2 oz./60 ml.)
1 part Triple Sec (½ oz./15 ml.)
1 part pineapple juice
 (½ oz./15 ml.)

Combine ingredients in cocktail shaker with cracked ice. Shake well and strain into chilled cocktail glass.

Hawaiian Orange Blossom   🍸

4 parts gin (2 oz./60 ml.)
2 parts Triple Sec (1 oz./30 ml.)
4 parts fresh orange juice
 (2 oz./60 ml.)
2 parts pineapple juice
 (1 oz./30 ml.)

Combine all ingredients with cracked ice in a cocktail shaker and shake well. Strain into chilled sour glass.

Hoffman House Cocktail   🍸

4 parts gin (2 oz./60 ml.)
1 part dry vermouth (½ oz./15 ml.)
3 dashes orange bitters
Spanish olive

Stir all ingredients, except olive, in a mixing glass. Strain into chilled cocktail glass and garnish with olive.

Homestead Cocktail   🍸

4 parts gin (2 oz./60 ml.)
2 parts sweet vermouth (1 oz./30 ml.)
Orange slice

Stir gin and vermouth with ice cubes in a mixing glass. Strain into chilled cocktail glass and garnish with orange slice.

Honolulu Cocktail   🍸

4 parts gin (2 oz./60 ml.)
2 parts pineapple juice
 (1 oz./30 ml.)
Fresh lemon juice (1 tsp.)
Fresh lime juice (1 tsp.)
Fresh orange juice (1 tsp.)
Dash orange bitters
Bar sugar (½ tsp.)

Combine all ingredients in a cocktail shaker with cracked ice and shake well. Strain into chilled cocktail glass.

Harlem Cocktail

Hudson Bay

4 parts gin (2 oz./60 ml.)
2 parts cherry brandy (1 oz./30 ml.)
151-proof rum (1 tbsp.)
1 part fresh orange juice
  (½ oz./15 ml.)
Fresh lime juice (1 tbsp.)

Combine all ingredients with cracked ice in a cocktail shaker. Shake well and strain into chilled cocktail glass.

Hula-Hula

4 parts gin (2 oz./60 ml.)
2 parts fresh orange juice
  (1 oz./30 ml.)
Triple Sec (1 tbsp.)

Combine all ingredients with cracked ice in a cocktail shaker. Strain into chilled cocktail glass.

Ideal Cocktail

4 parts gin (2 oz./60 ml.)
2 parts dry vermouth (1 oz./30 ml.)
Maraschino liqueur (½ tsp.)
Fresh lemon juice (1 tsp.)
Maraschino cherry

Combine all ingredients, except cherry, with cracked ice in a cocktail shaker. Shake well and pour into chilled cocktail glass. Garnish with cherry.

Imperial Cocktail

4 parts gin (2 oz./60 ml.)
2 parts dry vermouth (1 oz./30 ml.)
Maraschino liqueur (½ tsp.)
2 dashes Angostura bitters

Combine all ingredients in a mixing glass with ice cubes and stir well. Strain into chilled cocktail glass.

Inca Cocktail

4 parts gin (2 oz./60 ml.)
2 parts dry vermouth (1 oz./30 ml.)
2 parts sweet vermouth
  (1 oz./30 ml.)
2 parts dry sherry (1 oz./30 ml.)
Dash orange bitters
Dash Orgeat (almond) syrup

Combine all ingredients in a mixing glass with cracked ice and stir well. Strain into chilled cocktail glass.

Income Tax Cocktail

4 parts gin (2 oz./60 ml.)
Dry vermouth (1 tbsp.)
Sweet vermouth (1 tbsp.)
3 parts fresh orange juice
  (1½ oz./45 ml.)
3 dashes Angostura bitters

Combine all ingredients with cracked ice in a cocktail shaker. Shake well and strain into chilled cocktail glass.

Jamaica Glow

4 parts gin (2 oz./60 ml.)
1 part dry red wine (½ oz./15 ml.)
Dark rum (1 tbsp.)
1 part fresh orange juice
  (½ oz./15 ml.)

Combine all ingredients with cracked ice in a cocktail shaker. Shake well and strain into chilled cocktail glass.

James Bond Martini

6 parts gin (3 oz./90 ml.)
2 parts vodka (1 oz./30 ml.)
1 part Lillet blanc (½ oz./15 ml.)
Lemon twist

Combine liquid ingredients in a cocktail shaker with cracked ice and shake well. Strain into a chilled cocktail glass and garnish with lemon twist.

Jewel Cocktail

4 parts gin (2 oz./60 ml.)
3 parts green Chartreuse
  (1½ oz./45 ml.)
2 parts sweet vermouth
  (1 oz./30 ml.)
3 dashes orange bitters
Maraschino cherry

Combine liquid ingredients with cracked ice in a mixing glass and stir well. Strain into chilled cocktail glass and garnish with cherry.

Journalist

Jockey Club Cocktail

4 parts gin (2 oz./60 ml.)
White crème de cacao (½ tsp.)
1 part fresh lemon juice
  (½ oz./15 ml.)
Dash Angostura bitters

Combine all ingredients with cracked ice in a cocktail shaker. Shake well and strain into chilled cocktail glass.

Johnny Cocktail

4 parts sloe gin (2 oz./60 ml.)
2 parts Triple Sec (1 oz./30 ml.)
Pernod (1 tsp.)

Combine ingredients with cracked ice in a cocktail shaker. Shake well and strain into chilled cocktail glass.

Joulouville

4 parts gin (2 oz./60 ml.)
2 parts apple brandy (1 oz./30 ml.)
Sweet vermouth (1 tbsp.)
1 part fresh lemon juice
  (½ oz./15 ml.)
3 dashes grenadine

Combine all ingredients with cracked ice in a cocktail shaker. Shake well and strain into chilled cocktail glass.

Journalist

4 parts gin (2 oz./60 ml.)
Dry vermouth (1 tsp.)
Sweet vermouth (1 tsp.)
Triple Sec (1 tsp.)
Fresh lime juice (1 tsp.)
Dash Angostura bitters

Combine all ingredients with cracked ice in a cocktail shaker. Shake well and strain into chilled cocktail glass.

Judge, Jr.

4 parts gin (2 oz./60 ml.)
4 parts light rum (2 oz./60 ml.)
2 parts fresh lemon juice
  (1 oz./30 ml.)
Grenadine (2 tsp.)

Combine all ingredient with cracked ice in a cocktail shaker. Shake well and strain into chilled cocktail glass.

Judgette Cocktail

4 parts gin (2 oz./60 ml.)
3 parts peach brandy
  (1½ oz./45 ml.)
2 parts dry vermouth (1 oz./30 ml.)
Fresh lime juice (½ tsp.)

Combine ingredients with cracked
ice in a cocktail shaker. Shake
well and strain into chilled cocktail
glass.

KGB Cocktail

4 parts gin (2 oz./60 ml.)
1½ parts kirshwasser
  ¾ oz./22.5 ml.)
Apricot brandy (½ tsp.)
Lemon twist

Combine all ingredients, except
lemon, with cracked ice in a
cocktail glass. Shake well and
strain into chilled cocktail glass.
Garnish with lemon twist.

Knickerbocker Cocktail

4 parts gin (2 oz./60 ml.)
2 parts dry vermouth (1 oz./30 ml.)
Sweet vermouth (½ tsp.)
Lemon twist

Stir liquid ingredients with ice cubes
in a mixing glass. Strain into chilled
cocktail glass and garnish with
lemon twist.

Kup's Indispensable Cocktail

4 parts gin (2 oz./60 ml.)
1½ parts dry vermouth
  (¾ oz./22.5 ml.)
1½ parts sweet vermouth
  (¾ oz./22.5 ml.)
Orange twist

Combine liquid ingredients with
ice cubes in a mixing glass and
stir well. Strain into chilled cocktail
glass and garnish with orange twist.

Kyoto Cocktail

4 parts gin (2 oz./60 ml.)
2 parts melon liqueur (1 oz./30 ml.)
1 part dry vermouth (½ oz./15 ml.)
Fresh lemon juice (¼ tsp.)

Combine ingredients with cracked
ice in a cocktail shaker. Shake
well and strain into chilled cocktail
glass.

Lady Finger

4 parts gin (2 oz./60 ml.)
3 parts raspberry eau de vie
  (1½ oz./45 ml.)
2 parts cherry brandy (1 oz./30 ml.)

Combine ingredients with cracked
ice in a cocktail shaker. Shake
well and strain into chilled cocktail
glass.

Leap Frog Highball

4 parts gin (2 oz./60 ml.)
3 parts fresh lemon juice
  (1½ oz./45 ml.)
Ginger ale

Pour gin and lemon juice into a
chilled highball glass over ice
cubes. Fill with ginger ale and stir
gently.

Leap Year Cocktail

4 parts gin (2 oz./60 ml.)
1 parts sweet vermouth
 (½ oz./15 ml.)
1 part Grand Marnier (½ oz./15 ml.)
Fresh lemon juice (½ tsp.)

Combine ingredients with cracked
ice in a cocktail shaker. Shake
well and strain into chilled cocktail
glass.

Little Devil

4 parts gin (2 oz./60 ml.)
3 parts light rum (1½ oz./45 ml.)
2 parts Triple Sec (1 oz./30 ml.)
2 parts fresh lemon juice
 (1 oz./30 ml.)

Combine all ingredients with
cracked ice in a cocktail shaker.
Shake well and strain into chilled
cocktail glass.

London Cocktail

6 parts gin (3 oz./90 ml.)
Maraschino liqueur (½ tsp.)
5 dashes orange bitters
Bar sugar (½ tsp.)
Lemon twist

Combine all ingredients, except
lemon, with cracked ice in a
cocktail shaker. Shake well and
strain into chilled cocktail glass.
Garnish with lemon twist.

London French '75'

4 parts gin (2 oz./60 ml.)
2 parts fresh lemon juice
 (½ oz./15 ml.)
Bar sugar (½ tsp.)
Champagne or sparkling wine

Combine all ingredients, except
champagne, with cracked ice in
a cocktail shaker. Shake well and
pour into chilled collins glass. Fill
with cold champagne.

Lone Tree Cocktail

4 parts gin (2 oz./60 ml.)
1 part sweet vermouth
 (½ oz./15 ml.)
3 dashes orange bitters

Combine ingredients in a mixing
glass with ice cubes. Stir well and
strain into chilled cocktail glass.

Maiden's Blush

4 parts gin (2 oz./60 ml.)
Triple Sec (½ tsp.)
Grenadine (½ tsp.)
Fresh lemon juice (½ tsp.)

Combine all ingredients with
cracked ice in a cocktail shaker.
Shake well and strain into chilled
cocktail glass.

Maiden's Prayer

4 parts gin (2 oz./60 ml.)
2 parts Curaçao (1 oz./30 ml.)
1 part fresh lemon juice
 (½ oz./15 ml.)
Fresh orange juice (1 tbsp.)

Combine all ingredients with
cracked ice in a cocktail shaker
and shake well. Strain into chilled
cocktail glass.

Main Brace

4 parts gin (2 oz./60 ml.)
2 parts white Curaçao (1 oz./30 ml.)
2 parts white grape juice
 (1 oz./30 ml.)

Combine all ingredients with
cracked ice in a cocktail shaker
and shake well. Strain into chilled
cocktail glass.

GIN

Martini

6 parts gin (3 oz./90 ml.)
Dry vermouth (¼ tsp. or less)
Spanish olive

Combine gin and vermouth in a
mixing glass with ice cubes. Stir
well and pour into a chilled cocktail
glass. Garnish with olive.

NOTE: One of the numerous
variations on the Martini in
this book combines the gin
and vermouth with a splash of
Dubonnet. Garnish with a twist of
lemon instead of an olive.

Matinee

4 parts gin (2 oz./60 ml.)
2 parts sweet vermouth
  (1 oz./30 ml.)
1 part green Chartreuse
  (½ oz./15 ml.)
1 part fresh orange juice
  (½ oz./15 ml.)
Dash orange bitters

Combine all ingredients with
cracked ice in a cocktail shaker
and shake well. Strain into chilled
cocktail glass.

Maurice

4 parts gin (2 oz./60 ml.)
1 part dry vermouth (½ oz./15 ml.)
1 part sweet vermouth
  (½ oz./15 ml.)
2 parts fresh orange juice
  (1 oz./30 ml.)
Dash Angostura bitters

Combine all ingredients with
cracked ice in a cocktail shaker.
Shake well and strain into chilled
cocktail glass.

McClelland

4 parts sloe gin (2 oz./60 ml.)
2 parts white Curaçao (1 oz./30 ml.)
3 – 5 dashes orange bitters

Combine all ingredients with
cracked ice in a cocktail shaker
and shake well. Strain into chilled
cocktail glass.

Martini with an Olive

Mellon Cocktail

4 parts gin (2 oz./60 ml.)
1 part maraschino liqueur
  (½ oz./15 ml.)
1 part fresh lemon juice
  (½ oz./15 ml.)
Maraschino cherry
Lemon twist

Combine all ingredients, except
cherry and lemon twist, in a cocktail
shaker with cracked ice. Shake
well and strain into chilled cocktail
glass. Garnish with cherry and
lemon twist.

GIN

Merry Widow

4 parts gin (2 oz./60 ml.)
2 parts dry vermouth (1 oz./30 ml.)
1 part Pernod (½ oz./15 ml.)
3 – 5 dashes bitters
Lemon twist

Combine all ingredients, except lemon twist, with cracked ice in a cocktail shaker. Shake well and strain into chilled cocktail glass. Garnish with lemon twist.

Million-Dollar Cocktail

4 parts gin (2 oz./60 ml.)
2 parts sweet vermouth
  (1 oz./30 ml.)
2 parts pineapple juice (1 oz./30 ml.)
Grenadine (1 tsp.)

Combine all ingredients with cracked ice in a cocktail shaker. Shake vigorously and strain into chilled cocktail glass.

Mint Collins

6 parts gin (3 oz./90 ml.)
2 parts fresh lemon juice
  (1 oz./30 ml.)
Bar sugar (1 tsp.)
7 fresh mint leaves
Sparkling water
Lemon slice
Mint sprigs

Pour gin, lemon juice and sugar into a chilled collins glass. Drop in the mint leaves and crush them with a bar spoon. Add ice cubes and fill with sparkling water. Stir gently and garnish with lemon slice and mint sprigs.

Mississippi Mule

4 parts gin (2 oz./60 ml.)
1 part crème de cassis
  (½ oz./15 ml.)
1 part fresh lemon juice
  (½ oz./15 ml.)

Combine ingredients with cracked ice in a cocktail shaker. Shake well and pour into chilled old-fashioned glass.

Moldau

4 parts gin (2 oz./60 ml.)
2 parts slivovotz (1 oz./30 ml.)
1 part fresh orange juice
  (½ oz./15 ml.)
1 part fresh lemon juice
  (½ oz./15 ml.)

Combine all ingredients with cracked ice in a cocktail shaker. Shake well and strain into chilled cocktail glass.

Martini (variation)

Moll Cocktail

3 parts gin (1½ oz./45 ml.)
2 parts sloe gin (1 oz./30 ml.)
2 parts dry vermouth (1 oz./30 ml.)
Dash Angostura bitters

Combine all ingredients with
cracked ice in a cocktail shaker.
Shake well and strain into chilled
cocktail glass.

Montmarte

4 parts gin (2 oz./60 ml.)
1 part sweet vermouth
  (½ oz./15 ml.)
1 part white Curaçao (½ oz./15 ml.)

Combine ingredients with cracked
ice in a cocktail shaker and shake
well. Strain into chilled cocktail
glass.

Moon Shot

4 parts gin (2 oz./60 ml.)
6 parts clam juice (3 oz./90 ml.)
Dash Tabasco® sauce

Combine all ingredients in a mixing
glass with ice cubes and stir. Pour
into chilled old-fashioned glass.

Morning Joy

4 parts gin (2 oz./60 ml.)
3 parts crème de bananes
  (1½ oz./45 ml.)
6 parts fresh orange juice
  (3 oz./90 ml.)

Combine all ingredients with
cracked ice in a cocktail shaker.
Shake well and strain into chilled
sour glass.

Morro

4 parts gin (2 oz./60 ml.)
2 parts dark rum (1 oz./30 ml.)
1 part fresh lime juice
  (½ oz./15 ml.)
1 part pineapple juice
  (½ oz./15 ml.)
Bar sugar (½ tsp.)

Combine all ingredients with
cracked ice in a cocktail shaker.
Shake well and strain into a sugar-
rimmed old-fashioned glass over ice
cubes.

Moulin Rouge

4 parts sloe gin (2 oz./60 ml.)
1 part sweet vermouth
  (½ oz./15 ml.)
3 – 5 dashes Angostura bitters

Combine all ingredients with
cracked ice in a cocktail shaker.
Shake well and strain into chilled
cocktail glass.

Napoleon

4 parts gin (2 oz./60 ml.)
1 part white Curaçao (½ oz./15 ml.)
Dubonnet rouge (1 tsp.)
Amer Picon (1 tsp.)

Combine ingredients in mixing glass
with cracked ice and stir. Strain into
chilled cocktail glass.

Negroni

4 parts gin (2 oz./60 ml.)
2 parts Campari (1 oz./30 ml.)
1 part sweet vermouth (½ oz./15 ml.)
Orange twist

Combine all ingredients, except
orange twist, in a cocktail shaker
with cracked ice. Shake well and
strain into chilled old-fashioned
glass over ice cubes. Garnish with
orange twist.

New Love Cocktail

4 parts gin (2 oz./60 ml.)
Fresh lemon juice (½ tsp.)
Raspberry syrup (½ tsp.)
1 tsp. sweet vermouth

Combine ingredients with cracked ice in a cocktail shaker. Shake vigorously and strain into chilled cocktail glass.

New Orleans Gin Fizz

4 parts gin (2 oz./60 ml.)
2 parts fresh lemon juice
   (1 oz./30 ml.)
2 parts fresh lime juice (1 oz./30 ml.)
Sugar syrup (1 tsp.)
1 part half-and-half (½ oz./15 ml.)
1 egg white (or 1 tbsp. egg white
   substitute)
Sparkling water
Lime slice

Combine all ingredients, except sparkling water and lime slice, in a cocktail shaker with cracked ice. Shake vigorously. Strain into a chilled collins glass over ice cubes. Fill with sparkling water and stir gently. Garnish with lime slice.

Newbury

4 parts gin (2 oz./60 ml.)
3 parts sweet vermouth
   (1½ oz./45 ml.)
Triple Sec (¼ tsp.)
Lemon twist

Combine all ingredients, except lemon twist, with cracked ice in a cocktail shaker. Shake well and strain into chilled cocktail glass. Garnish with lemon twist.

Newport Cooler

4 parts gin (2 oz./60 ml.)
1 part brandy (½ oz./15 ml.)
1 part peach liqueur (½ oz./15 ml.)
Fresh lime juice (¼ tsp.)
Ginger ale

Pour all ingredients, except ginger ale, into a chilled collins glass over ice cubes. Fill with ginger ale and stir gently.

Nightmare

4 parts gin (2 oz./60 ml.)
2 parts Madeira (1 oz./30 ml.)
2 parts cherry brandy (1 oz./30 ml.)
Fresh orange juice (1 tsp.)

Combine ingredients with cracked ice in a cocktail shaker. Shake well and strain into chilled cocktail glass.

Normandy Cocktail

4 parts gin (2 oz./60 ml.)
2 parts Calvados (1 oz./30 ml.)
1 part apricot brandy (½ oz./15 ml.)
Fresh lemon juice (¼ tsp.)

Combine all ingredients with cracked ice in a cocktail shaker and shake well. Strain into chilled cocktail glass.

Octopus's Garden

6 parts gin (3 oz./90 ml.)
2 parts dry vermouth (1 oz./30 ml.)
Smoked baby octopus
Black olive

Combine liquid ingredients in a cocktail shaker with cracked ice and shake well. Strain into a chilled cocktail glass and garnish with olive and octopus.

Opal Cocktail

4 parts gin (2 oz./60 ml.)
1 part Triple Sec (½ oz./15 ml.)
2 parts fresh orange juice
  (1 oz./30 ml.)
Bar sugar (¼ tsp.)

Combine all ingredients with
cracked ice in a cocktail shaker.
Shake well and strain into chilled
cocktail glass.

Opera

4 parts gin (2 oz./60 ml.)
2 parts Dubonnet rouge
  (1 oz./30 ml.)
1 part maraschino liqueur
  (½ oz./15 ml.)

Stir ingredients with cracked ice in
a mixing glass. Strain into chilled
cocktail glass.

Orange Blossom Cocktail

4 parts gin (2 oz./60 ml.)
4 parts fresh orange juice
  (2 oz./60 ml.)
Orange slice

Combine all ingredients, except
orange slice, with cracked ice in
a cocktail shaker. Shake well and
strain into chilled cocktail glass.
Garnish with orange slice.

Orange Buck

4 parts gin (2 oz./60 ml.)
4 parts fresh orange juice
  (2 oz./60 ml.)
2 parts fresh lime juice
  (1 oz./30 ml.)
Ginger ale
Lime slice

Combine all ingredients, except
ginger ale and lime slice, with
cracked ice in a cocktail shaker.
Shake well and strain into a chilled
collins glass over ice cubes. Fill with
ginger ale and stir gently. Garnish
with lime slice.

Orange Oasis

4 parts gin (2 oz./60 ml.)
2 parts cherry brandy (1 oz./30 ml.)
8 parts fresh orange juice
  (½ cup or 4 oz./120 ml.)
Ginger ale

Combine all ingredients, except
ginger ale, with cracked ice in a
cocktail shaker. Strain over ice
cubes into a chilled highball glass.
Fill with ginger ale and stir gently.

Paisley Martini

6 parts gin (3 oz./90 ml.)
Dry vermouth (½ tsp.)
Scotch (½ tsp.)

Combine all ingredients with ice
cubes in a mixing glass. Stir well
and strain into a chilled cocktail
glass.

Pall Mall

4 parts gin (2 oz./60 ml.)
1 part dry vermouth (½ oz./15 ml.)
1 part sweet vermouth
  (½ oz./15 ml.)
White crème de menthe (1 tsp.)
Dash orange bitters

Combine all ingredients in a mixing
glass with ice cubes. Stir well and
strain into chilled cocktail glass.

Palm Beach Cocktail

4 parts gin (2 oz./60 ml.)
Sweet vermouth (1 tsp.)
4 parts grapefruit juice
  (2 oz./60 ml.)

Combine ingredients with cracked
ice in a cocktail shaker. Shake
well and strain into chilled cocktail
glass.

Parisian

4 parts gin (2 oz./60 ml.)
2 parts dry vermouth (1 oz./30 ml.)
1 part crème de cassis
 (½ oz./15 ml.)

Combine ingredients with cracked
ice in a cocktail shaker. Shake
well and strain into chilled cocktail
glass.

Park Avenue

4 parts gin (2 oz./60 ml.)
1 part sweet vermouth (½ oz./15 ml.)
1 part pineapple juice
 (½ oz./15 ml.)

Stir ingredients with cracked ice in
a mixing glass. Strain into chilled
cocktail glass.

Peach Blow Fizz

6 parts gin (3 oz./90 ml.)
2 parts fresh lemon juice
 (1 oz./30 ml.)
2 parts half-and-half (1 oz./30 ml.)
Sugar syrup (1 tsp.)
5 fresh strawberries, mashed
Sparkling water
Fresh peach wedge

Combine all ingredients, except
sparkling water and peach, with
cracked ice in a cocktail shaker.
Shake well and pour into chilled
highball glass. Fill with sparkling
water and stir gently. Garnish with
peach wedge.

Peace Train

3 parts gin (1½ oz./45 ml.)
2 parts Calvados (1 oz./30 ml.)
2 parts sweet vermouth
 (1 oz./30 ml.)
Yellow Chartreuse (1 tbsp.)

Combine all ingredients with
cracked ice in a cocktail shaker.
Shake well and strain into chilled
cocktail glass.

Peggy-O Cocktail

4 parts gin (2 oz./60 ml.)
1 part sweet vermouth
 (½ oz./15 ml.)
Dubonnet rouge (¼ tsp.)
Pernod (¼ tsp.)

Combine all ingredients with
cracked ice in a cocktail shaker
and shake well. Strain into chilled
cocktail glass.

Pegu Club Cocktail

4 parts gin (2 oz./60 ml.)
2 parts white Curaçao (1 oz./30 ml.)
Fresh lime juice (1 tbsp.)
Dash Angostura bitters
Dash orange bitters

Combine all ingredients with
cracked ice in a cocktail shaker.
Shake well and strain into chilled
cocktail glass.

Pen Dennis Club Cocktail

4 parts gin (2 oz./60 ml.)
2 parts apricot brandy (1 oz./30 ml.)
2 parts fresh lime juice
 (1 oz./30 ml.)
Sugar syrup (1 tsp.)
3 – 5 dashes bitters

Combine all ingredients with
cracked ice in a cocktail shaker.
Shake well and strain into chilled
cocktail glass.

Perfect Martini

6 parts gin (3 oz./90 ml.)
Dry vermouth (½ tsp.)
Sweet vermouth (½ tsp.)
Spanish olive

Combine liquid ingredients with ice cubes in a mixing glass and stir well. Strain into chilled cocktail glass and garnish with olive.

Peyton Place

3 parts sloe gin (1½ oz./45 ml.)
2 parts gin (1 oz./30 ml.)
5 parts grapefruit juice
 (2½ oz./75 ml.)
1 part sugar syrup (½ oz./15 ml.)
Club soda

Mix all ingredients, except soda, with cracked ice in a cocktail shaker. Pour into chilled collins glass. Fill with club soda. Stir gently.

Piccadilly Cocktail

4 parts gin (2 oz./60 ml.)
2 parts dry vermouth (1 oz./30 ml.)
Pernod (¼ tsp.)
Dash grenadine

Stir ingredients with ice in a mixing glass and strain into chilled cocktail glass.

Pink Lady

4 parts gin (2 oz./60 ml.)
Grenadine (1 tsp.)
Half-and-half (1 tsp.)
Fresh lemon juice (1 tsp.)
1 egg white (or 1 tbsp. egg white
 substitute)

Combine all ingredients with cracked ice in a cocktail shaker. Shake vigorously and strain into chilled cocktail glass.

Pink Pussycat

4 parts gin (2 oz./60 ml.)
Pineapple juice
Dash grenadine
Pineapple spear

Pour gin into a chilled highball glass over ice cubes. Fill with pineapple juice and add a dash of grenadine. Stir gently and garnish with pineapple spear.

Pink Rose

4 parts gin (2 oz./60 ml.)
Fresh lemon juice (1 tsp.)
Half-and-half (1 tsp.)
Grenadine (¼ tsp.)
1 egg white (or 1 tbsp. egg white
 substitute)

Combine all ingredients with cracked ice in a cocktail shaker. Shake well and strain into chilled cocktail glass.

Peyton Place

GIN

Pluggy's Favorite

4 parts gin (2 oz./60 ml.)
4 parts Pernod (2 oz./60 ml.)
4 parts water (2 oz./60 ml.)

Combine all ingredients with cracked ice in a cocktail shaker. Shake well and strain into chilled old-fashioned glass over ice cubes.

Polish Sidecar

4 parts gin (2 oz./60 ml.)
2 parts blackberry brandy
  (1 oz./30 ml.)
2 parts fresh lemon juice
  (1 oz./30 ml.)
Fresh blackberries

Combine all ingredients, except berries, with cracked ice in a cocktail shaker. Shake well and strain into chilled cocktail glass. Garnish with blackberries.

Pollyanna

6 parts gin (3 oz./90 ml.)
1 part sweet vermouth
  (½ oz./15 ml.)
Grenadine (½ tsp.)
3 orange slices
3 pineapple slices

Muddle fruit slices with all ingredients in a mortar and pestle. Pour ingredients into a cocktail shaker with cracked ice. Shake well and strain into chilled cocktail glass.

Pompano

4 parts gin (2 oz./60 ml.)
2 parts dry vermouth (1 oz./30 ml.)
4 parts grapefruit juice
  (2 oz./60 ml.)
Dash orange bitters

Combine all ingredients with cracked ice in a cocktail shaker. Shake well and strain into chilled cocktail glass.

Polish Sidecar

Post-Modern Lemonade

4 parts sloe gin (2 oz./60 ml.)
4 parts dry sherry (2 oz./60 ml.)
2 parts aquavit (1 oz./30 ml.)
6 parts fresh lemon juice
  (3 oz./90 ml.)
Slivovitz (1 tbsp.)
2 parts sugar syrup (1 oz./30 ml.)
Sparkling water
Lemon twist

Combine all ingredients, except lemon twist and sparkling water, with cracked ice in a cocktail shaker. Shake well and strain over ice cubes into chilled collins glass. Stir gently and garnish with lemon twist.

Prince's Smile

4 parts gin (2 oz./60 ml.)
2 parts apple brandy (1 oz./30 ml.)
2 parts apricot brandy (1 oz./30 ml.)
Fresh lemon juice (1 tsp.)

Combine all ingredients with cracked ice in a cocktail shaker. Shake well and strain into chilled cocktail glass.

Princeton Cocktail

6 parts gin (3 oz./90 ml.)
2 parts ruby port (1 oz./30 ml.)
3 – 5 dashes Angostura bitters
Lemon twist

Combine all ingredients with cracked ice in a cocktail shaker and shake well. Strain into chilled cocktail glass and garnish with lemon twist.

Queen Elizabeth

6 parts gin (3 oz./90 ml.)
1 part dry vermouth (½ oz./15 ml.)
Benedictine (2 tsp.)

Combine ingredients with ice cubes in a mixing glass and stir well. Strain into chilled cocktail glass.

Racquet Club Cocktail

4 parts gin (2 oz./60 ml.)
1½ parts dry vermouth
  (¾ oz./22.5 ml.)
Dash orange bitters

Combine all ingredients in a mixing glass with ice cubes. Stir well and strain into chilled cocktail glass.

Ramos Fizz

6 parts gin (3 oz./90 ml.)
1 part fresh lemon juice (½ oz./15 ml.)
1 part fresh lime juice
  (½ oz./15 ml.)
Bar sugar (1 tsp.)
Half-and-half (1 tsp.)
3 – 5 dashes orange flower water
1 egg white (or 1 tbsp. egg white
  substitute)
Sparkling water

Combine all ingredients, except egg white and sparkling water, with cracked ice in a cocktail shaker. Shake vigorously and pour into chilled collins glass. Fill with sparkling water and egg white and stir gently.

Red Cloud

4 parts gin (2 oz./60 ml.)
2 parts apricot liqueur (1 oz./30 ml.)
2 parts fresh lemon juice
  (1 oz./30 ml.)
Grenadine (1 tsp.)
Dash Angostura bitters

Combine all ingredients with cracked ice in a cocktail shaker. Shake well and strain into chilled cocktail glass.

Red Lion

4 parts gin (2 oz./60 ml.)
3 parts orange liqueur
  (1½ oz./45 ml.)
1 part fresh lemon juice
  (½ oz./15 ml.)
1 part fresh orange juice
  (½ oz./15 ml.)
Grenadine (½ tsp.)

Combine ingredients with cracked ice in a cocktail shaker. Shake well and strain into chilled cocktail glass.

Renaissance

4 parts gin (2 oz./60 ml.)
1 part fino sherry (½ oz./15 ml.)
1 part half-and-half (½ oz./15 ml.)
Freshly grated nutmeg

Combine all ingredients, except nutmeg, with cracked ice in a cocktail shaker. Shake well and strain into chilled old-fashioned glass over ice cubes. Sprinkle nutmeg on top.

Rendez-Vous

4 parts gin (2 oz./60 ml.)
2 parts cherry eau de vie
  (1 oz./30 ml.)
1 part Campari (½ oz./15 ml.)
Lemon twist

Combine all ingredients, except lemon twist, with cracked ice in a cocktail shaker. Shake well and strain into chilled cocktail glass. Garnish with lemon twist.

Resolute Cocktail

4 parts gin (2 oz./60 ml.)
2 parts apricot brandy (1 oz./30 ml.)
1 part fresh lemon juice
  (½ oz./15 ml.)

Combine ingredients with cracked ice in a cocktail shaker. Shake well and strain into chilled cocktail glass.

Road Runner

4 parts gin (2 oz./60 ml.)
1 part dry vermouth (½ oz./15 ml.)
Grenadine (1 tsp.)
Pernod (¼ tsp.)

Combine all ingredients with cracked ice in a cocktail shaker. Shake well and strain into chilled cocktail glass.

Rocky Green Dragon

4 parts gin (2 oz./60 ml.)
2 parts green Chartreuse
  (1 oz./30 ml.)
1 part cognac (½ oz./15 ml.)

Combine ingredients in a cocktail shaker with cracked ice. Shake well and strain into chilled cocktail glass.

Rolls Royce

6 parts gin (3 oz./90 ml.)
2 parts dry vermouth (1 oz./30 ml.)
2 parts sweet vermouth (1 oz./30 ml.)
Benedictine (¼ tsp.)

Combine all ingredients with ice cubes in a mixing glass. Stir well and strain into chilled cocktail glass.

Roman Cooler

4 parts gin (2 oz./60 ml.)
2 parts Punt e Mes (1 oz./30 ml.)
1 part fresh lemon juice
  (½ oz./15 ml.)
Sugar syrup (1 tsp.)
Sweet vermouth (½ tsp.)
Sparkling water
Orange twist

Combine all ingredients, except sparkling water and orange twist, with cracked ice in a cocktail shaker. Strain into a chilled highball glass over ice cubes. Fill with sparkling water and stir gently. Garnish with orange twist.

GIN

Rose Cocktail

4 parts gin (2 oz./60 ml.)
2 parts apricot brandy (1 oz./30 ml.)
2 parts dry vermouth (1 oz./30 ml.)
Grenadine (1 tsp.)
Fresh lemon juice (1 tsp.)
Lemon wedge
Bar sugar

Rim a chilled cocktail glass with sugar by moistening the rim with the lemon wedge and dipping it into a saucer with bar sugar. Discard the lemon wedge. Combine remaining ingredients with cracked ice in a cocktail shaker and shake well. Strain into the sugar-rimmed glass.

Roselyn Cocktail

4 parts gin (2 oz./60 ml.)
2 parts dry vermouth (1 oz./30 ml.)
Grenadine (1 tsp.)
Lemon twist

Combine all ingredients, except lemon twist, with ice cubes in a mixing glass. Stir well and strain into chilled cocktail glass. Garnish with lemon twist.

Ruby Fizz

6 parts sloe gin (3 oz./90 ml.)
3 parts fresh lemon juice
  (1½ oz./45 ml.)
Grenadine (1 tbsp.)
Sugar syrup (1 tsp.)
1 egg white (or 1 tbsp. egg white
  substitute)
Sparkling water

Combine all ingredients, except sparkling water, with cracked ice in a cocktail shaker. Shake well and strain into chilled highball glass over ice cubes. Fill with sparkling water and stir gently.

Saketini

6 parts gin (3 oz./90 ml.)
1 part sake (½ oz./15 ml.)
Lemon twist

Combine all ingredients, except lemon twist, with cracked ice in a cocktail shaker. Shake well and strain into chilled cocktail glass. Garnish with lemon twist.

San Sebastain

4 parts gin (2 oz./60 ml.)
1 part light rum (½ oz./15 ml.)
1 part Triple Sec (½ oz./15 ml.)
1 part fresh lemon juice
  (½ oz./15 ml.)
1 part grapefruit juice (½ oz./15 ml.)

Combine all ingredients with cracked ice in a cocktail shaker. Shake well and strain into chilled cocktail glass.

Self-Starter

4 parts gin (2 oz./60 ml.)
2 parts Lillet blanc (1 oz./30 ml.)
1 part apricot brandy (½ oz./15 ml.)
Pernod (¼ tsp.)

Combine all ingredients with cracked ice in a cocktail shaker and shake well. Strain into chilled cocktail glass.

Seventh Heaven

4 parts gin (2 oz./60 ml.)
1 part maraschino liqueur
  (½ oz./15 ml.)
1 part grapefruit juice (½ oz./15 ml.)
Fresh mint sprig

Combine all ingredients, except mint sprig, with cracked ice in a cocktail shaker and shake well. Strain into chilled cocktail glass and garnish with mint sprig.

Seville

4 parts gin (2 oz./60 ml.)
1 part fino sherry (½ oz./15 ml.)
1 part fresh lemon juice
  (½ oz./15 ml.)
1 part fresh orange juice
  (½ oz./15 ml.)
Sugar syrup (1 tbsp.)

Combine all ingredients with
cracked ice in a cocktail shaker.
Shake well and pour into chilled
old-fashioned glass.

Silicon Alley

4 parts gin (2 oz./60 ml.)
2 parts fresh lime juice
  (1 oz./30 ml.)
Scoop vanilla ice cream
Sparkling water

Combine all ingredients, except
sparkling water, in a blender with
cracked ice. Blend briefly until thick
and smooth and pour into chilled
highball glass. Fill with sparkling
water.

Silver Bullet

4 parts gin (2 oz./60 ml.)
2 parts Jagermeister (1 oz./30 ml.)
1 part fresh lemon juice
  (½ oz./15 ml)

Combine all ingredients with
cracked ice in a cocktail shaker.
Shake well and strain into chilled
cocktail glass.

Silver Cocktail

4 parts gin (2 oz./60 ml.)
2 parts dry vermouth (1 oz./30 ml.)
Maraschino liqueur (1 tsp.)
3 dashes orange bitters
Lemon twist

Combine all ingredients, except
lemon twist, with cracked ice in
a cocktail shaker. Shake well and
strain into chilled cocktail glass.
Garnish with lemon twist.

Silver Fizz

6 parts gin (3 oz./90 ml.)
3 parts fresh lemon juice
  (1½ oz./45 ml.)
Bar sugar (1 tsp.)
1 egg white (or 1 tbsp. egg white
  substitute)
Sparkling water

Combine all ingredients, except
sparkling water, with cracked ice in
a cocktail shaker. Shake well and
strain into chilled highball glass
over ice cubes. Fill with sparkling
water and stir gently.

Silver King Cocktail

4 parts gin (2 oz./60 ml.)
2 parts fresh lemon juice
  (1 oz./30 ml.)
Sugar syrup (1 tsp.)
1 egg white or (1 tbsp. egg white
  substitute)
Dash Angostura bitters

Combine all ingredients with
cracked ice in a cocktail shaker and
shake vigorously. Strain into chilled
cocktail glass.

Silver Streak

6 parts gin (3 oz./90 ml.)
3 parts Jagermeister (1½ oz./45 ml.)

Combine ingredients with cracked
ice in a cocktail shaker and shake
well. Strain into chilled cocktail
glass.

Singapore Sling

6 parts gin (3 oz./90 ml.)
2 parts cherry brandy (1 oz./30 ml.)
2 parts fresh lemon juice
 (1 oz./30 ml.)
Bar sugar (1 tsp.)
Sparkling water
Maraschino cherry
Orange slice

Combine all ingredients, except
sparkling water, brandy and fruit,
with cracked ice in a cocktail
shaker. Shake well and strain into
chilled collins glass over ice cubes.
Fill with sparkling water and float
brandy on top. Garnish with fruit.

Sloe Gin Cocktail

6 parts sloe gin (3 oz./90 ml.)
Dry vermouth (1 tsp.)
2 dashes Angostura bitters

Stir ingredients with ice cubes in a
mixing glass and strain into chilled
cocktail glass.

Sloe Gin Fizz

4 parts sloe gin (2 oz./60 ml.)
3 parts fresh lemon juice
 (1½ oz./45 ml.)
Sugar syrup (1 tsp.)
Sparkling water
Lemon slice

Combine all ingredients, except
sparkling water and lemon slice,
with cracked ice in a cocktail
shaker. Shake well and strain into
a chilled highball glass over ice
cubes. Fill with sparkling water, stir
gently and garnish with lemon slice.

Sloe Gin Rickey

4 parts sloe gin (2 oz./60 ml.)
2 parts fresh lime juice
 (1 oz./30 ml.)
Sparkling water
Lime slice

Pour sloe gin and lime juice into
a chilled highball glass over ice
cubes. Fill with sparkling water and
stir gently. Garnish with lime slice.

Sloe Screw

4 parts sloe gin (2 oz./60 ml.)
Fresh orange juice

Pour sloe gin into a chilled highball
glass over ice cubes. Fill with
orange juice and stir.

Smoky Martini

6 parts gin (3 oz./09 ml.)
1 part dry vermouth (½ oz./15 ml.)
1 tsp. scotch
Lemon twist

Combine liquid ingredients in a
mixing glass with cracked ice and
shake well. Strain into a chilled
cocktail glass and garnish with
twist.

Singapore Sling

GIN

Snowball

4 parts gin (2 oz./60 ml.)
2 parts Pernod (1 oz./30 ml.)
1 part half-and-half (½ oz./15 ml.)

Combine ingredients with cracked ice in a cocktail shaker. Shake well and strain into chilled cocktail glass.

Southern Bride

6 parts gin (3 oz./90 ml.)
Maraschino liqueur (1 tsp.)
4 parts grapefruit juice
  (2 oz./60 ml.)

Combine ingredients with cracked ice in a cocktail shaker. Shake well and strain into a chilled cocktail glass.

Southern Gin Cocktail

6 parts gin (3 oz./90 ml.)
1 part Triple Sec (½ oz./15 ml.)
3 dashes orange bitters
Lemon twist

Combine all ingredients, except lemon twist, with ice cubes in a mixing glass. Stir well and strain into chilled cocktail glass. Garnish with lemon twist.

Southside Cocktail

6 parts gin (3 oz./90 ml.)
3 parts fresh lemon juice
  (1½ oz./45 ml.)
Bar sugar (1 tsp.)
Fresh mint sprig

Combine all ingredients, except mint, with cracked ice in a cocktail shaker. Shake well and strain into chilled cocktail glass. Garnish with mint.

Sloe Screw

Spencer Cocktail

4 parts gin (2 oz./60 ml.)
2 parts apricot brandy (1 oz./30 ml.)
Fresh orange juice (½ tsp.)
Dash Angostura bitters
Maraschino cherry
Orange twist

Combine all ingredients, except fruit, with cracked ice in a cocktail shaker. Shake well and strain into chilled cocktail glass. Garnish with cherry and orange twist.

Star Daisy

4 parts gin (2 oz./60 ml.)
3 parts Calvados brandy
  (1½ oz./45 ml.)
3 parts fresh lemon juice
  (1½ oz./45 ml.)
Triple Sec (½ tsp.)
Sugar syrup (1 tsp.)

Combine ingredients with cracked ice in a cocktail shaker. Shake well and strain into chilled wine glass.

GIN

Strega Sour

4 parts gin (2 oz./60 ml.)
2 parts Strega (1 oz./30 ml.)
2 parts fresh lemon juice
  (1 oz./30 ml.)
Lemon slice

Combine all ingredients, except
lemon slice, in a cocktail shaker
with cracked ice. Shake well and
strain into chilled sour glass.
Garnish with lemon slice.

Suffering Bastard

4 parts gin (2 oz./60 ml.)
3 parts brandy (1½ oz./45 ml.)
1 part fresh lime juice
  (½ oz./15 ml.)
Sugar syrup (1 tsp.)
Angostura bitters (1 tbsp.)
Ginger beer
Cucumber slice
Mint sprig
Lime slice

Pour bitters into chilled collins glass
and swirl around until the inside
of the glass is coated. Discard the
excess. Fill glass with ice cubes
and add gin, brandy, lime juice, and
sugar syrup. Stir well and fill with
ginger beer. Stir gently and garnish
with cucumber slice, lime slice, and
mint sprig.

Sweet Martini

6 parts gin (3 oz./90 ml.)
1 part sweet vermouth
  (½ oz./15 ml.)
Dash orange bitters
Orange twist

Pour all ingredients, except orange
twist, with ice cubes in a mixing
glass. Stir well and strain into
chilled cocktail glass. Garnish with
orange twist.

Tailspin

4 parts gin (2 oz./60 ml.)
3 parts green Chartreuse
  (1½ oz./45 ml.)
3 parts sweet vermouth
  (1½ oz./45 ml.)
Dash orange bitters
Lemon twist
Maraschino cherry

Pour all ingredients, except cherry
and lemon twist, into a mixing glass
with ice cubes. Stir well and strain
into chilled cocktail glass. Garnish
with lemon twist and cherry.

Tango Cocktail

4 parts gin (2 oz./60 ml.)
2 parts dry vermouth (1 oz./30 ml.)
2 parts sweet vermouth
  (1 oz./30 ml.)
1 part Triple Sec (½ oz./15 ml.)

Combine ingredients with cracked
ice in a cocktail shaker. Shake
well and strain into chilled cocktail
glass.

Suffering Bastard

Ten-Gallon Cocktail

2 parts gin (1 oz./30 ml.)
2 parts coffee liqueur (1 oz./30 ml.)
2 parts sweet vermouth
  (1 oz./30 ml.)

Mix all ingredients with cracked ice in blender or cocktail shaker. Pour into chilled old-fashioned glass.

Thanksgiving
Special Cocktail

4 parts gin (2 oz./60 ml.)
3 parts apricot brandy
  (1½ oz./45 ml.)
2 parts dry vermouth (1 oz./30 ml.)
1 part fresh lemon juice
  (½ oz./15 ml.)
Maraschino cherry

Combine all ingredients, except cherry, with cracked ice in a cocktail shaker. Shake well and strain into chilled cocktail glass. Garnish with cherry.

Third Degree
Cocktail

6 parts gin (3 oz./90 ml.)
2 parts dry vermouth (1 oz./30 ml.)
1 part Pernod (½ oz./15 ml.)

Pour ingredients into mixing glass with ice cubes. Stir and strain into chilled cocktail glass.

Three Stripes
Cocktail

4 parts gin (2 oz./60 ml.)
2 parts dry vermouth
  (1 oz./30 ml.)
2 parts fresh orange juice
  (1 oz./30 ml.)

Combine all ingredients with cracked ice in a cocktail shaker and shake well. Strain into chilled cocktail glass.

Ten-Gallon Cocktail

Tidbit

4 parts gin (2 oz./60 ml.)
1 part fino sherry (½ oz./15 ml.)
1 scoop vanilla ice cream

Put all ingredients in a blender and blend until smooth. Pour into chilled highball glass.

Tom Collins

6 parts gin (3 oz./90 ml.)
4 parts fresh lemon juice
  (2 oz./60 ml.)
1 part sugar syrup
  (½ oz./15 ml.)
Sparkling water
Maraschino cherry
Orange slice

Combine all ingredients, except fruit and sparkling water, in a chilled collins glass filled with ice cubes. Fill with sparkling water and stir gently. Garnish with fruit.

Turf Cocktail

4 parts gin (2 oz./60 ml.)
2 parts dry vermouth (1 oz./30 ml.)
1 part Pernod (½ oz./15 ml.)
1 part fresh lemon juice
  (½ oz./15 ml.)
3 dashes Angostura bitters

Combine ingredients with cracked
ice in a cocktail shaker. Shake
well and strain into chilled cocktail
glass.

Tutti-Frutti

6 parts gin (3 oz./90 ml.)
2 parts amaretto (1 oz./30 ml.)
2 parts cherry liqueur (1 oz./30 ml.)
Chopped fresh apples (2 oz./60 ml.)
Chopped fresh pears (2 oz./60 ml.)
Chopped fresh peaches
  (2 oz./60 ml.)

Combine all ingredients in a blender
with cracked ice. Blend until smooth
and pour into chilled highball glass.

NOTE: If you must used canned
fruit, use the kind that is packed in
its own juice with no added sugar.

Tuxedo Cocktail

4 parts gin (2 oz./60 ml.)
3 parts dry vermouth
  (1½ oz./45 ml.)
Maraschino liqueur (½ tsp.)
3 dashes orange bitters
Maraschino cherry

Combine all ingredients, except
cherry, with ice cubes in a mixing
glass. Stir and strain into chilled
cocktail glass. Garnish with cherry.

Twin Six Cocktail

4 parts gin (2 oz./60 ml.)
2 parts sweet vermouth (1 oz./30 ml.)
Dash grenadine
1 egg white (or 1 tbsp. egg white
  substitute)

Combine ingredients with cracked
ice in a cocktail shaker. Shake
vigorously and strain into chilled
cocktail glass.

Ulanda Cocktail

4 parts gin (2 oz./60 ml.)
2 parts Triple Sec (1 oz./30 ml.)
Pernod (1 tsp.)

Combine ingredients with ice cubes
in a mixing glass and stir. Strain
into chilled cocktail glass.

Union Jack

4 parts gin (2 oz./60 ml.)
2 parts sloe gin (1 oz./30 ml.)
Grenadine (1 tsp.)

Combine ingredients with cracked
ice in a cocktail shaker. Shake
well and strain into chilled cocktail
glass.

Union League
Club

4 parts gin (2 oz./60 ml.)
2 parts ruby port (1 oz./30 ml.)
3 – 5 dashes orange bitters
Orange twist

Combine all ingredients, except
orange twist, with cracked ice in
a cocktail shaker. Shake well and
strain into chilled cocktail glass.
Garnish with orange twist.

Valencia Cocktail

4 parts gin (2 oz./60 ml.)
2 parts amontillado sherry
  (1 oz./30 ml.)
Lemon twist

Combine ingredients, except lemon twist, in mixing glass with ice cubes. Stir and strain into chilled cocktail glass. Garnish with lemon twist.

Velvet Kiss

4 parts gin (2 oz./60 ml.)
1 part crème de cassis
  (½ oz./15 ml.)
2 parts pineapple juice
  (1 oz./30 ml.)
2 parts half-and half
  (1 oz./30 ml.)
Dash grenadine

Combine ingredients with cracked ice in a cocktail shaker. Shake well and strain into chilled cocktail glass.

Verona Cocktail

4 parts gin (2 oz./60 ml.)
2 parts amaretto (1 oz./30 ml.)
1 part sweet vermouth
  (½ oz./15 ml.)
Fresh lemon juice (¼ tsp.)
Orange slice

Combine all ingredients, except orange, with cracked ice in a cocktail shaker. Shake well and strain into chilled old-fashioned glass over ice cubes. Garnish with orange slice.

Victor

4 parts gin (2 oz./60 ml.)
2 parts brandy (1 oz./30 ml.)
1 part sweet vermouth
  (½ oz./15 ml.)

Combine ingredients with cracked ice in a cocktail shaker. Shake well and strain into chilled cocktail glass.

Warsaw at Night Cocktail

4 parts berry vodka (2 oz./60 ml.)
2 parts blackberry brandy
  (1 oz./30 ml.)
1 part dry vermouth (½ oz./15 ml.)
Fresh lemon juice (1 tbsp.)

Combine ingredients with cracked ice in a cocktail shaker. Shake well and strain into chilled cocktail glass.

Wedding Belle Cocktail

4 parts gin (2 oz./60 ml.)
3 parts Dubonnet rouge
  (1½ oz./45 ml.)
1 part cherry eau de vie (½ oz./15 ml.)
1 part fresh orange juice
  (½ oz./15 ml.)

Combine ingredients with cracked ice in a cocktail shaker. Shake well and strain into chilled cocktail glass.

Wembly Cocktail

4 parts gin (2 oz./60 ml.)
1 part dry vermouth (½ oz./15 ml.)
Apricot brandy (1 tsp.)
Calvados (1 tsp.)

Combine all ingredients with cracked ice in a cocktail shaker. Shake well and strain into chilled cocktail glass.

White Lily

4 parts gin (2 oz./60 ml.)
3 parts Triple Sec (1½ oz./45 ml.)
3 parts light rum (1½ oz./45 ml.)
Pernod (¼ tsp.)

Combine all ingredients with
cracked ice in a cocktail shaker.
Shake well and strain into chilled
cocktail glass.

White Rose

4 parts gin (2 oz./60 ml.)
2 parts maraschino liqueur
 (1 oz./30 ml.)
4 parts fresh orange juice (2 oz./60 ml.)
2 parts fresh lime juice (1 oz./30 ml.)
Sugar syrup (1 tsp.)
1 egg white (or 1 tbsp. egg white
 substitute)

Combine ingredients with cracked
ice in a cocktail shaker. Shake
well and strain into chilled cocktail
glass.

White Way Cocktail

White Way Cocktail

4 parts gin (2 oz./60 ml.)
2 parts white crème de menthe
 (1 oz./30 ml.)

Combine ingredients with cracked
ice in a cocktail shaker. Shake
well and strain into chilled cocktail
glass.

Why Not?

4 parts gin (2 oz./60 ml.)
2 parts apricot brandy (1 oz./30 ml.)
2 parts dry vermouth (1 oz./30 ml.)
Fresh lemon juice (¼ tsp.)

Combine ingredients with cracked
ice in a cocktail shaker and shake
well. Strain linto chilled cocktail
glass.

Woodstock

4 parts gin (2 oz./60 ml.)
2 part fresh lemon juice
 (1 oz./30 ml.)
Maple syrup (1 tbsp.)
Dash orange bitters

Combine ingredients with cracked
ice in a cocktail shaker. Shake well
and strain linto chilled cocktail
glass.

Xanthia

4 parts gin (2 oz./60 ml.)
3 parts cherry brandy
 (1½ oz./45 ml.)
3 parts yellow Chartreuse
 (1½ oz./45 ml.)

Combine all ingredients with
cracked ice in a cocktail shaker.
Shake well and strain into chilled
cocktail glass.

Yale Cocktail

4 parts gin (2 oz./60 ml.)
1 part dry vermouth (½ oz./15 ml.)
Maraschino liqueur (¼ tsp.)
3 – 5 dashes Angostura bitters

Combine ingredients with cracked ice in a cocktail shaker. Shake well and strain into chilled cocktail glass.

Yellow Fingers

4 parts gin (2 oz./60 ml.)
2 parts blackberry brandy
   (1 oz./30 ml.)
2 parts crème de bananes
   (1 oz./30 ml.)
2 parts half-and-half (1 oz./30 ml.)

Combine all ingredients with cracked ice in a cocktail shaker. Shake well and strain into chilled cocktail glass.

LIQUEURS, WINES, & APERITIFS

Liqueurs, wines, and aperitifs are versatile and work well in cocktails. There are as many kinds of liqueur as there are fruits, herbs, and spices in the world. Most liqueurs are made by macerating the prominent ingredient—oranges, for example—in a neutral spirit, and then distilling it. Unlike flavored vodkas, sweeteners and sometimes coloring are added to liqueurs during distillation. Liqueurs are usually lower in alcohol than most hard liquor, although some may reach 100 proof. They are often served after a meal as a dessert. Aperitifs are served before a meal to stimulate the appetite. Their alcohol content is lower than hard liquor so as not to dull the taste buds before dinner. Some of the better know aperitifs are Campari, vermouth, and Lillet.

Wine and its relatives (port, sherry, Madeira, champagne) are usually served with dinner, or as an alternative to a cocktail. These grape-derived elixirs contribute to some lovely mixed drinks. Sangria is the classic wine cocktail. And, of course, what better way to drink Champagne than in a Bellini or Mimosa?

Adonis

6 parts dry sherry (3 oz./90 ml.)
2 parts sweet vermouth (1 oz./30 ml.)
Dash orange bitters
Orange peel

Mix sherry, vermouth and bitters in cocktail shaker with ice. Strain into chilled sherry glass. Twist orange peel over glass and drop.

Affinity

2 parts dry vermouth (1 oz./30 ml.)
2 parts sweet vermouth
 (1 oz./30 ml.)
2 parts scotch (1 oz./30 ml.)
3 – 6 dashes Angostura bitters

Stir all ingredients together in a mixing glass and strain into chilled cocktail glass.

Alabama Slammer

2 parts amaretto (1 oz./30 ml.)
2 parts Southern Comfort
 (1 oz./30 ml.)
1 part sloe gin (½ oz./15 ml.)
Splash of fresh lemon juice

Stir all ingredients except lemon juice in a highball glass over ice. Add the lemon juice.

Alhambra Royale

3 parts cognac (1½ oz./45 ml.)
Hot chocolate (1 cup)
1 wide slice of orange peel
Whipped cream (optional)

Fill mug nearly to the brim with hot chocolate. Twist the orange peel over the mug and drop in. Warm cognac in a ladle over hot water, ignite, and pour carefully while still flaming, into the mug. Stir. Top with a dollop of whipped cream if you wish.

Amaretto Coffee

1 cup hot coffee (8 oz.)
3 parts amaretto (1½ oz./45 ml.)
Whipped cream (optional)
Ground coriander

Pour amaretto into hot coffee and stir. Top with whipped cream if you like and sprinkle with ground coriander.

Amaretto Mist

4 parts amaretto (2 oz./60 ml.)
Lemon twist

Pack an old-fashioned glass with crushed ice. Pour the amaretto into the glass and garnish with lemon twist.

Amaretto Sour

Amaretto Sour

4 parts amaretto (2 oz./60 ml.)
2 parts fresh lemon juice
 (1 oz./30 ml.)
Orange slice

Shake amaretto and lemon juice well in a cocktail shaker. Strain into chilled sour glass. Garnish with orange slice.

Amaretto Stinger

4 parts amaretto (2 oz./60 ml.)
2 parts white crème de menthe
  (1 oz./30 ml.)

Shake ingredients well in cocktail
shaker. Strain over cracked ice into
chilled cocktail glass.

Amer Picon Cocktail

4 parts Amer Picon (2 oz./60 ml.)
2 parts fresh lime juice
  (1 oz./30 ml.)
Grenadine (1 tsp.)

Pour all ingredients into cocktail
shaker with cracked ice and shake
well. Strain into chilled cocktail
glass.

Americano

3 parts sweet vermouth
  (1½ oz./45 ml.)
3 parts Campari (1½ oz./45 ml.)
Sparkling water
Lemon peel

Pour vermouth and Campari into
a chilled highball glass over ice
cubes. Fill with sparkling water and
stir. Garnish with lemon peel.

Anatole Coffee

1 part cognac (½ oz./15 ml.)
1 part coffee liqueur (½ oz./15 ml.)
1 part Frangelico (½ oz./15 ml.)
12 parts iced coffee (6 oz./180 ml.)
Whipped cream
Chocolate shavings

Mix all ingredients, except whipped
cream and chocolate shavings, with
a little cracked ice in a blender.
Pour into chilled white wine glass.
Top with whipped cream and
sprinkle with chocolate shavings.

Andalusia

4 parts dry sherry (2 oz./60 ml.)
2 parts brandy (1 oz./30 ml.)
2 parts light rum (1 oz./30 ml.)
Angostura bitters (¼ tsp.)

Combine all ingredients in a mixing
glass with ice cubes. Stir well.
Strain into chilled cocktail glass.

Angel's Delight

½ part grenadine (¼ oz./7.5 ml.)
½ part Triple Sec (¼ oz./7.5 ml.)
½ part sloe gin (¼ oz./7.5 ml.)
½ part half-and half (¼ oz./7.5 ml.)

Pour ingredients into glass in order
given, carefully so each floats on
top of the previous one without
mixing.

Angel's Kiss

½ part white crème de cacao
  (¼ oz./7.5 ml.)
½ part brandy (¼ oz./7.5 ml.)
½ part sloe gin (¼ oz./7.5 ml.)
½ part half-and-half (¼ oz./7.5 ml.)

Pour ingredients into glass in order
given, carefully so each floats on
top of the previous one without
mixing.

Bellini

LIQUEURS, WINES, & APERITIFS

Angel's Tit !

½ part white crème de cacao
 (¼ oz./7.5 ml.)
½ part maraschino cherry liqueur
 (¼ oz./7.5 ml.)
½ part half-and-half (¼ oz./7.5 ml.)
Maraschino cherry

Pour ingredients into pony glass in
order given, carefully so each layer
floats on top of the previous one
with mixing. Chill for ½ hour before
serving. Top with cherry.

Annabelle Special

4 parts Benedictine (2 oz./60 ml.)
½ part dry vermouth (¼ oz./7.5 ml.)
½ part fresh lime juice (¼ oz./7.5 ml.)

Stir all ingredients in a mixing glass
with cracked ice. Strain into chilled
cocktail glass.

Appetizer

6 parts red aperitif wine (such as
 Dubonnet) (3 oz./90 ml.)
Juice of 1 orange, freshly squeezed

Mix wine and juice with cracked ice
in a mixing glass. Strain into chilled
cocktail glass.

B-52

1 part coffee liqueur (½ oz./15 ml.)
1 part Irish cream liqueur
 (½ oz./15 ml.)
1 part Grand Marnier (½ oz./15 ml.)

Pour this layered shooter carefully
to keep ingredients separate. In
shot glass, first pour coffee liqueur,
the Irish cream, and then the Grand
Marnier.

Bamboo Cocktail

4 parts dry sherry (2 oz./60 ml.)
1 part dry vermouth (½ oz./15 ml.)
Dash orange bitters

Stir all ingredients with ice cubes in
chilled cocktail glass.

Banshee

4 parts crème de bananes
 (2 oz./60 ml.)
2 parts white crème de cacao
 (1 oz./30 ml.)
1 part half-and-half (1 oz./30 ml.)

Combine all ingredients with
cracked ice in a shaker. Shake well.
Strain into chilled cocktail glass.

Barbarella

4 parts Cointreau (2 oz./60 ml.)
2 parts white Sambuca
 (1 oz./30 ml.)

Combine ingredients in cocktail
shaker with cracked ice and shake
well. Strain into chilled old-
fashioned glass.

Behind Bars

1 part Irish cream (½ oz./15 ml.)
1 part Kahlua (½ oz./15 ml.)
1 part Sambuca (½ oz./15 ml.)

Pour this layered shooter carefully.
In shot glass, pour the Irish cream.
Holding a butter knife against the
inside wall of the glass, pour the
Kahlua along the knife. Do this
again with the Sambuca.

Bellini !

Chilled champagne (Sparkling wine
 is acceptable in a pinch)
4 parts peach nectar (2 oz./60 ml.)
1 part fresh lemon juice
 (½ oz./15 ml.)

Pour the fruit juices into a chilled
champagne flute. Stir well. Add
champagne to the rim. Stir again
gently.

Berry Bomb

2 parts raspberry schnapps
  (1 oz./30 ml.)
1 part vodka (½ oz./15 ml.)
1 part Cointreau orange liqueur
  (½ oz./15 ml.)

In shot glass, pour the raspberry
schnapps first, add vodka, followed
by Cointreau. Serve in a shot glass.

Beverly Hills

4 parts Triple Sec (2 oz./60 ml.)
2 parts cognac (1 oz./30 ml.)
1 part coffee liqueur (½ oz./15 ml.)

Combine all ingredients in cocktail
shaker with cracked ice. Shake well.
Strain into chilled cocktail glass.

Bishop

4 parts fresh orange juice
  (2 oz./60 ml.)
4 parts fresh lemon juice
  (2 oz./60 ml.)
Bar sugar (1 tsp.)
Cabernet Sauvignon or other full-
  bodied red wine
Orange slice
Lemon Slice

Stir juices and sugar together in a
mixing glass. Strain over ice cubes
into chilled highball glass. Fill with
red wine. Stir again and garnish
with citrus slices.

Bittersweet Cocktail

3 parts dry vermouth
  (1½ oz./45 ml.)
3 parts sweet vermouth
  (1½ oz./45 ml.)
3 dashes Angostura bitters
3 dashes orange bitters
Orange twist

Combine all ingredients, except
cracked ice, in a cocktail shaker
and shake well. Strain over ice
cubes into a chilled old-fashioned
glass. Garnish with orange twist.

Black Velvet

Chilled champagne or Sparkling
  wine (½ pint/250 ml.)
Chilled stout or dark porter
  (½ pint/250 ml.)

Slowly pour both ingredients at the
same time into a chilled highball
glass. Do not stir.

Blanche

2 parts Pernod (1 oz./30 ml.)
2 parts Cointreau (1 oz./30 ml.)
1 parts white Curaçao
  (½ oz./15 ml.)

Combine all ingredients in cocktail
shaker with cracked ice and shake
well. Strain into chilled cocktail glass.

Blue Lady

5 parts blue Curaçao (2½ oz./75 ml.)
2 parts white crème de cacao
  (1 oz./30 ml.)
2 parts half-and-half (1 oz./30 ml.)

Combine all ingredients with
cracked ice in a cocktail shaker.
Shake well and strain into chilled
cocktail glass.

Bob Danby

6 parts Dubonnet rouge
  (3 oz./90 ml.)
3 parts brandy (1½ oz./45 ml.)

Stir both ingredients with ice cubes
in a mixing glass. Strain into chilled
cocktail glass.

Bocce Ball

4 parts amaretto (2 oz./60 ml.)
Fresh orange juice
Orange slice

Pour the amaretto and orange juice
into a chilled highball glass with
ice cubes. Stir. Garnish with orange
slice.

Brazil Cocktail

4 parts dry sherry (2 oz./60 ml.)
3 parts dry vermouth
  (1½ oz./45 ml.)
Dash Pernod
Dash Angostura bitters
Lemon twist

Combine all liquid ingredients in
a mixing glass with ice cubes and
stir well. Strain into chilled cocktail
glass and garnish with twist.

Brown Billy

2 parts chocolate liqueur
  (1 oz./30 ml.)
2 parts milk (1 oz./30 ml.)
1 dash amaretto

Pour the milk into a cocktail glass.
Then pour the liqueur on top and
add a dash of amaretto. Do not mix.

Buddha Punch

32 parts Gewürztraminer or Riesling
  wine (2 cups or 16 oz./480 ml.)
16 parts light rum (1 cup or
  8 oz./240 ml.)
16 parts fresh orange juice (1 cup
  or 8 oz./240 ml.)
8 parts fresh lemon juice (½ cup
  or 4 oz./120 ml.)
8 parts Triple Sec (½ cup or
  4 oz./120 ml.)
1 part cherry brandy (½ oz./15 ml.)
1 part sugar syrup (½ oz./15 ml.)
Several dashes bitters
Champagne or sparkling wine
  (1 bottle or 750 ml.)
Lime slices

Pre-chill all ingredients. Pour
everything, except champagne and
lime slices, into chilled punch bowl.
Stir. Just before serving, add the
champagne and a block of ice. Stir
gently and float lime slices on top.
Serves 20.

Burgundy Punch

Red Burgundy or Cabernet
  Sauvignon (2 bottles or 750 ml.)
16 parts cherry brandy (1 cup or
  8 oz./240 ml.)
16 parts port (1 cup or 8 oz./240 ml.)
32 parts fresh orange juice (1 pint
  or 16 oz./480 ml.)
8 parts fresh lemon juice (½ cup or
  4 oz./120 ml.)
2 parts sugar syrup (1 oz./30 ml.)
Orange slices

Pre-chill ingredients. Pour into
chilled punch bowl with a block
of ice. Stir well and garnish with
orange slices. Serves 20.

Cadiz

3 parts dry sherry (1½ oz./45 ml.)
2 parts blackberry brandy
  (1 oz./30 ml.)
1 part Triple Sec (½ oz./15 ml.)
1 part half-and-half (½ oz./15 ml.)

Combine all ingredients in a
cocktail shaker with cracked ice.
Shake well. Strain into chilled old-
fashioned glass.

Café Brulot

16 parts cognac
  (1 cup or 8 oz./240 ml.)
4 parts white Curaçao (2 oz./60 ml.)
64 parts hot black coffee
  (1 qt. or 32 oz./960 ml.)
2 cinnamon sticks
12 whole cloves
Peels of 2 lemons and 2 oranges cut
  into thin strips
4 sugar cubes

In a large punch bowl, mash
together the cinnamon, cloves, fruit
peel and sugar. Stir in the brandy
and Curaçao. Ignite and gradually
add hot coffee, stirring gently until
the flames are extinguished. Serve
in warmed mugs. Serves 6 – 8.

LIQUEURS, WINES, & APERITIFS

Café Diablo

4 parts cognac (2 oz./60 ml.)
2 parts Cointreau (1 oz./30 ml.)
2 parts white Curaçao (1 oz./30 ml.)
32 parts hot black coffee (1 pint or
  16 oz./480 ml.)
2 cinnamon sticks
8 whole cloves
6 coffee beans

Place all ingredients, except coffee,
in chafing dish. Warm the contents
over low, direct heat. Ignite. Add
the coffee and stir until flames
are extinguished. Serve in warmed
mugs. Serves 4.

Café Romano

2 parts white Sambuca (1 oz./30 ml.)
2 parts coffee liqueur (1 oz./30 ml.)
2 parts whole milk (1 oz./30 ml.)

Combine all ingredients in a
cocktail shaker with cracked ice
and shake well. Strain into chilled
cocktail glass.

Caipirinha

4 parts Cachaça (Brazilian sugar
  cane alcohol) or light rum
  (2 oz./60 ml.)
1 part fresh lime juice
  (½ oz./15 ml.)
Granulated sugar (1 tbsp.)
Lime rinds

Combine all ingredients in a
cocktail shaker with cracked ice.
Shake well. Strain into chilled old-
fashioned glass over ice cubes.

Campari-Soda

4 parts Campari (2 oz./60 ml.)
Pellegrino sparkling water
Lime wedge

Fill a highball glass with ice cubes
and pour the Campari into the
glass. Fill with Pellegrino water and
stir gently. Squeeze the lime over
the drink and drop it in.

Caipirinha

Capri

2 parts white crème de cacao
  (1 oz./30 ml.)
2 parts crème de bananes
  (1 oz./30 ml.)
2 parts whole milk (1 oz./30 ml.)

Shake all ingredients with cracked
ice in a cocktail shaker. Strain into
chilled old-fashioned glass over ice
cubes.

Cara Sposa

3 parts coffee liqueur
  (1½ oz./45 ml.)
2 parts Cointreau (1 oz./30 ml.)
2 parts whole milk (1 oz./30 ml.)

Combine all ingredients with
cracked ice in a blender. Blend until
smooth. Pour into chilled cocktail
glass.

Caribbean Champagne

Chilled champagne or Sparkling wine
Light rum (½ tsp.)
Crème de bananes (½ tsp.)
Banana slice

Pour rum and crème de bananes in a chilled champagne flute. Fill with champagne and stir gently. Garnish with banana slice.

Champagne Cocktail

1 sugar cube
Several dashes Angostura bitters
Chilled champagne
Lemon twist

Place sugar cube in bottom of chilled champagne flute. Douse with bitters. Fill with chilled champagne and stir. Garnish with lemon twist.

Champage Cocktail

Champagne Sorbet Punch

Champagne or Sparkling wine
  (2 bottles/750 ml. each)
White dessert wine
  (1 bottle/750 ml.)
Lemon sorbet (1 qt./1 l.)

Combine champagne and wine in a punch bowl with a block of ice. Stir gently. Add a block of ice and scoops of the sorbet. Serves 20 – 25.

Cherry Cooler

4 parts cherry brandy (2 oz./60 ml.)
Cola
Lemon slice

Pour cherry brandy and cola into a chilled highball glass over ice. Stir and garnish with lemon slice.

Cherry Fizz

4 parts cherry brandy (2 oz./60 ml.)
1 part fresh lemon juice
  (½ oz./15 ml.)
Bar sugar (½ tsp.)
Sparkling water
Maraschino cherry

Combine all ingredients, except water and cherry, in a cocktail shaker with cracked ice. Shake well. Strain over ice cubes into a chilled collins glass. Fill with sparkling water and stir gently. Garnish with cherry.

Chocolate Cocktail

6 parts port (3 oz./90 ml.)
1 part yellow chartreuse
  (1 oz./30 ml.)
1 part chocolate vodka
  (1 oz./30 ml.)
Grated semi-sweet chocolate
  (1 tbsp.)

Combine port, chartreuse, and vodka with cracked ice in a blender. Blend until smooth. Pour into chilled cocktail glass and sprinkle with chocolate.

Chocolate Cocktail

Chrysanthemum Cocktail

4 parts dry vermouth (2 oz./60 ml.)
3 parts Benedictine (1½ oz./45 ml.)
Pernod (¼ tsp.)
Orange twist

Combine the vermouth and Benedictine in a mixing glass with cracked ice and stir. Strain into chilled cocktail glass. Add the Pernod and stir. Drop the orange twist into the drink.

Claret Cobbler

8 parts chilled claret or Cabernet
  Sauvignon (4 oz./120 ml.)
Fresh lemon juice (1 tsp.)
Bar sugar (1 tsp.)
4 parts chilled sparkling water
  (2 oz./60 ml.)
Orange slice

In a chilled wine glass, dissolve sugar in lemon juice and water. Add claret and cracked ice. Stir gently and garnish with orange slice.

Claret Cup

32 parts claret or Cabernet
  Sauvignon (16 oz./480 ml.)
4 parts brandy (2 oz./60 ml.)
2 parts Cointreau (1 oz./30 ml.)
Bar sugar (3 tsp.)
16 parts sparkling water
  (8 oz./240 ml.)
Orange slices
Fresh mint sprigs

Stir all ingredients, except orange slices and mint sprigs, in a large pitcher with ice cubes. Garnish with fruit and mint. Serve in red wine glasses. Serves 3 – 4.

Claret Punch

Claret or Cabernet Sauvignon
  (3 bottles/750 ml. each)
32 parts brandy (16 oz./480 ml.)
16 parts Cointreau (8 oz./240 ml.)
Fresh lemon juice (24 oz./720 ml.)
Bar sugar (½ – 1 cup to taste/
  100–200 g.)
Sliced fruits in season

Stir all ingredients, except fruit, in a large punch bowl. Add one block of ice. Decorate with sliced seasonal fruits. Serves 15 – 20.

LIQUEURS, WINES, & APERITIFS

Coffee Cocktail

6 parts ruby port (3 oz./90 ml.)
2 parts brandy (1 oz./30 ml.)
2 – 3 dashes white Curaçao
Bar sugar (½ tsp.)
Freshly grated nutmeg

Combine all ingredients, except nutmeg, in a blender with cracked ice. Blend until smooth. Pour into chilled sour glass and sprinkle with nutmeg.

Coffee Grasshopper

3 parts coffee liqueur
  (1½ oz./45 ml.)
2 parts white crème de menthe
  (1 oz./30 ml.)
2 parts whole milk (1 oz./30 ml.)

Combine all ingredients with cracked ice in a cocktail shaker and shake well. Strain into chilled old-fashioned glass over ice cubes.

Combo

4 parts dry vermouth (2 oz./60 ml.)
Brandy (1 tsp.)
Cointreau (½ tsp.)
Bar sugar (½ tsp.)
Dash Angostura bitters

Shake all ingredients with cracked ice in a cocktail shaker. Strain into chilled old-fashioned glass over ice cubes.

Coney Island Baby

4 parts peppermint schnapps
  (2 oz./60 ml.)
2 parts dark crème de cacao
  (1 oz./30 ml.)
Seltzer

Combine schnapps and crème de cacao in a cocktail shaker with cracked ice. Shake well. Strain over ice cubes into a chilled highball glass. Fill with seltzer and stir gently.

Country Club Cooler

8 parts Lillet blanc (4 oz./120 ml.)
Grenadine (1 tsp.)
Sparkling water
Orange twist

Pour Lillet and grenadine into a chilled collins glass and stir. Add ice cubes and fill with sparkling water. Stir gently and garnish with orange twist.

Creamsicle

2 parts vanilla liqueur (1 oz./30 ml.)
2 parts vanilla vodka (1 oz./30 ml.)
8 parts fresh orange juice
  (4 oz./120 ml.)
4 parts half-and-half (2 oz./60 ml.)
Orange slice

Combine all ingredients, except orange slice, in a cocktail shaker with cracked ice. Shake well and strain over ice cubes into a chilled highball glass. Garnish with orange slice.

Creamsicle

Creamy Orange

2 parts cream sherry (1 oz./30 ml.)
2 parts fresh orange juice
  (1 oz./30 ml.)
1 part brandy (½ oz./15 ml.)
1 part whole milk (½ oz./15 ml.)

Combine all ingredients with
cracked ice in a cocktail shaker.
Shake well and strain into chilled
cocktail glass.

Crème de Menthe Frappe

4 parts green crème de menthe
  (2 oz./60 ml.)
Shaved ice

Fill an old-fashioned glass with
shaved ice. Add crème de menthe
and serve with short straw.

Daniel's Cocktail

4 parts ruby port (2 oz./60 ml.)
4 parts fresh orange juice
  (2 oz./60 ml.)
3 parts fresh lime juice
  (1½ oz./45 ml.)
Grenadine (2 tsp.)

Combine all ingredients with
cracked ice in a cocktail shaker
and shake well. Strain into chilled
cocktail glass.

Depth Charge

4 parts schnapps, flavor of your
  choice (2 oz./60 ml.)
Beer (1 pint or 16 oz./480 ml.)

Pour the schnapps, then the beer,
into a frosted mug.

Devil's Cocktail

4 parts ruby port (2 oz./60 ml.)
2 parts dry vermouth (1 oz./30 ml.)
Lemon juice (½ tsp.)

Stir ingredients with cracked ice in
a mixing glass. Strain into chilled
cocktail glass.

Diablo

4 parts white port (2 oz./60 ml.)
2 parts dry vermouth (1 oz./30 ml.)
Fresh lemon juice (¼ oz./7.5 ml.)
Lemon twist

Combine all ingredients, except
lemon twist, in a cocktail shaker
with cracked ice. Shake well and
strain onto chilled cocktail glass.
Garnish with lemon twist.

Diana

4 parts white crème de menthe
  (2 oz./60 ml.)
1 part cognac (½ oz./15 ml.)
Crushed ice

Pour the crème de menthe into a
snifter filled with crushed ice. Float
cognac on top.

Diplomat

4 parts dry vermouth (2 oz./60 ml.)
1 part sweet vermouth
  (½ oz./15 ml.)
Maraschino liqueur (½ tsp.)
3 dashes Angostura bitters
Lemon slice
Maraschino cherry

Combine liquid ingredients in a
mixing glass with cracked ice and
stir well. Strain into chilled cocktail
glass and garnish with fruit.

Dubonnet Fizz

4 parts Dubonnet rouge
 (2 oz./60 ml.)
2 parts cherry Heering (1 oz./30 ml.)
2 parts fresh orange juice
 (1 oz./30 ml.)
1 part fresh lemon juice
 (½ oz./15 ml.)
Sparkling water
Lemon slice

Combine all ingredients, except
sparkling water and lemon slice,
in a cocktail shaker with cracked
ice. Shake well. Strain into chilled
highball glass over ice cubes. Fill
with sparkling water and stir gently.
Garnish with lemon slice.

Duchess

4 parts Pernod (2 oz./60 ml.)
1 part dry vermouth (½ oz./15 ml.)
1 part sweet vermouth
 (½ oz./15 ml.)

Shake all ingredients with cracked
ice in a cocktail shaker. Strain into
chilled cocktail glass.

Ferrari

4 parts dry vermouth (2 oz./60 ml.)
2 parts amaretto (1 oz./30 ml.)
Dash orange bitters
Lemon twist

Combine all ingredients, except
lemon, in a cocktail shaker with
cracked ice. Shake well and strain
over ice cubes into a chilled old-
fashioned glass. Garnish with lemon
twist.

Fifth Avenue

3 parts dark crème de cacao
 (1½ oz./45 ml.)
3 parts apricot brandy
 (1½ oz./45 ml.)
1½ parts half-and-half
 (¾ oz./22.5 ml.)

Layer ingredients in the order given
into a pousse-café glass.

Flaming Angel

1 part shot Kahlua (½ oz./15 ml.)
1 part shot milk (½ oz./15 ml.)
1 part shot 150 proof rum
 (½ oz./15 ml.)

In a shot glass, pour the Kahlua,
then layer the milk on top, and end
with the rum. Light the rum and let
it burn briefly. Blow out and shoot.

Friar Tuck

4 parts Frangelico (2 oz./60 ml.)
4 parts fresh lemon (2 oz./60 ml.)
Grenadine (1 tsp.)
Orange slice

Combine all ingredients in a blender
with cracked ice. Blend until smooth
and pour into chilled old-fashioned
glass. Garnish with orange slice.

General Harrison's
Egg Nog

1 egg (or 2 tbsp. egg substitute)
Bar sugar (1 tsp.)
Dry red wine
Freshly ground nutmeg

Combine egg and sugar in a
cocktail shaker with cracked ice.
Shake vigorously. Strain into chilled
highball glass and fill with red wine.
Stir and sprinkle nutmeg on top.

NOTE: You may substitute hard
cider for wine.

Glad Eyes

4 parts Pernod (2 oz./60 ml.)
2 parts peppermint schnapps
 (1 oz./30 ml.)

Combine ingredients with cracked
ice in a mixing glass and stir well.
Strain into chilled cocktail glass.

Glogg

Dry red wine
  (2 bottles/50 ml. each)
Brandy (1 bottle/750 ml.)
Aquavit or plain vodka
  (1 pint or 16 oz./480 ml.)
25 whole cloves
20 crushed cardamom seeds
4 cinnamon sticks
Dried orange peel (2 oz./40 g.)
Blanched almonds (2 cups/350 g.)
Raisins (2 cups/350 g.)
Sugar cubes (1 pound or
  16 oz./400 g.)

Put all ingredients, except sugar
and aquavit, in a large kettle and
bring to a boil. Turn down heat
immediately and simmer for 15 – 20
minutes, stirring occasionally. Place
a rack or mesh strainer over the
kettle and spread the sugar cubes
over it. Saturate the sugar with the
aquavit or vodka. Ignite and let the
sugar melt into the glogg. Stir again.
Serve hot in heated mugs.
Serves 10.

Gluhwein

12 parts dry red wine
  (6 oz./180 ml.)
Lemon peel
Orange peel
1 cinnamon stick, broken in pieces
5 whole cloves
Pinch freshly ground nutmeg
Honey (1 tsp.)

Combine all ingredients in a
saucepan and stir until honey is
dissolved. Do not boil. Serve in a
heated mug.

Godchild

3 parts amaretto (1½ oz./45 ml.)
2 parts vanilla vodka (1 oz./30 ml.)
2 parts half-and-half (1 oz./30 ml.)

Combine all ingredients with
cracked ice in a blender and blend
until smooth. Serve in chilled
champagne flute.

Grasshopper

Grand Apple

4 parts Calvados (2 oz./60 ml.)
2 parts cognac (1 oz./30 ml.)
2 parts Grand Marnier (1 oz./30 ml.)

Combine ingredients in a mixing
glass with cracked ice. Stir well.
Strain over ice cubes into a chilled
old-fashioned glass.

Grasshopper

4 parts green crème de menthe
 (2 oz./60 ml.)
4 parts white crème de cacao
 (2 oz./60 ml.)
4 parts half-and-half (2 oz./60 ml.)

Combine all ingredients with cracked ice in a cocktail shaker and shake well. Strain into chilled cocktail glass.

Green Room

4 parts dry vermouth (2 oz./60 ml.)
2 parts brandy (1 oz./30 ml.)
Several dashes Triple Sec
Orange twist

Stir all ingredients, except orange twist, in a mixing glass with cracked ice. Strain into chilled cocktail glass and garnish with orange twist.

Hammerhead

4 parts amaretto (2 oz./60 ml.)
4 parts white Curaçao (2 oz./60 ml.)
4 parts gold rum (2 oz./60 ml.)
Dash Southern Comfort

Combine all ingredients with cracked ice in a cocktail shaker and shake well. Strain into chilled cocktail glass.

Heavenly Days

4 parts chocolate vodka
 (2 oz./60 ml.)
4 parts hazelnut syrup (2 oz./60 ml.)
4 parts fresh lemon juice
 (2 oz./60 ml.)
Grenadine (1 tsp.)
Sparkling water
Orange slice

Combine all ingredients, except orange slice and water, in a cocktail shaker with cracked ice. Shake well and pour over ice into a chilled highball glass. Fill with sparkling water and stir gently. Garnish with orange slice.

Hot Toddy

6 parts chosen liquor (3 oz./90 ml.)
2 parts honey or sugar syrup
 (1 oz./30 ml.)
2 parts fresh lemon juice
 (1 oz./30 ml.)
5 whole cloves
Ground cinnamon to taste
Lemon slice
Boiling water or hot tea
Freshly grated nutmeg
Cinnamon stick

Add all ingredients, except nutmeg, boiling water and cinnamon stick, to a warmed coffee mug. Fill with boiling water and stir. Garnish with cinnamon stick and nutmeg.

Hotel Plaza Cocktail

2 parts dry vermouth (1 oz./30 ml.)
2 parts sweet vermouth
 (1 oz./30 ml.)
2 parts gin (1 oz./30 ml.)
Maraschino cherry

Stir liquid ingredients with ice cubes in a mixing glass. Strain into chilled cocktail glass and garnish with cherry.

Hot Toddy

Kir Royale

Jade

Blue Curaçao (¼ tsp.)
Melon liqueur (¼ tsp.)
Fresh lime juice (¼ tsp.)
Dash Angostura bitters
Champagne or sparkling wine
Lime slice

Combine all ingredients, except champagne and lime slice, in a cocktail shaker with cracked ice. Shake well and strain into champagne flute. Fill with champagne and garnish with lime slice.

Jamaica Hop

4 parts coffee liqueur (2 oz./60 ml.)
2 parts white crème de cacao (1 oz./30 ml.)
4 parts half-and-half (2 oz./60 ml.)

Combine ingredients with cracked ice in a cocktail shaker. Shake well and strain into chilled cocktail glass.

Irish Dream

3 parts Irish cream liqueur (1½ oz./45 ml.)
1 pinch granulated sugar

Heat the Irish cream in a microwave oven (approx. 20 seconds on high). Rim shot glasses with sugar and pour Irish cream into shot glasses. Serve immediately.

Jamaican Coffee

4 parts coffee liqueur (2 oz./60 ml.)
3 parts light rum (1½ oz./45 ml.)
Hot black coffee
Whipped cream
Freshly ground allspice

Pour rum and liqueur into a mug of hot coffee. Stir. Top with whipped cream and sprinkle with ground allspice.

Ixtapa

4 parts coffee liqueur (2 oz./60 ml.)
2 parts silver tequila (1 oz./30 ml.)

Stir ingredients with cracked ice in a mixing glass and pour into chilled cocktail glass.

Kir

4 parts crème de cassis (2 oz./60 ml.)
White wine
Lemon twist

Pour cassis over ice cubes in a chilled wine glass. Fill with white wine and stir well. Garnish with lemon twist.

Kir Royale

4 parts crème de cassis
 (2 oz./60 ml.)
Champagne

Stir the cassis with cracked ice in a
mixing glass. Pour into chilled wine
glass and fill with cold champagne.
Stir gently.

Kirsch Rickey

4 parts kirshwasser (2 oz./60 ml.)
Fresh lime juice (1 tbsp.)
Sparkling water
2 pitted black cherries

Pour kirshwasser and lime juice
into a chilled highball glass filled
with ice cubes. Fill with sparking
water and stir gently. Garnish with
cherries.

Kiss Me Quick

4 parts Pernod (2 oz./60 ml.)
White Curaçao (½ tsp.)
3 – 5 dashes Angostura bitters
Sparkling water

Combine all ingredients, except
water, with cracked ice in a cocktail
shaker. Shake well and pour into
chilled highball glass. Fill with
sparkling water and stir gently.

Knockout Cocktail

4 parts dry vermouth (2 oz./60 ml.)
3 parts gin (1½ oz./45 ml.)
2 parts Pernod (1 oz./30 ml.)
White crème de menthe (2 tsp.)
Maraschino cherry

Combine liquid ingredients with
ice cubes in a mixing glass and
stir well. Strain into chilled cocktail
glass and garnish with cherry.

Liebfraumilch

4 parts white crème de cacao
 (2 oz./60 ml.)
4 parts half-and-half (2 oz./60 ml.)
4 parts fresh lime juice
 (2 oz./60 ml.)

Combine all ingredients with
cracked ice in a cocktail shaker.
Shake well and strain into chilled
cocktail glass.

Locomotive Light

12 parts dry red wine
 (6 oz./180 ml.)
1 part maraschino liqueur
 (½ oz./15 ml.)
1 part Triple Sec (½ oz./15 ml.)
1 part honey (½ oz./15 ml.)
Lemon slice
Ground cinnamon

Combine wine, liqueurs, and honey
in a saucepan. Stir until honey is
dissolved. Turn on burner and warm
until hot, stirring often. Do not boil.
Simmer and stir for about 1 minute.
Pour into heated coffee mug and
garnish with cinnamon and lemon
slice.

Kirsch Rickey

Lollipop

2 parts green Chartreuse
(1 oz./30 ml.)
2 parts cherry brandy (1 oz./30 ml.)
2 parts Triple Sec (1 oz./30 ml.)
Maraschino liqueur (1 tsp.)

Combine all ingredients with
cracked ice in a cocktail shaker.
Shake well and strain into chilled
cocktail glass.

London Dock

6 parts dry red wine (3 oz./90 ml.)
4 parts dark rum (2 oz./60 ml.)
2 parts honey (1 oz./30 ml.)
Lemon peel
Cinnamon stick
Freshly grated nutmeg
Boiling water

Dissolve honey with a little boiling
water in the bottom of a heated
coffee mug. Add remaining
ingredients, except cinnamon and
nutmeg, and fill with boiling water.
Use cinnamon stick to stir and
sprinkle with nutmeg.

London Fog

2 parts white crème de menthe
(1 oz./30 ml.)
2 parts Pernod (1 oz./30 ml.)
1 scoop vanilla ice cream

Combine ingredients with cracked
ice in a blender. Blend for a few
seconds at medium speed. Pour
into chilled pousse-café glass.

Manhattan Cooler

8 parts dry red wine
(½ cup or 4 oz./120 ml.)
4 parts fresh lemon juice
(2 oz./60 ml.)
Gold rum (¼ tsp.)
Sugar syrup (1 tbsp.)

Combine all ingredients in mixing
glass with cracked ice. Stir well and
strain into chilled highball glass
over ice cubes.

Mary Garden Cocktail

4 parts Dubonnet rouge (2 oz./60 ml.)
2 parts dry vermouth (1 oz./30 ml.)

Combine ingredients with cracked
ice in cocktail shaker and shake well.
Strain into chilled cocktail glass.

Merry Widow Fizz

4 parts Dubonnet rouge
(2 oz./60 ml.)
4 parts fresh orange juice
(2 oz./60 ml.)
2 parts fresh lemon juice (1 oz./30 ml.)
1 egg white (or 1 tbsp. egg white
substitute)
Sparkling water

Combine all ingredients, except egg
white, with cracked ice in a cocktail
shaker. Shake vigorously and strain
over ice cubes into a chilled collins
glass. Fill with sparkling water and
stir gently.

Mimosa

Chilled champagne or sparkling wine
Fresh orange juice

Half fill a chilled champagne flute
with orange juice. Add champagne
to the top and stir gently.

Mimosa

Mint Tulip

2 parts white crème de menthe
  (1 oz./30 ml.)
1 part vodka (½ oz./15 ml.)
1 mint leaf

Lay mint leaf in the bottom of the
shot glass. Add vodka first and let
sit for several minutes to absorb
mint. Fill with the crème de menthe
and serve.

Mocha Mint

3 parts coffee liqueur
  (1½ oz./45 ml.)
3 parts white crème de cacao
  (1½ oz./45 ml.)
3 parts white crème de menthe
  (1½ oz./45 ml.)

Combine ingredients with cracked
ice in a cocktail shaker. Shake
well and strain into chilled cocktail
glass.

Mulled Wine

12 parts dry red wine
  (6 oz./180 ml.)
2 parts ruby port (1 oz./30 ml.)
2 parts brandy (1 oz./30 ml.)
Cinnamon stick
Freshly grated nutmeg (to taste)
3 whole cloves
Lemon twist

Combine all ingredients in a sauce
pan. Warm over medium heat (do
not boil) and pour into heated
coffee mug.

Negus Punch

Ruby port (1 bottle - 750 ml.)
Zest of one whole lemon
8 sugar cubes
2 cinnamon sticks
1 whole nutmeg, crushed
7 whole cloves
Ground allspice (½ tsp.)
1 part fresh lemon juice
  (½ oz./15 ml.)
Boiling water

Put lemon zest and sugar cubes in
a large warmed pitcher. Add enough
water to dissolve sugar. Add spices,
lemon juice and wine. Stir well and
add two cups of boiling water right
before serving. Serves 10 – 12.

Nineteen

6 parts dry vermouth (3 oz./90 ml.)
1 part gin (½ oz./15 ml.)
1 part cherry eau de vie
  (½ oz./15 ml.)
Pernod (¼ tsp.)
Sugar syrup (¼ tsp.)

Combine all ingredients with
cracked ice in a cocktail shaker.
Shake well and strain into chilled
cocktail glass.

Nineteen Pick-Me-Up

4 parts Pernod (2 oz./60 ml.)
2 parts gin (1 oz./30 ml.)
Sugar syrup (¼ tsp.)
3 – 5 dashes Angostura bitters
3 – 5 dashes orange bitters
Sparkling water

Combine all ingredients, except
sparkling water, with cracked ice in
a cocktail shaker. Shake well and
strain over ice cubes into chilled
highball glass. Fill with sparkling
water and stir gently.

Nutcracker

4 parts crème de noisette
   (2 oz./60 ml.)
4 parts amaretto (2 oz./60 ml.)
4 parts half-and-half (2 oz./60 ml.)

Combine all ingredients with
cracked ice in a cocktail shaker.
Shake well and strain into chilled
cocktail glass.

Peppermint Patty

Nutty Colada

6 part amaretto (3 oz./90 ml.)
2 parts gold rum (1 oz./30 ml.)
2 parts coconut milk (1 oz./30 ml.)
Coconut syrup (1 tbsp.)
4 parts pineapple juice
   (2 oz./60 ml.)
Crème de noyaux (¼ tsp.)
Pineapple spear

Combine all ingredients, except
pineapple spear, with cracked ice in
a blender. Blend until slushy. Pour
into chilled collins glass and garnish
with pineapple spear.

Orange and Black

1 part chocolate liqueur
   (½ oz./15 ml.)
1 part triple sec (½ oz./15 ml.)

Pour both ingredients in a shot
glass. Stir lightly, and serve.

Ostend Fizz

4 parts kirshwasser (2 oz./60 ml.)
2 parts crème de cassis
   (1 oz./30 ml.)
2 parts fresh lemon juice
   (1 oz./30 ml.)
Sparkling water
Lemon slice

Combine all ingredients, except
water and lemon slice, with cracked
ice in a cocktail shaker. Shake well
and pour into chilled collins glass
over ice cubes. Fill with sparkling
water and stir gently. Garnish with
lemon slice.

Pacific Pacifier

3 parts Cointreau (1½ oz./45 ml.)
2 parts crème de bananes
   (1 oz./30 ml.)
2 parts half-and-half (1 oz./30 ml.)

Combine all ingredients with
cracked ice in a cocktail shaker.
Shake well and strain into chilled
old-fashioned glass over ice cubes.

LIQUEURS, WINES, & APERITIFS

Pernod Cocktail

Pantomime

6 parts dry vermouth (3 oz./90 ml.)
3 – 5 dashes grenadine
3 – 5 dashes Orgeat (almond) syrup
1 egg white (or 1 tbsp. egg white substitute)

Combine ingredients in a blender with cracked ice. Blend until smooth and strain into chilled cocktail glass.

Paradox

3 parts Irish cream (1½ oz./45 ml.)
3 parts lime juice (1½ oz./45 ml.)

Hold one shot of Irish cream in your mouth, and take one shot of lime juice. Mix the blend in your mouth for full experience.

Peach Hobbler

4 parts peach schnapps
  (2 oz./60 ml.)
2 parts lime juice (1 oz./30 ml.)

Mix ingredients over ice in a cocktail shaker and strain into shot glass.

Peaches and Cream

4 parts peach liqueur (2 oz./60 ml.)
4 parts half-and-half (2 oz./60 ml.)

Combine ingredients with cracked ice in a cocktail shaker. Shake well and strain into chilled old-fashioned glass over ice cubes.

Peachy Melba

6 parts strawberry vodka
  (3 oz./90 ml.)
6 parts peach nectar (3 oz./90 ml.)
1 part grenadine (½ oz./15 ml.)
1 parts fresh lemon juice
  (½ oz./15 ml.)
1 part fresh lime juice
  (½ oz./15 ml.)
Peach slice

Combine all ingredients, except peach slice, with cracked ice in a cocktail shaker. Shake well and pour into chilled old-fashioned glass. Garnish with peach.

Peppermint Patty

4 parts white crème de cacao
  (2 oz./60 ml.)
4 parts white crème de menthe
  (2 oz./60 ml.)
2 parts half-and-half (1 oz./30 ml.)

Combine all ingredients with cracked ice in a cocktail shaker and shake well. Pour into chilled old-fashioned glass.

Pernod Cocktail

4 part Pernod (2 oz./60 ml.)
1 part water (½ oz./15 ml.)
Sugar syrup (¼ tsp.)
3 – 5 dashes Angostura bitters

Fill an old-fashioned glass with crushed ice, sugar syrup, bitters and water. Stir well and add Pernod. Stir again.

Pernod Frappe

6 parts Pernod (3 oz./90 ml.)
1 part anisette (½ oz./15 ml.)
2 parts half-and-half (1 oz./30 ml.)
1 egg white (or 1 tbsp. egg white
  substitute)

Combine ingredients with cracked
ice in a cocktail shaker. Shake
vigorously and strain into chilled
wine glass.

Phoebe Snow

4 parts Dubonnet rouge (2 oz./60 ml.)
4 parts Pernod (2 oz./60 ml.)

Combine all ingredients with
cracked ice in a cocktail shaker.
Shake well and strain into chilled
cocktail glass.

Picon

4 parts Amer Picon (2 oz./60 ml.)
4 parts sweet vermouth
  (2 oz./60 ml.)

Combine ingredients with cracked
ice in a cocktail shaker. Shake
well and strain into chilled cocktail
glass.

Picon Fizz

4 parts Amer Picon (2 oz./60 ml.)
1 part grenadine (½ oz./15 ml.)
1 part brandy (½ oz./15 ml.)
Sparkling water

Pour Amer Picon and grenadine
into a chilled highball glass over
ice cubes and stir well. Fill with
sparkling water and stir gently. Float
brandy on top.

Pimm's Cup

4 parts Pimm's Cup No. 1
  (2 oz./60 ml.)
Cointreau (1 tsp.)
4 parts fresh lime juice (2 oz./60 ml.)
Sugar syrup (1 tsp.)
Lemon-lime soda
2 thin cucumber slices
Fresh mint sprig
Lime slice

Combine sugar syrup and lime juice
in a chilled collins glass. Fill with ice
cubes. Add Pimm's and Cointreau.
Fill with lemon-lime soda and stir
gently. Garnish with cucumber, mint
and lime slice.

Pink Squirrel

2 parts dark crème de cacao
  (1 oz./30 ml.)
2 parts crème de noyaux
  (1 oz./30 ml.)
2 parts half-and-half (1 oz./30 ml.)

Combine all ingredients with
cracked ice in a cocktail shaker.
Shake well and strain into chilled
cocktail glass.

Phoebe Snow

Plaza Cocktail

2 parts dry vermouth (1 oz./30 ml.)
2 parts sweet vermouth
 (1 oz./30 ml.)
2 parts gin (1 oz./30 ml.)

Combine all ingredients with ice cubes in a mixing glass and stir. Strain into chilled cocktail glass.

Port Milk Punch

6 parts ruby port (3 oz./90 ml.)
16 parts milk (1 cup or 8 oz.)
Sugar syrup (1 tsp.)
Freshly grated nutmeg

Combine all ingredients, except nutmeg, with cracked ice in a cocktail shaker. Shake well and strain into chilled collins glass. Sprinkle with nutmeg.

Pimm's Cup

Port Wine Cobbler

6 parts ruby port (3 oz./90 ml.)
Bar sugar (1 tsp.)
4 parts sparkling water
 (2 oz./60 ml.)
Orange slice
Maraschino cherry

Dissolve sugar in sparkling water in the bottom of a chilled red wine glass. Fill with shaved ice and add port. Stir and garnish with fruit.

Port Wine Cocktail

6 parts ruby port (3 oz./90 ml.)
Brandy (1 tsp.)

Stir ingredients with ice cubes in a mixing glass. Strain into chilled cocktail glass.

Port Wine Sangaree

6 parts ruby port (3 oz./90 ml.)
Brandy (1 tbsp.)
Bar sugar (½ tsp.)
Water (1 tsp.)
Sparkling water

Dissolve sugar in water in the bottom of a chilled highball glass. Add the port and fill glass with ice cubes. Fill with sparkling water almost to the top. Stir gently and float brandy on top.

Pousse-Café

1 part grenadine (½ oz./15 ml.)
1 part white crème de cacao
 (½ oz./15 ml.)
1 part maraschino liqueur
 (½ oz./15 ml.)
1 part white Curaçao (½ oz./15 ml.)
1 part green crème de menthe
 (½ oz./15 ml.)
1 part brandy (½ oz./15 ml.)

Pour ingredients in the order given, slowly and carefully into a pousse-café glass so each ingredient forms a separate layer.

Pousse L'Amour

1 part maraschino liqueur
  (½ oz./15 ml.)
1 egg yolk
1 part Benedictine (½ oz./15 ml.)
1 part cognac (½ oz./15 ml.)

Pour ingredients, in the order given,
slowly and carefully into a pousse-
café glass so each ingredient forms
a separate layer.

Queen Elizabeth Wine

4 parts Benedictine (2 oz./60 ml.)
2 parts dry vermouth (1 oz./30 ml.)
2 parts fresh lemon juice (1 oz./30 ml.)
Lemon twist

Combine all ingredients, except
lemon twist, with ice cubes in a
mixing glass. Stir well and strain
into chilled cocktail glass. Garnish
with lemon twist.

Red Apple Dusk

4 parts Calvados (2 oz./60 ml.)
4 parts apple juice (2 oz./60 ml.)
4 parts grapefruit juice
  (2 oz./60 ml.)
Grenadine (3 – 5 dashes)

Combine all ingredients with
cracked ice in a cocktail shaker.
Shake well and strain into chilled
cocktail glass.

Reform Cocktail

4 parts fino sherry (2 oz./60 ml.)
2 parts sweet vermouth (1 oz./30 ml.)
3 – 5 dashes Angostura bitters

Combine ingredients with ice cubes
in a mixing glass. Stir well and
strain into chilled cocktail glass.

Regent's Punch

Sweet white wine (Riesling,
  Sauterne, etc.) (1 bottle/750 ml.)
Madeira (2 bottles/750 ml. each)
Triple Sec (1 bottle/750 ml.)
Cognac (1 bottle/750 ml.)
Champagne or sparkling wine
  (3 bottles/750 ml. each)
Dark rum (1 pint or 16 oz./480 ml.)
Strong black iced tea (1 pint or
  16 oz./480 ml.)
Fresh lemon juice (1 cup or
  8 oz./240 ml.)
Orange juice (3 cups or 24 oz./
  750 ml.)
Bar sugar (¼ cup/50 g.)
Sparkling water (2 qt. or 2 l.)

Chill ingredients for at least two
hours. Pour all ingredients, except
champagne and sparkling water,
into a very large punch bowl and
stir. Add one cake of ice. Before
serving, add champagne and
sparkling water. Stir gently.
Serves 80.

Roman Snowball

6 parts white Sambuca
  (3 oz./90 ml.)
5 coffee beans

Pour Sambuca into a champagne
flute half-filled with crushed ice.
Add coffee beans and serve with
a straw. Chew the beans after they
have been steeping for a while.

LIQUEURS, WINES, & APERITIFS

Rose

4 parts dry vermouth (2 oz./60 ml.)
2 parts cherry brandy or eau de vie
 (1 oz./30 ml.)
1 tsp. raspberry syrup
Fresh raspberries
Fresh mint spring

Combine all liquid ingredients
in a cocktail mixer and stir. Pour
over cracked iced into a highball
glass and garnish with mint and
raspberries.

Rosy Fingered Dawn

2 parts Punta e Mes
2 parts fresh lemon juice
 (1 oz./30 ml.)
2 parts fresh lime juice
 (1 oz./30 ml.)
4 parts fresh orange juice
 (2 oz./60 ml.)
1 part coconut cream (½ oz./15 ml.)
Grenadine (1 tsp.)
Orgeat (almond) syrup (1 tsp.)

Combine all ingredients with
cracked ice in a blender and blend
until smooth. Pour into a chilled
cocktail glass.

Rumstufian

16 parts ale (1 cup or 8 oz./240 ml.)
4 parts gin (2 oz./60 ml.)
4 parts fino sherry (2 oz./60 ml.)
Sugar (1 tsp.)
2 egg yolks
Lemon twist
Cinnamon stick
5 whole cloves
Dash allspice
Freshly grated nutmeg

Beat eggs and sugar in a bowl.
Set aside. In a saucepan, combine
all remaining ingredients, except
nutmeg, and heat until almost at
a boil. Add egg mixture, stirring
constantly with a wire whisk for
about 45 seconds. Serve in heated
mug and sprinkle with nutmeg.

Russian Coffee

4 parts coffee liqueur (2 oz./60 ml.)
2 parts vanilla vodka (1 oz./30 ml.)
3 parts half-and-half
 (1½ oz./45 ml.)

Combine all ingredients in a blender
with cracked ice. Blend until
smooth and pour into chilled brandy
snifter.

Sally's Summer Cooler

6 parts peppermint schnapps
 (3 oz./90 ml.)
2 parts fresh lime juice (1 oz./30 ml.)
Sparkling water
Lime slice

Pour schnapps and lime juice into
chilled collins glass with ice cubes.
Fill with sparkling water and stir
gently. Garnish with lime slice.

San Francisco Cocktail

3 parts dry vermouth
 (1½ oz./45 ml.)
3 parts sweet vermouth
 (1½ oz./45 ml.)
3 parts sloe gin (1½ oz./45 ml.)
3 – 5 dashes Angostura bitters
3 – 5 dashes orange bitters
Maraschino cherry

Combine all ingredients, except
cherry, with cracked ice in a
cocktail shaker. Shake well and
strain into chilled cocktail glass.

Sanctuary

4 parts Dubonnet rouge (2 oz./60 ml.)
2 parts Amer Picon (1 oz./30 ml.)
2 parts Triple Sec (1 oz./30 ml.)
Lemon twist

Combine all ingredients, except lemon twist, with cracked ice in a cocktail shaker and shake well. Strain into chilled cocktail glass and garnish with lemon twist.

Sangria

Dry red wine (2 bottles - 750 ml. each)
8 parts Triple Sec (4 oz./120 ml.)
6 parts brandy (3 oz./90 ml.)
6 parts fresh orange juice
   (3 oz./90 ml.)
4 parts fresh lemon juice
   (2 oz./60 ml.)
4 parts fresh lime juice
   (2 oz./60 ml.)
Sugar syrup (½ cup or 4 oz./
   120 ml.)
Lemon slices
Lime slices
Orange slices

Chill all ingredients for at least one hour. Pour into punch bowl and stir. Add a large cake of ice and float fruit slices on top. Serves 20.

Savoy Hotel

1½ parts dark crème de cacao
   (¾ oz./22.5 ml.)
1½ parts Benedictine
   (¾ oz./22.5 ml.)
1½ part cognac (¾ oz./22.5 ml.)

Pour ingredients, in order given, slowly and carefully into a chilled pousse-café glass so that each ingredient forms a separate layer.

Shandy Gaff

Beer
Ginger ale

Pour equal parts simultaneously into a chilled collins glass.

Sherry Cobbler

8 parts Amontillado sherry (½ cup
   or 4 oz./120 ml.)
White Curaçao (¼ tsp.)
Sugar syrup (¼ tsp.)
Lemon twist
Pineapple spear

Fill a wine glass with crushed ice and add the Curaçao and syrup. Stir well until a frost appears on the glass. Add the sherry and stir again. Garnish with lemon twist and pineapple spear.

Sherry Cocktail

6 parts Amontillado sherry
   (3 oz./90 ml.)
3 dashes Angostura bitters
Orange twist

Stir ingredients with ice cubes in a mixing glass. Strain into chilled cocktail glass and garnish with orange twist.

Sherry Eggnog

6 parts cream sherry (3 oz./90 ml.)
Bar sugar (½ tsp.)
1 whole egg or 2 tbsp. egg
   substitute
Milk
Freshly grated nutmeg

Combine all ingredients, except milk and nutmeg, with cracked ice in a cocktail shaker. Shake vigorously. Strain into chilled collins glass, fill with milk and stir well. Sprinkle nutmeg on top.

Sangria

Sloshed Shirley Temple

4 parts cream sherry (2 oz./60 ml.)
2 parts fresh lemon juice
  (1 oz./30 ml.)
1 part sugar syrup (½ oz./15 ml.)
1 part grenadine (½ oz./15 ml.)
Ginger ale
Maraschino cherry
Orange slice

Combine all ingredients, except fruit and ginger ale, with cracked ice in a cocktail shaker. Shake well and strain into chilled old-fashioned glass over ice cubes. Fill with ginger ale and stir gently. Garnish with fruit.

Sherry Sangaree

4 parts fino sherry (2 oz./60 ml.)
Ruby port (1 tbsp.)
Bar sugar (½ tsp.)
Water (1 tsp.)
2 parts sparkling water
  (1 oz./30 ml.)

In the bottom of a chilled old-fashioned glass, dissolve sugar in water, add sherry and stir. Fill glass with ice cubes and sparkling water. Float port on top.

Slippery Nipple

4 parts white Sambuca
  (2 oz./60 ml.)
2 parts Irish cream liqueur
  (1 oz./30 ml.)
Dash grenadine

Pour Sambuca into chilled cocktail glass. Float Irish cream on top and drop grenadine on top in the center of the drink.

Sherry Twist

4 parts cream sherry (2 oz./60 ml.)
2 parts brandy (1 oz./30 ml.)
1 part dry vermouth (½ oz./15 ml.)
1 part white Curaçao (½ oz./15 ml.)
Fresh lemon juice (1 tsp.)
Orange twist

Combine all ingredients, except orange twist, with cracked ice in a cocktail shaker. Shake well and strain into chilled cocktail glass. Garnish with orange twist.

Sloe Vermouth

4 parts dry vermouth (2 oz./60 ml.)
2 parts sloe gin (1 oz./30 ml.)
1 part fresh lemon juice
  (½ oz./15 ml.)

Combine all ingredients with cracked ice in a cocktail shaker. Shake well and strain into chilled cocktail glass.

Smiler Cocktail

2 parts dry vermouth (1 oz./30 ml.)
2 parts sweet vermouth
 (1 oz./30 ml.)
2 parts gin (1 oz./30 ml.)
Dash Angostura bitters
Fresh orange juice (½ tsp.)

Combine all ingredients with
cracked ice in a cocktail shaker.
Shake well and strain into chilled
cocktail glass.

Sombrero

4 parts coffee liqueur (2 oz./60 ml.)
2 parts half-and-half (1 oz./30 ml.)

Pour liqueur into chilled old-
fashioned glass over ice cubes.
Float half-and-half on top.

Sombrero

Soyer au Champagne

Cognac (¼ tsp.)
Maraschino liqueur (¼ tsp.)
Triple Sec (¼ tsp.)
Vanilla ice cream (2 heaping tbsp.)
Champagne or sparkling water
Maraschino cherry

Mix ice cream with cognac and
liqueurs in a chilled wine glass. Fill
with champagne and stir gently.
Garnish with cherry.

Spritzer

6 parts red or white wine
 (3 oz./90 ml.)
Sparkling water
Lemon twist

Pour wine into chilled wine glass
over ice cubes. Fill with sparkling
water and garnish with lemon twist.

Stars and Stripes

1½ parts cherry Heering
 (¾ oz./22.5 ml.)
1½ parts half-and-half
 (¾ oz./22.5 ml.)
1½ parts blue Curaçao
 (¾ oz./22.5 ml.)

Pour ingredients carefully, in order
given, into chilled pousse café
glass, so that each ingredient forms
a separate layer.

Straight Law Cocktail

6 parts amontillado sherry
 (3 oz./90 ml.)
2 parts gin (1 oz./30 ml.)

Combine ingredients with ice cubes
in a mixing glass and stir. Strain
into chilled cocktail glass.

LIQUEURS, WINES, & APERITIFS

Tamarindo Hop

4 parts ruby port (2 oz./60 ml.)
4 parts tamarind syrup
  (2 oz./60 ml.)
2 parts grenadine (1 oz./30 ml.)
Grapefruit juice

Combine all ingredients, except
grapefruit juice, with cracked ice in
a cocktail shaker. Shake well and
pour into a chilled collins glass over
ice cubes. Fill with grapefruit juice
and stir.

Tempter Cocktail

4 parts ruby port (2 oz./60 ml.)
3 parts apricot brandy
  (1½ oz./45 ml.)

Pour ingredients into a mixing glass
and stir with ice cubes. Strain into
chilled cocktail glass.

Tiger Tail

4 parts Pernod (2 oz./60 ml.)
8 parts fresh orange juice
  (4 oz./120 ml.)
Cointreau (¼ tsp.)
Lime wedge

Combine all ingredients, except
lime wedge, with cracked ice in a
blender. Blend until smooth and
pour into chilled wine glass. Garnish
with lime wedge.

Tintoretto

4 parts Poire William or pear eau
  de vie (2 oz./60 ml.)
Pureed ripe Anjou pear (¼ cup)
Champagne or sparkling wine

Puree pear in food processor or
food mill and pour into chilled wine
glass. Add the brandy and top off
with champagne. Stir gently.

Spritzer

Toasted Almond

4 parts coffee liqueur (2 oz./60 ml.)
3 parts amaretto (1½ oz./45 ml.)
4 parts half-and-half (2 oz./60 ml.)

Combine ingredients with cracked
ice in a cocktail shaker. Shake well
and strain into chilled old-fashioned
glass over ice cubes.

Tropical Cocktail

4 parts white crème de cacao
  (2 oz./60 ml.)
3 parts maraschino liqueur
  (1½ oz./45 ml.)
2 parts dry vermouth
  (1½ oz./45 ml.)
Dash Angostura bitters

Combine all ingredients with
cracked ice in a cocktail shaker.
Shake well and strain into chilled
cocktail glass.

Union Square Cafe's Campari Citrus Cooler

6 parts Campari (3 oz./90 ml.)
2 parts fresh lime juice (1 oz./30 ml.)
Aranciata orange soda (1 bottle or 8 oz./240 ml.)
Orange wedge

Pour Campari and lime juice into a chilled collins glass over ice cubes. Fill with orange soda and stir. Garnish with an orange wedge.

Vermouth Cassis

4 parts dry vermouth (2 oz./60 ml.)
2 parts crème de cassis
Sparkling water

Pour vermouth and cassis into chilled highball glass over ice cubes and stir. Fill with sparkling water and stir gently.

Vermouth Cocktail

3 parts dry vermouth (1½ oz./45 ml.)
3 parts sweet vermouth (1½ oz./45 ml.)
Dash Angostura bitters
Maraschino cherry

Combine all ingredients, except cherry, with ice cubes in a mixing glass. Stir and strain into chilled cocktail glass. Garnish with cherry.

Victory

4 parts Pernod (2 oz./60 ml.)
2 parts grenadine (1 oz./30 ml.)
Sparkling water

Combine all ingredients, except sparkling water, in a cocktail shaker with cracked ice. Pour into chilled highball glass and fill with sparkling water. Stir gently.

Vieux Carré

4 parts cognac (2 oz./60 ml.)
2 parts rye (1 oz./30 ml.)
1 part dry vermouth (½ oz./15 ml.)
1 part sweet vermouth (½ oz./15 ml.)
Dash Angostura bitters
Dash orange bitters
Lemon twist

Combine liquid ingredients with cracked ice in a cocktail shaker and shake well. Strain into a cocktail glass and garnish with lemon twist.

Washington Cocktail

4 parts dry vermouth (2 oz./60 ml.)
2 parts brandy (1 oz./30 ml.)
Sugar syrup (½ tsp.)
Dash Angostura bitters

Combine ingredients with cracked ice in a cocktail shaker. Shake well and strain into chilled cocktail glass.

Wassail Bowl

Ale (6 12-oz./0.33-l. bottles)
Cream sherry (1 cup or 8 oz./240 ml.)
Bar sugar (½ cup/100 g.)
Allspice (½ tsp.)
Ground cinnamon (1 tsp.)
Freshly ground nutmeg (2 tsp.)
Powdered ginger (¼ tsp.)
Lemon slice

In a large saucepan or stock pot, heat the sherry and one bottle of ale. Do not boil. Add sugar and spices and stir until dissolved. Add remaining ale and stir. Let stand at room temperature for about 3 hours. Pour into punch bowl and garnish with lemon slices.
Serves 10.

LIQUEURS, WINES, & APERITIFS

Weep-No-More

4 parts Dubonnet rouge
   (2 oz./60 ml.)
3 parts brandy (1½ oz./45 ml.)
Maraschino liqueur (1 tsp.)
2 parts fresh lime juice
   (1 oz./30 ml.)

Combine ingredients with cracked
ice in a cocktail shaker. Shake
well and strain into chilled cocktail
glass.

Whispers of the Frost

2 parts ruby port (1 oz./30 ml.)
2 parts fino sherry (1 oz./30 ml.)
2 parts bourbon (1 oz./30 ml.)
Sugar syrup (½ tsp.)
Lemon twist

Combine all ingredients with
cracked ice in a cocktail shaker.
Shake well and strain into chilled
cocktail glass.

Wobbling Zombie

6 parts dry white wine
   (3 oz./90 ml.)
4 parts fresh lime juice
   (2 oz./60 ml.)
4 parts fresh orange juice
   (2 oz./60 ml.)
4 parts pineapple juice
   (2 oz./60 ml.)
4 parts guava nectar (2 oz./60 ml.)
2 parts grenadine (1 oz./30 ml.)
1 part Orgeat (almond) syrup
   (½ oz./15 ml.)
Fresh mint sprig
Pineapple spear

Combine all ingredients, except
mint and pineapple spear, with
cracked ice in a blender. Blend until
smooth. Pour into chilled collins
glass and garnish with pineapple
and mint sprig.

Xeres Cocktail

6 parts manzanilla sherry
   (3 oz./90 ml.)
Dash orange bitters
Orange twist

Stir ingredients, except for orange
twist, with cracked ice in a mixing
glass and strain into cocktail glass.
Garnish with orange twist.

Yodel

6 parts Fernet Branca
   (3 oz./90 ml.)
8 parts fresh orange juice
   (4 oz./120 ml.)
Sparkling water

Pour liqueur and juice into chilled
highball glass over ice cubes. Stir
and fill with sparkling water.

Zaza Cocktail

4 parts Dubonnet rouge
   (2 oz./60 ml.)
2 parts gin (1 oz./30 ml.)
Dash orange bitters
Orange twist

Combine all ingredients, except
orange twist, with cracked ice in
a cocktail shaker. Shake well and
strain into chilled cocktail glass.
Garnish with orange twist.

NON-ALCOHOLIC

The original edition of *The New York Bartender's Guide* included several recipes for drinks without alcohol. It seemed reasonable then to expect any well-stocked bar to include the ingredients for a variety of non-alcoholic drinks. Ten years later, it is absolutely essential, and the best bars and bartenders can make even the pickiest non-drinkers feel at home. Parties of sensible drinkers out on the town often choose a "designated driver" to handle the driving and, hopefully, help the revelers avoid those morning-after regrets. The next time you host, make room on your drinks menu for these non-drinking stalwarts. The iconic drinks are all here, including the New York classic, the Egg Cream. And, yes, it really does taste better with Fox's U-Bet Syrup!

Baby Bellini

Chilled sparkling cider
4 parts peach nectar (2 oz./60 ml.)
2 parts fresh lemon juice
 (1 oz./30 ml.)

Pour the fruit juices into a chilled
champagne flute. Stir well. Add
cider to the rim. Stir again gently.

Beachcomber

10 parts guava nectar
 (5 oz./150 ml.)
2 parts raspberry syrup (1 oz./30 ml.)
4 parts fresh lime juice (2 oz./60 ml.)

Combine all ingredients with
cracked ice in a cocktail shaker.
Shake well and pour into chilled
collins glass.

Beachcomber

Black and Tan

Chilled ginger ale
Chilled ginger beer
Lime wedge

Pour equal parts of each beverage
into a chilled pilsner glass. Do not
stir. Garnish with lime wedge.

Brazilian Chocolate

Unsweetened chocolate
 (1 solid oz./30 g.)
Sugar (¼ cup/50 g.)
Salt (dash)
16 parts boiling water (8 oz./
 240 ml.)
16 parts hot half-and-half
 (8 oz./240 ml.)
24 parts strong hot coffee
 (12 oz./360 ml.)
Vanilla extract (1 tsp.)
Grated cinnamon (½ tsp.)

Melt chocolate, sugar, and salt in a
microwave or a double boiler. Stir
in boiling water and continue to
heat until mixture is hot and well
blended. Add hot half-and-half and
coffee. Stir well and add vanilla and
cinnamon. Serve in heated coffee
mugs. Serves 4.

Café au Lait

Hot coffee
Hot milk
Sugar (optional)

Combine equal parts of each liquid
in a heated coffee mug. Sweeten
to taste.

California Smoothie

1 banana, sliced thin
Fresh strawberries (½ cup)
Pitted dates, chopped (½ cup)
3 parts honey (1½ oz./45 ml.)
16 parts cold fresh orange juice
  (8 oz./240 ml.)
Cracked ice

Combine fruits and honey in a
blender and blend until smooth.
Add orange juice and cracked ice
and blend until smooth. Pour into
chilled collins glass.

Chicken Shot

4 parts chilled chicken bouillon
  (2 oz./60 ml.)
4 parts chilled beef bouillon
  (2 oz./60 ml.)
1 part fresh lemon juice
  (½ oz./15 ml.)
Tabasco® sauce to taste
Worcestershire sauce to taste
Freshly ground pepper to taste
Celery salt to taste

Combine all ingredients in a mixing
glass with cracked ice. Stir well.
Pour into chilled old-fashioned
glass.

Clam Digger

16 parts Clamato juice (8 oz./240 ml.)
2 parts fresh lime juice (1 oz./30 ml.)
Tabasco® sauce (3 – 5 dashes)
Worcestershire sauce (3 – 5 dashes)
Freshly ground pepper to taste
Celery salt to taste
White horseradish (¼ tsp.)
Celery stalk
Lime wedge

Combine all ingredients with
cracked ice in a cocktail shaker and
shake well. Strain into chilled collins
glass over ice cubes and garnish
with lime wedge and celery stalk.

Egg Nog

Coco Cola

4 parts coconut milk (2 oz./60 ml.)
2 parts fresh lime juice (1 oz./30 ml.)
Cola
Lime wedge

Combine coconut milk and lime
juice in a cocktail shaker and shake
well. Pour over ice into a chilled
highball glass. Fill with cola and
garnish with lime wedge.

Egg Cream

2 parts chocolate syrup (1 oz./30 ml.)
7 parts cold milk (3½ oz./105 ml.)
Seltzer

Put syrup in the bottom of collins
glass. Add milk and stir. Add seltzer
and stir vigorously so a foamy head
appears.

NON-ALCOHOLIC

Egg Nog

16 parts milk (8 oz./240 ml.)
1 egg, coddled
Sugar (1 tbsp.)
Almond extract (¼ tsp.)
Vanilla extract (¼ tsp.)
Whipped cream
Freshly grated nutmeg

Beat the egg well and pour into cocktail shaker with cold milk, sugar and extracts. Shake well and pour into chilled mug. Top with whipped cream and sprinkle nutmeg on top.

Faux Kir

2 parts raspberry syrup (1 oz./30 ml.)
White grape juice
Lemon twist

Pour syrup over ice cubes in a chilled wine glass. Fill with white grape juice and stir well. Garnish with lemon twist.

Faux Kir Royale

3 parts raspberry syrup (1½ oz./45 ml.)
Sparkling white grape juice or cider

Stir the syrup with cracked ice in a mixing glass. Pour into chilled wine glass and fill with cold sparkling cider. Stir gently.

Fruit Juice Spritzer

6 parts fruit juice of your choice
 (3 oz./90 ml.)
Sparkling water
Lemon twist

Pour juice into chilled wine glass over ice cubes. Fill with sparkling water and garnish with lemon twist.

Gazpacho Cocktail

12 parts tomato juice
 (6 oz./180 ml.)
2 parts fresh lemon juice (1 oz./30 ml.)
2 cucumber slices chopped
1 scallion white part only, sliced
Garlic clove, crushed
Oregano (⅛ tsp.)
Tabasco sauce (3 – 5 dashes)
Freshly ground pepper to taste
Salt to taste
Cucumber slice, whole
Avocado slice

Combine all ingredients, except whole cucumber and avocado slices, in a blender with cracked ice and blend until smooth. Pour into chilled collins glass and garnish with cucumber and avocado slices.

Guacamole Cocktail

1 California avocado, diced
10 parts chilled tomato juice
 (5 oz./150 ml.)
4 parts chilled fresh lime juice
 (2 oz./60 ml.)
1 small green chile, chopped
1 garlic clove, minced
Salt to taste
Freshly ground black pepper to taste
Lime wedge

Combine all ingredients, except lime wedge, in a blender. Blend until smooth but not too watery. Chill mixture for 1 hour and pour into chilled collins glass. Garnish with lime wedge.

Hawaiian Lemonade

6 parts pineapple juice (3 oz./90 ml.)
Fresh lemonade
Pineapple spear

Pour pineapple juice into a chilled collins glass over ice cubes. Fill with lemonade and stir. Garnish with pineapple spear.

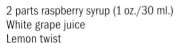

Hot Tot Toddy

Hot tea
2 parts honey (1 oz./30 ml.)
2 parts fresh lemon juice (1 oz./30 ml.)
5 whole cloves
Ground cinnamon to taste
Lemon slice
Freshly grated nutmeg
Cinnamon stick

Mull all ingredients, except nutmeg, tea and cinnamon stick, in the bottom of a warmed coffee mug. Fill with hot tea and stir. Garnish with cinnamon stick and nutmeg.

Iced Tea

Loose tea of your choice
  (2 heaping tsp.)
12 parts water (6 oz./180 ml.)
Sugar to taste
Fresh mint sprig
Lemon wedge

Put tea in a heated ceramic tea pot and add boiling water. Steep for 5 minutes. Stir and strain into a chilled collins glass filled with ice cubes. Add more ice if necessary. Add sugar to taste and garnish with mint and lemon.

Italian Soda

2 parts Italian syrup of your choice
  (1 oz./30 ml.) *
Sparkling water
Lemon or lime slice

Add syrup to a chilled collins glass filled with ice cubes. Add sparkling water and stir gently. Garnish with slice of lemon or lime. If you prefer a sweeter soda, use more syrup.

*NOTE: Italian syrups come in a variety of flavors and are widely available at specialty food stores, natural groceries, and cafés. Flavors vary from Orgeat (almond) and hazelnut to almost all fruits, as well as peppermint and other unusual and refreshing choices.

Knick's Victory Cooler

4 parts apricot nectar (2 oz./60 ml.)
Raspberry soda
Orange peel
Fresh raspberries

Pour apricot nectar into a chilled collins glass almost filled with ice cubes. Fill with raspberry soda. Stir gently and garnish with orange peel and a few fresh raspberries.

Lemonade

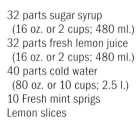

32 parts sugar syrup
  (16 oz. or 2 cups; 480 ml.)
32 parts fresh lemon juice
  (16 oz. or 2 cups; 480 ml.)
40 parts cold water
  (80 oz. or 10 cups; 2.5 l.)
10 Fresh mint sprigs
Lemon slices

Pour lemon juice into pitcher and add cold water. Add one cup of the sugar syrup and mint sprigs and stir. Taste and add more sugar syrup if necessary. Stir well and add several ice cubes. Float several lemon slices on top. Serves 10.

NOTE: To make pink lemonade, add ½ cup of raspberry or strawberry syrup and decrease the amount of sugar syrup accordingly. To make Limeade, substitute fresh lime juice for lemon juice.

NON-ALCOHOLIC

Margie's Mimosa

Chilled sparkling white grape juice
Fresh orange juice
Lemon slice

Fill half a chilled champagne flute with orange juice. Pour grape juice to the rim and stir gently. Garnish with lemon.

Mulled Cider Warmer

Apple cider (1 qt./1 l.)
2 parts honey (1 oz./30 ml.)
Ground allspice (¼ tsp.)
Cardamom seeds (5)
Freshly ground cinnamon (½ tsp.)
Ground ginger (¼ tsp.)
Freshly ground nutmeg (¼ tsp.)
8 whole cloves
Dried orange peel (1 tbsp.)
Cinnamon sticks

Combine all ingredients except cinnamon sticks in a saucepan. Heat and stir over high heat until the honey dissolves. Reduce heat and simmer for about 15 minutes or longer. Pour into warmed coffee mugs and garnish with cinnamon sticks. Serves 6.

Pepper Pot

8 parts pineapple juice (4 oz./120 ml.)
2 parts Orgeat (almond) syrup
  (1 oz./30 ml.)
2 parts fresh lemon juice
  (1 oz./30 ml.)
Tabasco® sauce (3 – 5 dashes)
Cayenne pepper to taste
Curry powder

Combine all ingredients, except the curry powder, in a cocktail shaker with cracked ice. Shake well and pour into chilled highball glass. Sprinkle curry powder on top.

Quick Pick

Iced tea, unsweetened
4 parts peppermint syrup
  (2 oz./60 ml.)
Lime wedge
Fresh mint sprig

Pour syrup and iced tea into a chilled collins glass filled with ice cubes. Squeeze the lime wedge over drink and drop in. Stir and garnish with mint sprig.

Refrigerator Tea

Loose tea of your choice
  (4 heaping tsp.)
10 – 15 crushed fresh mint leaves
  (optional)
60 parts water (30 oz./1 l.)
Sugar to taste

Combine tea and water in a glass jar and cover. Refrigerate overnight. Strain into chilled collins glasses filled with ice cubes and sweeten to taste.

Safe Sex on the Beach

4 parts peach nectar (2 oz./60 ml.)
6 parts cranberry juice
  (3 oz./90 ml.)
6 parts pineapple juice
  (3 oz./90 ml.)
Maraschino cherry

Pour all ingredients, except cherry, into a chilled collins glass filled with ice cubes and stir well. Garnish with cherry.

NON-ALCOHOLIC

Sangrita Seca

32 parts tomato juice
  (16 oz./480 ml.)
16 parts cup fresh orange juice
  (8 oz./240 ml.)
6 parts fresh lime juice (3 oz./90 ml.)
1 jalapeño pepper, seeded and
  chopped fine
1 part Tabasco® sauce
  (½ oz./15 ml.)
Worcestershire sauce (2 tsp.)
White pepper (½ tsp.)
Celery salt to taste

Pour all ingredients into a large
pitcher. Chill for at least one hour
(the longer you chill this, the spicier
it gets). When ready to serve, strain
into a fresh pitcher. Serve over ice
in chilled highball glasses. Serves
6 – 8.

Sparkling Peach Melba

Frozen raspberries (¼ cup)
8 parts peach nectar (4 oz./120 ml.)
Sparkling water

Puree the raspberries and strain
out the seeds. Combine with peach
nectar in a cocktail shaker and
shake well. Pour into chilled collins
glass and fill with sparkling water.
Stir gently.

Spiced Iced Coffee

64 parts strong hot black coffee
  (32 oz./1 l.)
4 cinnamon sticks
12 whole cloves
Ground nutmeg (½ tsp.)
Ground ginger (½ tsp.)
Peels of 2 lemons and 2 oranges cut
  into thin strips
4 sugar cubes

In heat proof pitcher, mash together
cinnamon, cloves, fruit peels, and
sugar. Add hot coffee, stir, and chill
in refrigerator. Pour over ice into
chilled highball glasses. Serves
6 – 8.

Strawberry/ Banana Kefir

1 banana, sliced
Fresh strawberries (1 cup)
2 parts honey (1 oz./30 ml.)
16 parts vanilla yogurt
  (8 oz./240 ml.)
16 parts apple juice (8 oz./240 ml.)

Combine all ingredients, except
apple juice, in a blender and blend
until smooth. Slowly pour apple
juice while continuing to blend
at low speed until desired liquid
consistency is achieved. Chill in a
pitcher and serve in chilled highball
glasses garnished with fresh
strawberries. Serves 4.

NOTE: Using the honey/yogurt/juice
combinations, you may create other
fruit kefirs.

Sun Tea

Loose tea of your choice (2 tbsp.)
64 parts water (32 oz./1 l.)
Peel of one lemon
Sugar to taste
Lemon wedges

Combine tea, water and lemon
peel in a glass jar and cover. Set in
direct sunlight for at least 4 hours.
Strain into pitcher and chill. Serve
over ice cubes in collins glasses
garnished with lemon wedges and
sugar to taste.

NON-ALCOHOLIC

Tomato Cocktail

32 parts tomato juice
 (16 oz./480 ml.)
2 parts red wine vinegar
 (1 oz./30 ml.)
Salt (½ tsp.)
Paprika (⅛ tsp.)
Basil (½ tsp.)
Freshly ground pepper (½ tsp.)
1 whole cucumber, peeled and
 pureed
4 lime wedges

Combine all ingredients, except lime wedges, in a glass pitcher and stir well. Chill and serve over ice cubes in highball glasses garnished with lime wedges.

Virgin Island

6 parts pineapple juice
 (3 oz./90 ml.)
2 parts coconut cream
 (1 oz./30 ml.)
2 parts fresh lime juice
 (1 oz./30 ml.)
Orgeat (almond) syrup (½ tsp.)
Pineapple spear

Combine all ingredients, except pineapple spear, in a blender with cracked ice. Blend until slushy and pour into chilled highball glass. Garnish with pineapple spear.

Virgin Mary

8 parts tomato juice (4 oz./120 ml.)
2 parts fresh lime juice
 (1 oz./30 ml.)
White horseradish (¼ tsp.)
Tabasco® sauce (3 – 5 dashes)
Worcestershire sauce (3 – 5 dashes)
Freshly ground pepper to taste
Salt to taste
Lime wedge

Combine all ingredients, except lime wedge, with cracked ice in a cocktail shaker. Shake well and pour into chilled highball glass. Garnish with lime wedge.

Wonderful Town

4 parts peppermint syrup
 (2 oz./60 ml.)
2 parts chocolate syrup (1 oz./30 ml.)
Sparkling water
Fresh mint sprig

Mix syrups in the bottom of a chilled highball glass. Fill glass with ice cubes and top off with sparkling water. Stir gently and garnish with mint.

NOTE: Use a thin chocolate syrup, such as Fox's U-Bet.

Zesty Cooler

2 parts fresh lime juice
 (1 oz./30 ml.)
Ginger beer
Lime wedge

Pour lime juice into a chilled beer mug over ice cubes. Fill with ginger beer and stir gently. Garnish with lime wedge.

NON-ALCOHOLIC

RUM

Rum dates back to the seventeenth century and its history—filled with tales of pirates, rum runners, politics, and intrigue—is very much intertwined with the history of sugar and of slavery in America. This fermented sugarcane juice has a literary history as well. When you sip your Floridita or Daiquiri, imagine sitting with Hemingway in Key West, or, better yet, in pre-Castro Cuba. Most rum originates in the Caribbean and is aged in charred wooden casks for at least three years. Jamaica is known for its dark rum, while Puerto Rico's rum is usually golden colored. Some wonderful dark rums from Barbados are aged for as long as thirty years, and their richness is best savored neat. White rum, sometimes called silver rum, is a popular choice for mixed drinks. It has a light clean taste and, unlike other rums, is aged in new wooden casks, and so remains clear. Flavored rum's popularity is growing. Along with coconut rum and spiced rum, both of which have been available for several years, you can now experiment with banana rum, orange rum, apple rum, and more.

Acapulco

4 parts light rum (2 oz./60 ml.)
1 part Cointreau or Triple Sec
  (½ oz./15 ml.)
1 part fresh lime juice
  (½ oz./15 ml.)
Bar sugar (1 tsp.)
1 egg white
1 sprig fresh mint

Combine rum, Cointreau, lime juice, sugar and egg white into a cocktail shaker half filled with ice cubes. Shake well. Strain into a glass almost filled with ice cubes. Garnish with mint.

American Flyer

3 parts light rum (1½ oz./45 ml.)
Fresh lime juice (1 tbsp.)
Sugar syrup (½ tsp.)
Champagne or sparkling wine

Combine the rum, lime juice and sugar syrup in a cocktail shaker with cracked ice. Shake well. Strain into a chilled white wine glass and top off with champagne.

Ankle Breaker

4 parts 151-proof rum (2 oz./60 ml.)
2 parts cherry brandy (1 oz./30 ml.)
2 parts fresh lime juice
  (1 oz./30 ml.)
Sugar syrup (1 tsp.) (optional)

Combine all ingredients with cracked ice in a cocktail shaker. Shake well. Strain into chilled old-fashioned glass.

Apple Daiquiri

4 parts light rum (2 oz./60 ml.)
1½ parts Calvados (¾ oz./22.5 ml.)
1 part lemon juice (½ oz./15 ml.)
Sugar syrup (1 tsp.) (use more
  or less, depending on desired
  sweetness)
Apple slice

Combine all ingredients, except apple wedge, in a cocktail shaker with cracked ice. Shake well. Strain into chilled cocktail glass. Garnish with apple slice.

Apricot Lady

3 parts light rum (1½ oz./45 ml.)
2 parts apricot brandy (1 oz./30 ml.)
Triple Sec (½ tsp.)
Fresh lime juice (1 tbsp.)
1 egg white (or 1 tbsp. egg white
  substitute)
Orange slice

Combine all ingredients, except orange slice, with cracked ice in a cocktail shaker and shake well. Strain over ice cubes into a chilled old-fashioned glass. Garnish with orange slice.

Arawak Cup

4 parts dark rum (2 oz./60 ml.)
1 part pineapple juice
  (½ oz./15 ml.)
1 part passion fruit syrup
  (½ oz./15 ml.)
1 part fresh lime juice
  (½ oz./15 ml.)
Orgeat (almond) syrup (1 tsp.)
Pineapple spear

Combine all ingredients, except pineapple spear, with cracked ice in a cocktail shaker. Shake well. Strain into chilled cocktail glass. Garnish with pineapple spear.

RUM

Backhoe

1 part 150 proof rum (½ oz./15 ml.)
1 part whiskey (½ oz./15 ml.)
1 part tequila (½ oz./15 ml.)

Mix ingredients over ice in a
cocktail shaker and strain into a
shot glass.

Bahama Mama

2 parts dark rum (1 oz./30 ml.)
2 parts white rum (1 oz./30 ml.)
2 parts gold rum (1 oz./30 ml.)
2 parts coconut liqueur
  (1 oz./30 ml.)
4 parts fresh orange juice
  (2 oz./60 ml.)
4 parts pineapple juice
  (2 oz./60 ml.)
1 part fresh lemon juice
  (½ oz./15 ml.)
2 dashes grenadine
Maraschino cherry
Orange slice

Combine all liquid ingredients with
ice cubes in a cocktail shaker.
Shake well. Pour into chilled collins
glass and garnish with fruit.

Bali Hai

4 parts light rum (2 oz./60 ml.)
2 parts Aguardiente (1 oz./30 ml.)
4 parts fresh lemon juice
  (2 oz./60 ml.)
4 parts fresh lime juice
  (2 oz./60 ml.)
Orgeat (almond) syrup (1 tsp.)
Grenadine (1 tsp.)
Champagne or sparkling wine

Combine all ingredients, except
champagne, with cracked ice in a
cocktail shaker. Shake well. Pour
into chilled collins glass. Top off
with cold champagne.

Banana Daiquiri

4 parts light rum (2 oz./60 ml.)
1 part Triple Sec (½ oz./15 ml.)
1 part fresh lime juice
  (½ oz./15 ml.)
1 part half-and-half (½ oz./15 ml.)
Bar sugar (1 tsp.)
¼ sliced banana
Lime slice

Put all ingredients, except for lime
slice, into a blender with about ½
cup cracked ice. Blend at low speed
until smooth. Pour into chilled
balloon wine glass and garnish with
slice of lime.

Banana Milk Shake

4 parts light rum (2 oz./60 ml.)
2 parts banana liqueur
  (1 oz./30 ml.)
4 parts whole milk (2 oz./60 ml.)
Dash grenadine
Banana slice
Freshly ground nutmeg

Combine liquid ingredients in
cocktail shaker with cracked ice.
Shake well. Strain into chilled
cocktail glass, garnish with banana
and sprinkle nutmeg on top.

Banana Rum Frappe

2 parts light rum (1 oz./30 ml.)
1 part banana liqueur (½ oz./15 ml.)
1 part fresh orange juice
  (½ oz./15 ml.)
Banana slice

Combine all ingredients, except
banana, in a blender with cracked
ice. Blend at high speed for about
ten seconds or until smooth.

RUM

Barbados Planter's Punch

6 parts gold rum (3 oz./90 ml.)
2 parts fresh lime juice
 (1 oz./30 ml.)
Bar sugar (½ tsp.)
Dash orange bitters
Sparkling water
Banana slice
Orange slice
Maraschino cherry
Freshly grated nutmeg

Combine all ingredients, except the fruit and nutmeg, with cracked ice in a cocktail shaker. Shake well. Pour into chilled collins glass. Garnish with the fruit and the nutmeg.

Barbary Coast

2 parts light rum (1 oz./30 ml.)
1 part gin (½ oz./15 ml.)
1 part scotch (½ oz./15 ml.)
1 part white crème de cacao
 (½ oz./15 ml.)
1 part half-and-half (½ oz./15 ml.)

Shake all ingredients together with cracked ice in a cocktail shaker. Strain into chilled cocktail glass.

Batida de Piña

6 parts light rum (3 oz./90 ml.)
Fresh crushed pineapple
 (⅔ cup/160 ml.) (if you must use canned pineapple, use the kind that's packed in juice)
Bar sugar (½ tsp.)
Sprig of fresh mint

Combine all ingredients, except mint, in a blender with cracked ice. Blend at high speed until smooth but not watery. Pour into chilled double old-fashioned glass. Garnish with mint sprig.

Bayou Bomb

1 part 150 proof rum (½ oz./15 ml.)
1 part bourbon whiskey
 (½ oz./15 ml.)

Pour ingredients into a shot glass in the order listed and shoot!

Beach Bum

4 parts light rum (2 oz./60 ml.)
1½ parts Triple Sec (¾ oz./22.5 ml.)
1½ parts fresh lime juice
 (¾ oz./22.5 ml.)
Dash of grenadine

Rim a chilled cocktail glass with sugar by rubbing with a lime wedge and dipping into sugar. Combine all ingredients in cocktail shaker and shake well. Strain into the glass.

Beachcomber's Gold

4 parts light rum (2 oz./60 ml.)
1 part dry vermouth (½ oz./15 ml.)
1 part sweet vermouth (½ oz./15 ml.)

Combine ingredients with cracked ice in cocktail shaker. Shake well. Strain into chilled cocktail glass filled with crushed ice.

Bee's Kiss

4 parts white rum (2 oz./60 ml.)
Honey (1 tsp.)
Whole milk (1 tsp.)

Combine all ingredients with cracked ice and shake vigorously in cocktail shaker. Strain over ice cubes in chilled cocktail glass.

RUM

Black Stripe

Bee's Knees

4 parts gold rum (2 oz./60 ml.)
1 part fresh orange juice
 (½ oz./15 ml.)
1 part fresh lime juice
 (½ oz./15 ml.)
Bar sugar (½ tsp.)
3 – 5 dashes white Curaçao
Orange peel

Combine all ingredients, except the orange peel, in a cocktail shaker with cracked ice. Shake well. Strain into chilled cocktail glass and garnish with orange peel.

Black Devil

4 parts light rum (2 oz./60 ml.)
1 part dry vermouth (½ oz./15 ml.)
Pitted black olive

Stir rum and vermouth in mixing glass with cracked ice. Strain into chilled cocktail glass and drop in the olive.

Black Maria

4 parts light rum (2 oz./60 ml.)
4 parts coffee liqueur (2 oz./60 ml.)
8 parts cold black coffee
 (4 oz./120 ml.)
Bar sugar (1 tsp.)

Stir ingredients in a large brandy snifter. Add cracked ice.

Black Stripe

6 parts dark rum (3 oz./90 ml.)
Molasses (2 tsp.)
8 parts boiling water
 (½ cup or 4 oz./120 ml.)
Lemon twist
Cinnamon stick
Freshly ground nutmeg

Dissolve molasses in the mug with a little boiling water. Add cinnamon stick and lemon twist and the remaining boiling water. Float rum on top and flame for a few seconds. Stir to extinguish flames. Sprinkle nutmeg on top.

Blow Me Down

3 parts 150 proof rum (1½ oz./45 ml.)
2 dashes Tabasco® sauce

Pour rum into shot glass. Add Tabasco to the top. Serve at room temperature.

Blue Hawaiian

4 parts light rum (2 oz./60 ml.)
4 parts blue Curaçao (2 oz./60 ml.)
4 parts cream of coconut
 (2 oz./60 ml.)
8 parts pineapple juice
 (4 oz./120 ml.)
Pineapple spear
Maraschino cherry

Combine all liquid ingredients in a blender with cracked ice and blend at high speed for about ten seconds. Pour into chilled highball glass and garnish with cherry and pineapple spear.

RUM

Blue Mountain

4 parts dark rum (2 oz./60 ml.)
2 parts vanilla vodka (1 oz./30 ml.)
2 parts coffee liqueur
  (1 oz./30 ml.)
8 parts fresh orange juice
  (½ cup or 4 oz./120 ml.)

Combine all ingredients with
cracked ice in a cocktail shaker and
shake well. Strain into chilled old-
fashioned glass.

Bolero

4 parts light rum (2 oz./60 ml.)
1 part Calvados (½ oz./15 ml.)
1 part sweet vermouth
  (½ oz./15 ml.)
Dash Angostura bitters

Combine all ingredients in a mixing
glass with cracked ice. Stir well.
Strain over ice cubes into a chilled
old-fashioned glass.

Bongo Cola

4 parts gold rum (2 oz./60 ml.)
2 parts coffee liqueur (1 oz./30 ml.)
4 parts pineapple juice
  (2 oz./60 ml.)
Dash of kirshwasser
Dash of fresh lemon juice
Cola
Maraschino cherry

Combine all ingredients, except cola
and cherry, in a cocktail shaker with
cracked ice. Shake well. Pour into
chilled collins glass over ice cubes.
Top off with cola. Stir gently and
garnish with cherry.

Borinqueño

4 parts white rum (2 oz./60 ml.)
2 parts fresh lime juice
  (1 oz./30 ml.)
2 parts fresh orange juice
  (1 oz./30 ml.)
Passion fruit syrup (1 tbsp.)
151-proof rum (1 tsp.)

Combine ingredients with cracked
ice in a blender. Blend at low speed
for about 10 seconds. Pour into
chilled old-fashioned glass.

Boston Cooler

4 parts light rum (2 oz./60 ml.)
1 part fresh lemon juice
  (½ oz./15 ml.)
Bar sugar (½ tsp.)
Sparkling water
Lemon twist

Combine rum, lemon juice and
sugar in a cocktail shaker with
cracked ice Shake well. Strain over
ice cubes into a chilled highball
glass. Stir. Add sparkling water and
lemon twist.

RUM

Blue Hawaiian

Boston Sidecar

3 parts light rum (1½ oz./45 ml.)
1 part brandy (½ oz./15 ml.)
1 part Triple Sec (½ oz./15 ml.)
1 part fresh lemon juice
 (½ oz./15 ml.)

Combine all ingredients in a cocktail shaker with ice cubes. Shake well. Strain into chilled cocktail glass.

Bushranger

4 parts light rum (2 oz./60 ml.)
3 parts Dubonnet rouge
 (1½ oz./45 ml.)
Dash Angostura bitters
Lemon twist

Combine all ingredients, except lemon peel, in a cocktail shaker with cracked ice. Shake well. Strain into chilled cocktail glass and garnish with lemon peel.

Caipirissima

6 parts light rum (3 oz./90 ml.)
2 parts fresh lime juice
 (1 oz./30 ml.)
Granulated sugar (1 tbsp.)
Lime rinds

Combine all ingredients in a cocktail shaker with cracked ice. Shake well. Strain into chilled old-fashioned glass over ice cubes.

Calm Voyage

3 parts light rum (1½ oz./45 ml.)
2 parts Strega (½ oz./15 ml.)
Passion fruit syrup (1 tbsp.)
Fresh lemon juice (1 tbsp.)

Combine all ingredients in a blender with cracked ice. Blend at low speed until smooth and pour into chilled champagne flute.

Cantaloupe Cup

Calypso

4 parts gold rum (2 oz./60 ml.)
2 parts pineapple juice
 (1 oz./30 ml.)
1 part fresh lemon juice
 (½ oz./15 ml.)
Falernum (1 tsp.)
Dash Angostura bitters
Freshly grated nutmeg

Combine all ingredients, except nutmeg, with cracked ice in a cocktail shaker. Shake well and strain into chilled cocktail glass. Sprinkle with nutmeg.

Cantaloupe Cup

4 parts light rum (2 oz./60 ml.)
1 part fresh lime juice
 (½ oz./15 ml.)
1 part fresh orange juice
 (½ oz./15 ml.)
Diced ripe cantaloupe (⅓ cup)
Bar sugar (½ tsp.)
Cantaloupe slice

Combine all ingredients, except cantaloupe slice, in a blender with cracked ice. Blend until smooth. Pour into chilled old-fashioned glass and garnish with cantaloupe slice.

Cardinal

4 parts light rum (2 oz./60 ml.)
1 part amaretto (½ oz./15 ml.)
1 part Triple Sec (½ oz./15 ml.)
2 parts fresh lime juice
 (1 oz./30 ml.)
Grenadine (½ tsp.)
Lime slice

Combine all ingredients, except lime slice, in a cocktail shaker with cracked ice. Pour into chilled old-fashioned glass and garnish with lime slice.

Casa Blanca

4 parts light rum (2 oz./60 ml.)
1 part Triple Sec (½ oz./15 ml.)
1 part cherry liqueur (½ oz./15 ml.)
1 part fresh lime juice
 (½ oz./15 ml.)

Combine all ingredients with cracked ice in a cocktail shaker and shake well. Strain into chilled cocktail glass.

Cat's Claw

1 part rum (½ oz./15 ml.)
1 part vodka (½ oz./15 ml.)
1 part Triple Sec (½ oz./15 ml.)
1 part crème de menthe (white)
 (½ oz./15 ml.)

Mix ingredients with ice in a cocktail shaker and strain into shot glass.

Chamborlada

4 parts light rum (2 oz./60 ml.)
2 parts dark rum (1 oz./30 ml.)
6 parts pineapple juice
 (3 oz./90 ml.)
4 parts coconut cream
 (2 oz./60 ml.)
4 parts Chambord (2 oz./60 ml.)

Combine all ingredients, except Chambord, with cracked ice in a blender. Blend until smooth. Pour the Chambord into the bottom of the balloon wine glass. Then pour the piña colada mixture on top of that, keeping it layered. Top off the piña colada mixture with a little more Chambord.

Cherry Daiquiri

4 parts light rum (2 oz./60 ml.)
1 part cherry liqueur (½ oz./15 ml.)
1 part fresh lime juice
 (½ oz./15 ml.)
Kirshwasser (¼ tsp.)
Lime twist

Combine all ingredients, except lime twist, in a cocktail shaker with cracked ice. Shake well and strain into chilled cocktail glass. Garnish with lime twist.

Cherry Rum

4 parts light rum (2 oz./60 ml.)
2 parts cherry brandy (1 oz./30 ml.)
1 part whole milk (½ oz./15 ml.)

Combine all ingredients with cracked ice in a cocktail shaker and shake well. Strain into chilled cocktail glass.

RUM

Chamborlada

Chi-Chi

4 parts light rum (2 oz./60 ml.)
1 part blackberry brandy
 (½ oz./15 ml.)
Pineapple juice

Stir rum and pineapple juice together in a chilled highball glass almost filled with ice cubes. Float brandy on top.

Chi Chi

Chicago Fizz

3 parts gold rum (1½ oz./45 ml.)
2 parts ruby port (1 oz./30 ml.)
1 part fresh lemon juice (½ oz./15 ml.)
Bar sugar (½ tsp.)
1 egg white (or 1 tbsp. egg white substitute)
Sparkling water

Combine all ingredients, except sparkling water, with cracked ice in a cocktail shaker. Shake vigorously. Strain into chilled collins glass over ice cubes and fill with sparkling water. Stir gently.

Chinese Cocktail

4 parts dark rum (2 oz./60 ml.)
Grenadine (1 tbsp.)
3 – 5 dashes white Curaçao
3 – 5 dashes maraschino liqueur
Dash Angostura bitters

Combine all ingredients with cracked ice in a cocktail shaker and shake well. Strain into chilled cocktail glass.

Continental Cocktail

4 parts light rum (2 oz./60 ml.)
1 part green crème de menthe
 (½ oz./15 ml.)
1 part fresh lime juice
 (½ oz./15 ml.)
Bar sugar (½ tsp.)

Combine all ingredients with cracked ice in a cocktail shaker and shake well. Strain into chilled cocktail glass.

Corkscrew

4 parts light rum (2 oz./60 ml.)
1 part dry vermouth (½ oz./15 ml.)
1 part peach liqueur (½ oz./15 ml.)
Lime slice

Combine all ingredients, except lime, in a cocktail shaker with cracked ice. Shake well. Strain into chilled cocktail glass and garnish with lime slice.

Creole

4 parts light rum (2 oz./60 ml.)
Fresh lemon juice (1 tsp.)
Tabasco® sauce to taste
Freshly ground pepper to taste
Salt to taste
Beef bouillon (or any of your choice)

Combine rum, lemon juice and Tabasco sauce with cracked ice in a cocktail shaker and shake well. Strain into chilled old-fashioned glass over ice cubes. Fill with bouillon and stir. Season with salt and pepper.

RUM

Crimson

4 parts gin (2 oz./60 ml.)
1 part ruby port (½ oz./15 ml.)
Fresh lime juice (2 tsp.)
Grenadine (1 tsp.)

Shake all ingredients, except port, with cracked ice in a cocktail shaker. Strain into chilled cocktail glass and float port on top.

Cuba Libre

4 parts light rum (2 oz./60 ml.)
Cola
Lime wedge

Pour the rum and cola into a chilled highball glass filled with ice cubes. Stir and garnish with lime.

Cuban Special

4 parts light rum (2 oz./60 ml.)
Triple Sec (1 tsp.)
2 parts fresh lime juice
  (1 oz./30 ml.)
Pineapple juice (1 tbsp.)
Pineapple spear

Combine all ingredients with cracked ice in a cocktail shaker and shake well. Strain into chilled cocktail glass and garnish with pineapple spear.

Cubano

4 parts light rum (2 oz./60 ml.)
2 parts fresh lime juice
  (1 oz./30 ml.)
Bar sugar (½ tsp.)

Combine all ingredients with cracked ice in a cocktail shaker. Shake well and strain into chilled cocktail glass.

Culross

4 parts light rum (2 oz./60 ml.)
1 part apricot brandy (½ oz./15 ml.)
1 part Lillet blanc (½ oz./15 ml.)
Fresh lemon juice (1 tsp.)

Combine ingredients with cracked ice in a cocktail shaker. Shake well and strain into chilled cocktail glass.

Curaçao Cooler

4 parts dark rum (2 oz./60 ml.)
3 parts white Curaçao (1½ oz./45 ml.)
2 parts fresh lime juice
  (1 oz./30 ml.)
Sparkling water
Orange slice

Combine all ingredients, except sparkling water and orange slice, in a cocktail shaker with cracked ice. Shake well. Pour into chilled highball glass and fill with sparkling water. Stir gently and garnish with orange slice.

Cuba Libre

RUM

Curaçao Cooler

Daiquiri

4 parts light rum (2 oz./60 ml.)
1½ parts fresh lime juice
 (¾ oz./22.5 ml.)
Sugar syrup (½ tsp.)

Combine all ingredients with
cracked ice in a cocktail shaker.
Shake well. Strain into chilled
cocktail glass.

RUM

Derby Daiquiri

4 parts light rum (2 oz./60 ml.)
2 parts fresh orange juice
 (1 oz./30 ml.)
1 part fresh lime juice
 (½ oz./15 ml.)
Bar sugar (1 tsp.)

Combine all ingredients with
cracked ice in a blender. Blend at
low speed until smooth. Pour into
chilled champagne flute.

Derby Special

4 parts light rum (2 oz./60 ml.)
1 part Cointreau (½ oz./15 ml.)
2 parts fresh orange juice
 (1 oz./30 ml.)
1 part fresh lime juice
 (½ oz./15 ml.)

Combine all ingredients in a blender
with cracked ice. Blend until
smooth and thick. Pour into chilled
cocktail glass.

Devil's Tail

4 parts light rum (2 oz./60 ml.)
2 parts raspberry vodka
 (1 oz./30 ml.)
Apricot brandy (2 tsp.)
1 part fresh lime juice
 (½ oz./15 ml.)
Grenadine (2 tsp.)
Lime twist

Combine all ingredients, except lime
twist, with cracked ice in a blender.
Blend at low speed until smooth.
Pour into chilled champagne flute
and garnish with lime twist.

El Presidente

4 parts light rum (2 oz./60 ml.)
2 parts fresh lime juice (1 oz./30 ml.)
Grenadine (1 tsp.)
Pineapple juice (1 tsp.)

Shake ingredients with cracked
ice in cocktail shaker. Strain into
chilled cocktail glass.

Eye-Opener

4 parts light rum (2 oz./60 ml.)
Pernod (1 tsp.)
Cointreau (1 tsp.)
White crème de cacao (1 tsp.)
Bar sugar (½ tsp.)

Shake all ingredients vigorously with
cracked ice in a cocktail shaker.
Strain into chilled sour glass.

Fair and Warmer

4 parts light rum (2 oz./60 ml.)
1 part sweet vermouth
 (½ oz./15 ml.)
3 dashes white Curaçao
Lemon twist

Shake all ingredients, except lemon, with cracked ice in a cocktail shaker. Strain into chilled cocktail glass and garnish with lemon twist.

Fern Gulley

4 parts dark rum (2 oz./60 ml.)
3 parts light rum (1½ oz./45 ml.)
1 part amaretto (½ oz./15 ml.)
1 part coconut cream (½ oz./15 ml.)
2 parts fresh orange juice
 (1 oz./30 ml.)
2 parts fresh lime juice
 (1 oz./30 ml.)

Combine all ingredients with cracked ice in a blender. Blend at low speed until smooth. Pour into chilled red wine glass.

Eye-Opener

Fireman's Sour

4 parts light rum (2 oz./60 ml.)
3 parts fresh lime juice
 (1½ oz./45 ml.)
Bar sugar (½ tsp.)
Grenadine (1 tbsp.)
Lemon slice
Maraschino cherry

Combine all ingredients, except fruit, with cracked ice in a cocktail shaker. Shake well and strain into chilled sour glass. Garnish with cherry and lemon.

Fish House Punch

Dark rum (2 l.)
Cognac (1 l.)
8 parts peach brandy
 (4 oz./120 ml.)
Fresh lemon juice (1 l.)
Bottled spring water (non-
 sparkling) (2 l.)
Bar sugar (1½ cups/300 g. or
 to taste)
Fresh peach slices

In a chilled punch bowl, dissolve sugar in water and lemon juice. Stir in remaining ingredients. Add large block of ice and garnish with peach slices. Serves 40.

Floridita

4 parts rum light (2 oz./60 ml.)
3 parts fresh lime juice
 (1½ oz./45 ml.)
1 part simple syrup (½ oz./15 ml.)
1 tbsp. Maraschino liqueur

Shake all ingredients with ice and strain into a chilled cocktail glass.

RUM

Floridita Dos

4 parts light rum (2 oz./60 ml.)
1 part sweet vermouth
  (½ oz./15 ml.)
1 part fresh lime juice
  (½ oz./15 ml.)
1 tbsp. white crème de cacao
1 tsp. Grenadine

Shake all ingredients in a cocktail shaker. Strain into chilled cocktail glass.

Fog Cutter

4 parts light rum (2 oz./60 ml.)
2 parts brandy (1 oz./30 ml.)
2 parts gin (1 oz./30 ml.)
Sweet sherry (1 tsp.)
3 parts fresh lemon juice
  (1½ oz./45 ml.)
2 parts fresh orange juice
  (1 oz./30 ml.)
Orgeat (almond) syrup (1 tsp.)

Combine all ingredients, except sherry, with cracked ice in a cocktail shaker and shake well. Strain over ice cubes into chilled collins glass. Float sherry on top.

Fort Lauderdale

4 parts light rum (2 oz./60 ml.)
1 part sweet vermouth (½ oz./15 ml.)
2 parts fresh lime juice (1 oz./30 ml.)
2 parts fresh orange juice
  (1 oz./30 ml.)
Orange slice

Combine all ingredients, except orange slice, with cracked ice in a cocktail shaker. Shake well and strain into chilled old-fashioned glass over ice cubes. Garnish with orange.

Frozen Daiquiri

Frozen Berkeley

4 parts light rum (2 oz./60 ml.)
1 part brandy (½ oz./15 ml.)
Passion fruit syrup (1 tbsp.)
Fresh lime juice (1 tbsp.)

Combine all ingredients with ½ cup of crushed ice in a blender. Blend until slushy and pour into chilled champagne flute.

Frozen Daiquiri

4 parts light rum (2 oz./60 ml.)
2 parts fresh lime juice
  (1 oz./30 ml.)
Bar sugar (1 tsp.)
Lime slice

Combine all ingredients, except lime slice, with ½ cup of cracked ice in a blender. Blend at low speed until slushy and pour into chilled champagne flute. Garnish with lime slice.

RUM

Frozen Mint Daiquiri

4 parts light rum (2 oz./60 ml.)
1 part fresh lime juice
  (½ oz./15 ml.)
6 fresh mint leaves
Bar sugar (1 tsp.)

Combine all ingredients with
½ cup of cracked ice in a blender
and blend until slushy. Pour into
chilled old-fashioned glass.

Frozen Peach Daiquiri

4 parts light rum (2 oz./60 ml.)
2 parts fresh lime juice
  (1 oz./30 ml.)
Sugar syrup (1 tsp.)
4 parts fresh peaches, chopped fine
  (2 oz./60 ml.)
Fresh peach slice

Combine all ingredients, except
peach slice, in a blender with ½ cup
cracked ice. Blend until slushy and
pour into cocktail glass. Garnish
with peach slice.

Frozen Pineapple Daiquiri

4 parts light rum (2 oz./60 ml.)
2 parts fresh lime juice
  (1 oz./30 ml.)
Pineapple syrup (½ tsp.)
4 parts fresh pineapple, chopped
  fine (2 oz./60 ml.)
Pineapple spear

Combine all ingredients, except
pineapple spear, with ½ cup
cracked ice in a blender. Blend
until slushy and pour into a cocktail
glass. Garnish with pineapple spear.

Gauguin

4 parts light rum (2 oz./60 ml.)
1 part fresh lemon juice
  (½ oz./15 ml.)
1 part fresh lime juice
  (½ oz./15 ml.)
1 part passion fruit syrup
  (½ oz./15 ml.)
Maraschino cherry

Combine all ingredients, except
cherry, in a blender with cracked ice.
Blend at low speed until smooth.
Pour into chilled old-fashioned glass
and garnish with cherry.

Golden Gate

4 parts light rum (2 oz./60 ml.)
2 parts gin (1 oz./30 ml.)
2 parts white crème de cacao
  (1 oz./30 ml.)
4 parts fresh lemon juice
  (2 oz./60 ml.)
151-proof rum (1 tsp.)
Orgeat (almond) syrup (1 tsp.)
Orange slice

Combine all ingredients, except
orange slice, in a cocktail shaker
with cracked ice. Shake well and
pour into chilled old-fashioned
glass. Garnish with orange slice.

Grand Occasion

4 parts light rum (2 oz./60 ml.)
1 part Grand Marnier (½ oz./15 ml.)
1 part white crème de cacao
  (½ oz./15 ml.)
1 part lemon juice (½ oz./15 ml.)

Combine all ingredients with
cracked ice and shake well. Strain
into chilled cocktail glass.

RUM

Gumdrop Martini

4 parts lemon-flavored rum
  (2 oz./60 ml.)
2 parts vodka (1 oz./30 ml.)
1 part Southern Comfort
  (½ oz./15 ml.)
½ tsp. dry vermouth
1 part fresh lemon juice (½ oz./15 ml.)
Gumdrops
Lemon slice

Rim a chilled cocktail glass with bar
sugar. Combine liquid ingredients
with cracked ice in a cocktail shaker
and shake well. Strain into the
chilled cocktail glass and garnish
with lemon slice and gumdrops.

Happy Apple

4 parts gold rum (2 oz./60 ml.)
6 parts apple cider (3 oz./90 ml.)
1 part fresh lemon juice (½ oz./15 ml.)
Lime twist

Combine all ingredients, except lime
twist, with cracked ice in a cocktail
shaker. Shake well and pour into
chilled old-fashioned glass. Garnish
with lime twist.

Havana Banana Fizz

4 parts light rum (2 oz./60 ml.)
5 parts pineapple juice
  (2½ oz./75 ml.)
3 parts fresh lime juice (1½ oz./45 ml.)
3 – 5 dashes Peychaud's bitters
⅓ banana, sliced
Bitter lemon soda

Combine all ingredients, except
soda, with cracked ice in a blender.
Blend at low speed until smooth.
Pour into a chilled old-fashioned
glass, fill with bitter lemon soda
and stir.

Havana Club

6 parts light rum (3 oz./90 ml.)
1 part dry vermouth (½ oz./15 ml.)

Combine ingredients with cracked
ice in a mixing glass. Stir well and
strain into chilled cocktail glass.

Havana Cocktail

4 parts light rum (2 oz./60 ml.)
4 parts pineapple juice (2 oz./60 ml.)
1 part fresh lemon juice
  (½ oz./15 ml.)

Combine all ingredients with
cracked ice in a cocktail shaker.
Shake well and strain into chilled
cocktail glass.

Honey Bee

4 parts light rum (2 oz./60 ml.)
1 part honey (½ oz./15 ml.)
1 part fresh lemon juice
  (½ oz./15 ml.)

Combine all ingredients in a
cocktail shaker with cracked ice
and shake well. Strain into chilled
cocktail glass.

Hot Buttered Rum

Hop Toad

4 parts light rum (2 oz./60 ml.)
3 parts apricot brandy
 (1½ oz./45 ml.)
2 parts fresh lime juice (1 oz./30 ml.)

Combine all ingredients in a mixing glass with ice cubes and stir well. Strain into chilled cocktail glass.

Hot Buttered Rum

4 parts dark rum (2 oz./60 ml.)
Brown sugar (1 tsp.)
Pat of butter
Boiling water
Freshly ground nutmeg

Put sugar into warmed mug and fill two-thirds with boiling water. Add rum and stir. Float butter on top and sprinkle with nutmeg.

Hurricane

3 parts dark rum (1½ oz./45 ml.)
3 parts light rum (1½ oz./45 ml.)
2 parts passion fruit syrup
 (1 oz./30 ml.)
Fresh lime juice (1 tbsp.)

Shake all ingredients with cracked ice in a cocktail shaker. Strain into chilled cocktail glass.

Independence Swizzle

4 oz. dark rum (2 oz./60 ml.)
3 parts fresh lime juice
 (1½ oz./45 ml.)
Honey (1 tsp.)
3 – 5 dashes Angostura bitters
Lime slice

Dissolve honey in a little warm water. Stir it with remaining ingredients, except lime slice, in a chilled old-fashioned glass filled with crushed ice. Garnish with lime slice and serve with swizzle stick.

Hurricane

Isle of the Blessed Coconut

4 parts light rum (2 oz./60 ml.)
1 part fresh lemon juice
 (½ oz./15 ml.)
1 part fresh lime juice
 (½ oz./15 ml.)
1 part fresh orange juice
 (½ oz./15 ml.)
Cream of coconut (1 tsp.)
Orgeat (almond) syrup (1 tsp.)

Combine all ingredients with cracked ice in a blender and blend until smooth. Pour into a chilled cocktail glass.

Isle of Pines

4 parts light rum (2 oz./60 ml.)
1 part fresh lime juice
 (½ oz./15 ml.)
Peppermint schnapps (1 tsp.)
6 fresh mint leaves

Combine all ingredients with cracked ice in a blender. Blend until slushy and pour into chilled cocktail glass.

RUM

Jamaica Egg Cream

4 parts dark rum (2 oz./60 ml.)
2 parts gin (1 oz./30 ml.)
2 parts half-and-half (1 oz./30 ml.)
Fresh lemon juice (1 tbsp.)
Bar sugar (1 tsp.)
Sparkling water

Combine all ingredients, except
water, in a cocktail shaker with
cracked ice and shake well. Pour
into chilled highball glass and fill
with sparkling water. Stir gently.

Jamaica Mule

4 parts light rum (2 oz./60 ml.)
2 parts dark rum (1 oz./30 ml.)
2 parts 151-proof rum (1 oz./30 ml.)
2 parts Falernum (1 oz./30 ml.)
2 parts fresh lime juice
  (1 oz./30 ml.)
Ginger beer
Pineapple spear
Slice candied ginger

Combine all ingredients, except
ginger beer, pineapple and ginger,
with cracked ice in a cocktail
shaker. Shake well and strain into
chilled collins glass. Fill with ginger
beer and stir gently. Garnish with
pineapple spear and ginger.

Jolly Roger

4 parts light rum (2 oz./60 ml.)
2 parts Drambuie (1 oz./30 ml.)
2 parts fresh lime juice
  (1 oz./30 ml.)
Scotch (¼ tsp.)
Sparkling water

Combine all ingredients, except
sparkling water, with cracked ice in
a cocktail shaker. Shake well and
pour into chilled highball glass. Fill
with sparkling water and stir gently.

Josiah's Bay Float

Josiah's Bay Float

2 parts gold rum (1 oz./30 ml.)
1 part Strega (½ oz./15 ml.)
2 parts pineapple juice
  (1 oz./30 ml.)
Lime juice (2 tsp.)
Sugar syrup (2 tsp.)
Champagne or sparkling wine
Lime slice
Maraschino cherry
Pineapple shell, carved out
  (optional)

Mix all ingredients, except
champagne, lime, and cherry, with
cracked ice in a cocktail shaker or
blender. Pour into chilled collins
glass or pineapple shell. Fill with
champagne. Stir gently and garnish
with lime slice and cherry.

RUM

Kamehameha Rum Punch

4 parts light rum (2 oz./60 ml.)
2 parts dark rum (1 oz./30 ml.)
Blackberry brandy (2 tsp.)
4 parts pineapple juice (2 oz./60 ml.)
2 parts Orgeat (almond) syrup
  (1 oz./30 ml.)
2 parts fresh lime juice
  (1 oz./30 ml.)
Fresh lemon juice (1 tsp.)
Pineapple spear

Combine all ingredients, except dark rum and pineapple spear, in a cocktail shaker with cracked ice. Shake well and pour into chilled highball glass. Float dark rum on top and garnish with pineapple spear.

Kingston Cocktail

4 parts dark rum (2 oz./60 ml.)
1½ parts coffee liqueur
  (¾ oz./22.5 ml.)
Fresh lime juice (2 tsp.)

Combine ingredients with cracked ice in a cocktail shaker. Shake well and strain into chilled cocktail glass.

Knickerbocker Special Cocktail

4 parts light rum (2 oz./60 ml.)
Triple Sec (½ tsp.)
Raspberry syrup (1 tsp.)
Pineapple syrup (1 tsp.)
Fresh lime juice (1 tsp.)
Fresh orange juice (1 tsp.)
Pineapple spear

Combine liquid ingredients with cracked ice in a cocktail shaker and shake well. Strain into chilled cocktail glass and garnish with pineapple.

La Bomba

4 parts light rum (2 oz./60 ml.)
2 parts apricot brandy (1 oz./30 ml.)
2 parts Pernod (1 oz./30 ml.)
2 parts Triple Sec (1 oz./30 ml.)
2 parts fresh lemon juice
  (1 oz./30 ml.)
Pineapple spear

Combine all ingredients, except pineapple, in a cocktail shaker with cracked ice. Shake well and strain into chilled old-fashioned glass. Garnish with pineapple spear.

Lallah Rookh

4 parts light rum (2 oz./60 ml.)
2 parts cognac (1 oz./30 ml.)
1 part vanilla extract (½ oz./15 ml.)
Bar sugar (½ tsp.)
Whipped cream

Combine all ingredients, except whipped cream, with cracked ice in a blender. Blend at low speed until smooth. Pour into chilled wine glass and top with whipped cream.

Lexington Ave. Express

4 parts 151-proof rum (2 oz./60 ml.)
2 parts fresh lime juice
  (1 oz./30 ml.)
Grenadine (1 tsp.)

Combine ingredients with cracked ice in a cocktail shaker. Shake well and strain into a chilled old-fashioned glass over ice cubes.

RUM

Limbo Cocktail

4 parts light rum (2 oz./60 ml.)
1 part crème de bananes
 (½ oz./15 ml.)
2 parts fresh orange juice
 (1 oz./30 ml.)

Combine all ingredients with cracked ice in a cocktail shaker and shake well. Strain into chilled cocktail glass.

Mai Tai

Limey

4 parts light rum (2 oz./60 ml.)
2 parts lime liqueur (1 oz./30 ml.)
1 part Triple Sec (½ oz./15 ml.)
Fresh lime juice (1 tbsp.)
Lime twist

Combine all ingredients, except lime twist, in a blender with cracked ice. Blend until slushy and pour into chilled red wine glass. Garnish with lime slice.

Little Dix Mix

4 parts dark rum (2 oz./60 ml.)
1 part crème de bananes
 (½ oz./15 ml.)
1 part fresh lime juice
 (½ oz./15 ml.)
Triple Sec (1 tsp.)

Combine all ingredients with cracked ice in a cocktail shaker. Shake well and pour into chilled old-fashioned glass.

Little Princess

4 parts light rum (2 oz./60 ml.)
2 parts sweet vermouth
 (1 oz./30 ml.)

Combine ingredients with cracked ice in a mixing glass. Stir well and strain into chilled cocktail glass.

Louisiana Planter's Punch

4 parts gold rum (2 oz./60 ml.)
2 parts bourbon (1 oz./30 ml.)
2 parts cognac (1 oz./30 ml.)
Pernod (¼ tsp.)
5 dashes Peychaud's bitters
1 part sugar syrup (½ oz./15 ml.)
2 parts fresh lemon juice
 (1 oz./30 ml.)
Sparkling water
Lemon slice
Orange slice

Combine all ingredients, except sparkling water and fruit, in a cocktail shaker with cracked ice. Shake well and strain into chilled highball glass over ice cubes. Fill with sparkling water and stir gently. Garnish with fruit slices.

RUM

Mahukona

4 parts light rum (2 oz./60 ml.)
1 part white Curaçao (½ oz./15 ml.)
1 part fresh lemon juice
  (½ oz./15 ml.)
Orgeat (almond) syrup (½ tsp.)
5 dashes orange bitters
Pineapple spear

Combine all ingredients except
pineapple spear with cracked ice
in a blender. Blend until smooth
and pour into chilled highball glass.
Garnish with pineapple spear.

Mai Kai No

4 parts light rum (2 oz./60 ml.)
4 parts dark rum (2 oz./60 ml.)
1 part 151-proof rum (½ oz./15 ml.)
4 parts fresh lime juice (2 oz./60 ml.)
2 parts passion fruit syrup
  (1 oz./30 ml.)
1 part Orgeat (almond) syrup
  (½ oz./15 ml.)
Sparkling water
Pineapple spear

Combine all ingredients, except
sparkling water and pineapple
spear, with cracked ice in a cocktail
shaker. Shake well and pour into a
chilled collins glass over ice cubes.
Fill with sparkling water. Stir gently
and garnish with pineapple spear.

Mai Tai

4 parts dark rum (2 oz./60 ml.)
4 parts light rum (2 oz./60 ml.)
2 parts Curaçao (1 oz./30 ml.)
2 parts fresh lime juice
  (1 oz./30 ml.)
Grenadine (1 tbsp.)
Orgeat (almond) syrup (1 tbsp.)
Pineapple spear
Orchid and paper umbrella
  (optional)

Combine all ingredients with
cracked ice in a cocktail shaker
and shake well. Strain into a chilled
highball glass over ice cubes.
Garnish with pineapple and other
decorations.

Mandeville

4 parts dark rum (2 oz./60 ml.)
4 parts light rum (2 oz./60 ml.)
Pernod (1 tbsp.)
Grenadine (½ tsp.)
Fresh lemon juice (1 tbsp.)
1 part cola (½ oz./15 ml.)

Combine all ingredients with
cracked ice in a cocktail shaker.
Shake well and strain into a chilled
old-fashioned glass over ice cubes.

Mary Pickford

4 parts light rum (2 oz./60 ml.)
Maraschino liqueur (½ tsp.)
4 parts pineapple juice (2 oz./60 ml.)
Grenadine (½ tsp.)

Combine ingredients with cracked
ice in a cocktail shaker. Shake
well and strain into chilled cocktail
glass.

Miami

4 parts light rum (2 oz./60 ml.)
2 parts peppermint schnapps
  (1 oz./30 ml.)
Fresh lime juice (¼ tsp.)

Combine all ingredients with
cracked ice in a cocktail shaker.
Shake well and strain into chilled
cocktail glass.

Mister Pip's St. Thomas Special

4 parts dark rum (2 oz./60 ml.)
Passion fruit syrup (1 tbsp.)
Fresh orange juice
Freshly ground nutmeg

Stir rum and syrup with cracked
ice in a mixing glass. Strain into a
chilled collins glass over ice cubes.
Fill with orange juice and stir.
Sprinkle nutmeg on top.

Mojito

4 parts light rum (2 oz./60 ml.)
2 parts fresh lime juice
 (1 oz./30 ml.)
Bar sugar (1 tsp.)
5 – 7 fresh mint leaves
Dash Angostura bitters

Combine all ingredients with
cracked ice in a cocktail shaker
and shake well. Strain into chilled
cocktail glass.

Mulled Cider

4 parts gold rum (2 oz./60 ml.)
12 parts apple cider (6 oz./180 ml.)
Honey (1 tsp.)
Cinnamon stick
Freshly grated nutmeg (to taste)
3 whole cloves
Lemon twist

Combine all ingredients in a sauce
pan. Warm over medium heat,
stirring occasionally. Do not boil.
Pour into heated coffee mug.

Myrtle Bank Punch

4 parts 151-proof rum (2 oz./60 ml.)
2 parts maraschino liqueur
 (1 oz./30 ml.)
3 parts fresh lime juice
 (1½ oz./45 ml.)
Grenadine (1 tsp.)
Bar sugar (½ tsp.)

Combine all ingredients, except
maraschino liqueur, in a blender
with cracked ice. Blend until smooth
and pour into chilled highball glass.
Float liqueur on top.

Navy Grog

2 parts dark rum (1 oz./30 ml.)
2 parts light rum (1 oz./30 ml.)
2 parts 86-proof Demerara rum
 (1 oz./30 ml.)
1 part guava juice (½ oz./15 ml.)
1 part fresh lime juice
 (½ oz./15 ml.)
1 part pineapple juice
 (½ oz./15 ml.)
1 part Orgeat (almond) syrup
 (½ oz./15 ml.)
Tamarind syrup (1 tbsp.)
Lime slice

Combine all ingredients, except lime
slice, with cracked ice in a blender.
Blend until slushy and pour into
chilled highball glass. Garnish with
lime slice.

Nevada Cocktail

4 parts dark rum (2 oz./60 ml.)
4 parts grapefruit juice
 (2 oz./60 ml.)
1 part fresh lime juice
 (½ oz./15 ml.)
Bar sugar (½ tsp.)
Dash Angostura bitters

Combine ingredients with cracked
ice in a cocktail shaker. Shake
well and strain into chilled cocktail
glass.

Night Cap

New Orleans Buck

4 parts light rum (2 oz./60 ml.)
2 parts fresh lime juice (1 oz./30 ml.)
2 parts fresh orange juice
  (1 oz./30 ml.)
Ginger ale
Lime slice

Combine all ingredients, except ginger ale and lime slice, with cracked ice in a cocktail shaker. Shake well and strain into a chilled collins glass over ice cubes. Fill with ginger ale and stir gently. Garnish with lime slice.

Night Cap

4 parts light rum (2 oz./60 ml.)
Sugar syrup (1 tsp.)
Warm milk
Freshly grated nutmeg

Pour rum and syrup into a heated coffee mug. Fill mug with warm milk and stir. Sprinkle nutmeg on top.

Nirvana

4 parts dark rum (2 oz./60 ml.)
1 part grenadine (½ oz./15 ml.)
1 part tamarind syrup (½ oz./15 ml.)
Sugar syrup (1 tsp.)
Grapefruit juice

Combine all ingredients, except grapefruit juice, with cracked ice in a cocktail shaker. Shake well and pour into a chilled collins glass over ice cubes. Fill with grapefruit juice and stir.

Ocho Rios

4 parts dark rum (2 oz./60 ml.)
2 parts guava nectar (1 oz./30 ml.)
2 parts fresh lime juice
  (1 oz./30 ml.)
Falernum (1 tsp.)
2 parts half-and-half (1 oz./30 ml.)

Combine ingredients with cracked ice in a blender. Blend at low speed until smooth. Pour into chilled champagne flute.

Outrigger

4 parts gold rum (2 oz./60 ml.)
1 part white Curaçao (½ oz./15 ml.)
1 part apricot liqueur (½ oz./15 ml.)
2 parts fresh lime juice
  (1 oz./30 ml.)
Lime slice

Combine all ingredients, except lime slice, in a cocktail shaker with cracked ice and shake well. Strain into a chilled old-fashioned glass over ice cubes and garnish with lime slice.

Pago Pago

6 parts gold rum (3 oz./90 ml.)
White crème de cacao (1 tsp.)
Chartreuse (1 tsp.)
2 parts fresh lime juice
  (1 oz./30 ml.)
2 parts pineapple juice
  (1 oz./30 ml.)

Combine all ingredients with cracked ice in a cocktail shaker. Shake well and pour into chilled old-fashioned glass.

RUM

Pain Killer

6 parts dark rum (3 oz./90 ml.)
2 parts pineapple juice
 (1 oz./30 ml.)
2 parts orange juice (1 oz./30 ml.)
1 part coconut cream (½ oz./15 ml.)
2 – 3 dashes nutmeg
Maraschino cherry

Combine all liquid ingredients with
cracked ice in a cocktail shaker.
Shake well and pour into a highball
glass over ice. Top off with nutmeg
and maraschino cherry.

Palmetto Cocktail

4 parts light rum (2 oz./60 ml.)
2 parts dry vermouth (1 oz./30 ml.)
3 dashes Angostura bitters

Stir ingredients with ice cubes in
a mixing glass. Strain into chilled
cocktail glass.

Pancho Villa

4 parts light rum (2 oz./60 ml.)
2 parts gin (1 oz./30 ml.)
2 parts apricot brandy (1 oz./30 ml.)
Cherry brandy (1 tbsp.)
Pineapple juice (1 tbsp.)

Combine all ingredients with
cracked ice in a cocktail shaker.
Shake well and strain into chilled
cocktail glass.

Passionate Daiquiri

4 parts light rum (2 oz./60 ml.)
2 parts fresh lime juice
 (1 oz./30 ml.)
1 part passion fruit syrup
 (½ oz./15 ml.)

Combine ingredients with cracked
ice in a cocktail shaker and shake
well. Strain into chilled cocktail
glass.

Peach Daiquiri

4 parts light rum (2 oz./60 ml.)
2 parts fresh lime juice
 (1 oz./30 ml.)
Bar sugar (½ tsp.)
½ fresh peach, peeled and diced

Combine ingredients with cracked
ice in a blender. Blend until slushy
and pour into chilled balloon wine
glass.

Pilot Boat

4 parts dark rum (2 oz./60 ml.)
2 parts crème de bananes
 (1 oz./30 ml.)
4 parts fresh lime juice
 (2 oz./60 ml.)

Combine ingredients with cracked
ice in a cocktail shaker. Shake
well and strain into chilled cocktail
glass.

Piña Colada for Friends

16 parts light rum (1 cup or
 8 oz./240 ml.)
4 parts dark rum (2 oz./60 ml.)
10 parts coconut cream
 (5 oz./150 ml.)
20 parts pineapple juice
 (10 oz./300 ml.)
4 parts half-and-half (2 oz./60 ml.)
4 pineapple spears

Combine all ingredients, except
pineapple spears, in a blender with
cracked ice. Blend until smooth.
Pour into chilled collins glasses
and garnish with pineapple spears.
Serves 4.

RUM

Piña Colada

4 parts light rum (2 oz./60 ml.)
2 parts dark rum (1 oz./30 ml.)
6 parts pineapple juice
 (3 oz./90 ml.)
4 parts coconut cream
 (2 oz./60 ml.)
Pineapple spear

Combine all ingredients, except pineapple spear, with cracked ice in a blender. Blend until smooth and pour into chilled collins glass. Garnish with pineapple spear.

Pineapple Daiquiri

4 parts light rum (2 oz./60 ml.)
1 part Triple Sec (½ oz./15 ml.)
6 parts pineapple juice
 (3 oz./90 ml.)
1 part fresh lime juice
 (½ oz./15 ml.)
Pineapple spear

Combine all ingredients, except pineapple spear, with cracked ice in a blender. Blend until slushy and pour into chilled wine glass.

Piña Colada

Pineapple Fizz

4 parts light rum (2 oz./60 ml.)
6 parts pineapple juice
 (3 oz./90 ml.)
Sugar syrup (1 tsp.)
Sparkling water

Combine all ingredients, except sparkling water, with cracked ice in a cocktail shaker and shake well. Pour into chilled collins glass over ice cubes. Fill with sparkling water and stir gently.

Pink Creole

4 parts light rum (2 oz./60 ml.)
1 part fresh lime juice
 (½ oz./15 ml.)
Grenadine (1 tsp.)
Half-and-half (1 tsp.)
Black cherry soaked in rum

Combine all ingredients, except cherry, in a cocktail shaker with cracked ice. Shake well and strain into chilled cocktail glass. Garnish with cherry.

Pink Veranda

2 parts gold rum (1 oz./30 ml.)
2 parts dark rum (1 oz./30 ml.)
4 parts cranberry juice
(2 oz./60 ml.)
1 part fresh lime juice
 (½ oz./15 ml.)
Sugar syrup (1 tsp.)
½ egg white

Combine all ingredients with cracked ice in a cocktail shaker. Shake vigorously and pour into chilled old-fashioned glass.

RUM

Pirate's Julep

6 parts gold rum (3 oz./90 ml.)
White Curaçao (1 tsp.)
Orgeat (almond) syrup (1 tsp.)
3 – 5 dashes Peychaud's bitters
10 mint leaves
Fresh mint sprig

Muddle mint leaves in a chilled
highball glass with Orgeat (almond)
syrup. Add bitters, fill glass with
crushed ice and pour in rum. Stir
until glass frosts. Float Curaçao on
top and garnish with mint sprig.

Plantation Punch

4 parts dark rum (2 oz./60 ml.)
2 parts Southern Comfort
  (1 oz./30 ml.)
2 parts fresh lemon juice
  (1 oz./30 ml.)
Ruby port (1 tsp.)
Brown sugar (1 tsp.)
Sparkling water
Lemon slice
Orange slice

Combine all ingredients, except
port, water and fruit, with cracked
ice in a cocktail shaker. Shake well
and pour into chilled collins glass.
Fill almost to the rim with sparkling
water and float port on top. Garnish
with fruit.

Planter's Cocktail

4 parts dark rum (2 oz./60 ml.)
2 parts fresh lemon juice
  (1 oz./30 ml.)
Sugar syrup (1 tsp.)

Combine ingredients with cracked ice
in a cocktail shaker and shake well.
Strain into chilled cocktail glass.

Planter's Punch

Planter's Punch

4 parts dark rum (2 oz./60 ml.)
4 parts light rum (2 oz./60 ml.)
2 parts fresh lime juice
  (1 oz./30 ml.)
2 parts fresh lemon juice
  (1 oz./30 ml.)
Triple Sec (¼ tsp.)
Dash grenadine
Bar sugar (1 tsp.)
Sparkling water
Lime slice
Maraschino cherry
Orange slice
Pineapple spear

Combine all ingredients, except
sparkling water and fruit, with
cracked ice in a cocktail shaker.
Shake well and strain into a chilled
collins glass over ice cubes. Fill
with sparkling water and stir gently.
Garnish with fruit.

RUM

Poker Cocktail

6 parts light rum (3 oz./90 ml.)
2 parts sweet vermouth
    (1 oz./30 ml.)

Combine ingredients with cracked ice in a cocktail shaker. Shake well and strain into chilled cocktail glass.

Polynesian Sour

4 parts light rum (2 oz./60 ml.)
1 part guava nectar (½ oz./15 ml.)
1 part fresh lemon juice
    (½ oz./15 ml.)
1 part fresh orange juice
    (½ oz./15 ml.)

Combine all ingredients with cracked ice in a blender. Blend until smooth and pour into chilled cocktail glass.

Port Antonio

2 parts gold rum (1 oz./30 ml.)
2 parts dark rum (1 oz./30 ml.)
1 part coffee liqueur (½ oz./15 ml.)
1 part fresh lime juice
    (½ oz./15 ml.)
Falernum (1 tsp.)
Lime slice

Combine all ingredients, except lime slice, with cracked ice in a cocktail shaker. Shake well and pour into chilled old-fashioned glass. Garnish with lime slice.

Presidente Cocktail

4 parts light rum (2 oz./60 ml.)
1 part dry vermouth (½ oz./15 ml.)
1 part Triple Sec (½ oz./15 ml.)
Dash grenadine
Lemon twist

Combine all ingredients, except lemon twist, with cracked ice in a cocktail shaker. Shake well and strain into chilled cocktail glass. Garnish with lemon twist.

Quarter Deck Cocktail

4 parts dark rum (2 oz./60 ml.)
2 parts cream sherry (1 oz./30 ml.)
Fresh lime juice (1 tbsp.)

Combine all ingredients with cracked ice in a cocktail shaker and shake well. Strain into chilled cocktail glass.

Presidente Cocktail

RUM

Rampart Street Parade

4 parts light rum (2 oz./60 ml.)
2 parts crème de bananes
  (1 oz./30 ml.)
1 part Southern Comfort
  (½ oz./15 ml.)
2 parts fresh lime juice
  (1 oz./30 ml.)

Combine all ingredients with
cracked ice in a cocktail shaker.
Shake well and strain into chilled
cocktail glass.

Robson Cocktail

4 parts dark rum (2 oz./60 ml.)
1 part fresh lemon juice
  (½ oz./15 ml.)
1 part fresh orange juice
(½ oz./15 ml.)
Grenadine (1 tbsp.)

Combine all ingredients with
cracked ice in a cocktail shaker
and shake well. Strain into chilled
cocktail glass.

Rum Buck

4 parts light rum (2 oz./60 ml.)
2 parts fresh lime juice
  (1 oz./30 ml.)
Ginger ale
Lime slice

Combine rum and lime juice with
cracked ice in a cocktail shaker.
Shake well and pour into chilled
collins glass. Fill with ginger ale and
stir gently. Garnish with lime slice.

Rum Cobbler

4 parts light rum (2 oz./60 ml.)
4 parts sparkling water
  (2 oz./60 ml.)
Bar sugar (1 tsp.)
Pineapple spear
Lime slice
Orange slice

Dissolve sugar in sparkling water in
the bottom of a chilled wine glass.
Fill glass with crushed ice and add
rum. Stir and garnish with fruits.

Rum Collins

6 parts light rum (3 oz./90 ml.)
3 parts fresh lime juice
  (1½ oz./45 ml.)
Bar sugar (1 tsp.)
Sparkling water
Lemon slice
Maraschino cherry

Combine all ingredients, except
sparkling water and fruit, with
cracked ice in a cocktail shaker.
Shake well and strain into chilled
collins glass over ice cubes. Fill
with sparkling water and stir gently.
Garnish with fruit.

Rum Cooler

6 parts light rum (3 oz./90 ml.)
Sugar syrup (1 tsp.)
Ginger ale
Orange twist

Pour rum and sugar syrup into a
chilled collins glass. Fill with ice
cubes and ginger ale. Stir gently
and garnish with orange twist.

RUM

Rum Daisy

4 parts gold rum (2 oz./60 ml.)
2 parts fresh lemon juice
  (2 oz./60 ml.)
Bar sugar (1 tsp.)
Grenadine (½ tsp.)
Maraschino cherry
Orange slice

Combine all ingredients, except fruit, with cracked ice in a cocktail shaker. Shake well and strain into chilled old-fashioned glass over ice cubes. Garnish with fruit.

Rum Dubonnet

4 parts light rum (2 oz./60 ml.)
1 part Dubonnet rouge
  (½ oz./15 ml.)
1 part fresh lemon juice
  (½ oz./15 ml.)

Combine ingredients with cracked ice in a cocktail shaker. Shake well and strain into chilled cocktail glass.

Rum Fix

4 parts gold rum (2 oz./60 ml.)
2 parts fresh lemon juice
  (1 oz./30 ml.)
1 part water (½ oz./15 ml.)
Bar sugar (1 tsp.)
Maraschino cherry
Lemon slice

Combine sugar, lemon juice and water in a cocktail shaker with cracked ice. Shake well and strain into a chilled highball glass filled with crushed ice. Add rum and stir well. Garnish with fruit.

Rum Martini

6 parts light rum (3 oz./90 ml.)
Dry vermouth (½ tsp.)
Dash orange bitters

Combine ingredients with ice cubes in a mixing glass. Stir well and strain into chilled cocktail glass.

Rum Old Fashioned

4 parts light rum (2 oz./60 ml.)
151-proof Demerara rum (1 tbsp.)
Sugar syrup (½ tsp.)
Dash Angostura bitters
Lime twist

Put bitters and syrup in chilled old-fashioned glass. Stir and add ice cubes. Add light rum and stir again. Float Demerara rum on top and garnish with lime twist.

Rum Punch

6 parts dark rum (3 oz./90 ml.)
2 parts fresh lime juice
  (1 oz./30 ml.)
Brown sugar (2 tbsp.)
Bar sugar (1 tbsp.)
Grenadine (1 tsp.)

Combine all ingredients with cracked ice in a blender. Blend until smooth and pour into chilled collins glass.

Rum Runner Mojito

6 parts light rum (3 oz./90 ml.)
2 parts Demerara rum (1 oz./30 ml.)
Juice of one small lime
6 - 8 fresh mint leaves
2 sugar cubes
Club soda

In a cocktail shaker, muddle sugar cubes with the mint leaves and some cracked ice. Add the light rum and shake well. Pour into a highball glass over ice cubes. Add the club soda, then float the Demerara rum on top.

RUM

Rum Screwdriver

4 parts dark rum (2 oz./60 ml.)
Fresh orange juice

Pour rum into chilled highball glass
over ice cubes. Fill with orange juice
and stir.

Scorpion

Rum Sour

4 parts light rum (2 oz./60 ml.)
2 parts fresh lemon juice
 (1 oz./30 ml.)
Bar sugar (1 tsp.)
Lemon slice
Maraschino cherry

Combine all ingredients, except
fruit, with cracked ice in a cocktail
shaker. Shake well and strain into
chilled sour glass. Garnish with
fruit.

Rum Swizzle

4 parts dark rum (2 oz./60 ml.)
3 parts fresh lime juice
 (1½ oz./45 ml.)
2 dashes Angostura bitters
Bar sugar (1 tsp.)
Sparkling water

Combine all ingredients, except
sparkling water, in a cocktail shaker
with cracked ice. Strain over ice
cubes into chilled collins glass. Fill
with sparkling water and stir gently.
Serve with a swizzle stick.

San Juan

4 parts light rum (2 oz./60 ml.)
Brandy (1 tbsp.)
3 parts grapefruit juice
 (1½ oz./45 ml.)
Coconut milk (1 tbsp.)
Fresh lime juice (1 tbsp.)

Combine all ingredients, except
brandy, with cracked ice in a
blender. Blend until smooth and
pour into chilled wine glass. Float
brandy on top.

Santiago Cocktail

4 parts light rum (2 oz./60 ml.)
4 parts fresh lime juice
 (2 oz./60 ml.)
Dash grenadine
Sugar syrup (½ tsp.)

Combine ingredients with cracked
ice in a cocktail shaker. Shake
well and strain into chilled cocktail
glass.

RUM

Saxon Cocktail

4 parts light rum (2 oz./60 ml.)
2 parts fresh lime juice
  (1 oz./30 ml.)
Grenadine (¼ tsp.)
Orange twist

Combine all ingredients, except
orange twist, with cracked ice in
a cocktail shaker. Shake well and
strain into chilled cocktail glass.
Garnish with orange twist.

Scorpion

4 parts gold rum (2 oz./60 ml.)
2 parts brandy (1 oz./30 ml.)
1 part Orgeat (almond) syrup
  (½ oz./15 ml.)
3 parts fresh lemon juice
  (1½ oz./45 ml.)
4 parts fresh orange juice
  (1½ oz./45 ml.)
Orange slice
Lemon slice

Combine all ingredients, except fruit,
with cracked ice in a blender. Blend
until smooth and pour into chilled
wine glass. Garnish with fruit.

September Morn

6 parts light rum (3 oz./90 ml.)
2 parts fresh lime juice
  (1 oz./30 ml.)
Grenadine (1 tsp.)
1 egg white

Combine ingredients with cracked
ice in a cocktail shaker. Shake
vigorously and strain into chilled
cocktail glass.

Sevilla

4 parts light rum (2 oz./60 ml.)
4 parts ruby port (2 oz./60 ml.)
Sugar (½ tsp.)
1 whole egg

Combine ingredients with cracked
ice and shake vigorously. Strain into
chilled wine glass.

Shanghai Cocktail

4 parts dark rum (2 oz./60 ml.)
1 part Pernod (½ oz./15 ml.)
2 parts fresh lemon juice
  (1 oz./30 ml.)
Grenadine (¼ tsp.)

Combine all ingredients with
cracked ice in a cocktail shaker
and shake well. Strain into chilled
cocktail glass.

Shark Bite

4 parts dark rum (2 oz./60 ml.)
6 parts fresh orange juice
  (3 oz./90 ml.)
2 parts fresh lemon juice
  (1 oz./30 ml.)
2 parts grenadine (1 oz./30 ml.)

Combine all ingredients with
cracked ice in a blender. Blend until
smooth and pour into chilled wine
glass.

Shark's Tooth

4 parts 151-proof rum (2 oz./60 ml.)
2 parts fresh lime juice
  (1 oz./30 ml.)
2 parts fresh lemon juice
  (1 oz./30 ml.)
Dash grenadine
Sugar syrup (¼ tsp.)
Sparkling water
Lime wedge

Combine all ingredients, except
sparkling water and lime, with
cracked ice in a cocktail shaker.
Shake well and pour into chilled
highball glass. Fill with sparkling
water and garnish with lime wedge.

RUM

Sir Walter Raleigh Cocktail

4 parts dark rum (2 oz./60 ml.)
3 parts brandy (1½ oz./45 ml.)
1 part grenadine (½ oz./15 ml.)
1 part white Curaçao (½ oz./15 ml.)
1 part fresh lemon juice
  (½ oz./15 ml.)

Combine ingredients with cracked ice in a cocktail shaker and shake well. Strain into chilled cocktail glass.

Sloppy Joe's Cocktail

4 parts light rum (2 oz./60 ml.)
3 parts dry vermouth
  (1½ oz./45 ml.)
Grenadine (½ tsp.)
Triple Sec (½ tsp.)
3 parts fresh lime juice
  (1½ oz./45 ml.)

Combine all ingredients with cracked ice in a cocktail shaker. Shake well and strain into chilled cocktail glass.

Spanish Town Cocktail

6 parts light rum (3 oz./90 ml.)
1 part Triple Sec (½ oz./15 ml.)

Combine ingredients in a mixing glass with ice cubes and stir. Strain into chilled cocktail glass.

Strawberry Colada

Strawberry Colada

6 parts gold rum (3 oz./90 ml.)
2 parts coconut cream
  (1 oz./30 ml.)
8 parts pineapple juice
  (4 oz./120 ml.)
6 fresh strawberries
Pineapple spear

Combine all ingredients, except pineapple spear and one strawberry, in a blender with cracked ice. Blend until smooth and pour into chilled collins glass. Garnish with pineapple and remaining strawberry.

Strawberry Daiquiri

4 parts light rum (2 oz./60 ml.)
2 parts fresh lime juice
  (1 oz./30 ml.)
Sugar syrup (1 tsp.)
7 large fresh strawberries (if it's not the season, frozen are fine)

Combine all ingredients, except for one strawberry, with cracked ice in a blender. Blend until smooth and pour into chilled cocktail glass. Garnish with remaining strawberry.

RUM

Sundowner

4 parts gold rum (2 oz./60 ml.)
2 parts fresh lime juice
  (1 oz./30 ml.)
Maraschino liqueur (¼ tsp.)
White Curaçao (¼ tsp.)
Tonic water
Lime slice

Combine all ingredients, except
tonic and lime slice, with cracked
ice in a cocktail shaker. Strain into
chilled highball glass over ice cubes
and fill with tonic water. Stir gently
and garnish with lime slice.

Surfers on Acid

4 parts coconut rum (2 oz./60 ml.)
2 parts Jagermeister (1 oz./30 ml.)
6 parts pineapple juice
  (3 oz./90 ml.)
⅛ tsp. fresh limejuice
Mint spring

Shake all ingredients, except for
mint spring, with cracked ice in a
cocktail shaker. Strain into an old-
fashioned glass over ice cubes and
garnish with a sprig of mint.

Swamp Water

4 parts dark rum (2 oz./60 ml.)
1 part blue Curaçao (½ oz./15 ml.)
3 parts fresh orange juice
  (1½ oz./45 ml.)
1 part fresh lemon juice
  ½ oz./15 ml.)

Combine all ingredients with
cracked ice in a cocktail shaker.
Shake well and strain into chilled
old-fashioned glass over ice cubes.

Tahiti Club

6 parts gold rum (3 oz./90 ml.)
1 part maraschino liqueur
  (½ oz./15 ml.)
2 parts pineapple juice
  (1 oz./30 ml.)
1 part fresh lemon juice
  (½ oz./15 ml.)
1 part fresh lime juice
  (½ oz./15 ml.)
Orange slice

Combine all ingredients, except
orange slice, with cracked ice in a
cocktail shaker. Pour into chilled
old-fashioned glass and garnish
with orange slice.

Three Miller Cocktail

4 parts light rum (2 oz./60 ml.)
2 parts brandy (1 oz./30 ml.)
1 part grenadine (½ oz./15 ml.)
1 part fresh lemon juice
  (½ oz./15 ml.)

Combine ingredients with ice in a
cocktail shaker. Shake well and
strain into chilled cocktail glass.

RUM

Swamp Water

Tiger's Milk

4 parts gold rum (2 oz./60 ml.)
3 parts cognac (1½ oz./45 ml.)
10 parts milk (5 oz./150 ml.)
Sugar syrup (1 tsp.)
Ground cinnamon

Combine all ingredients, except
cinnamon, with cracked ice in
a blender. Blend until smooth
and pour into chilled wine glass.
Sprinkle cinnamon on top.

Tom and Jerry

4 parts light rum (2 oz./60 ml.)
2 parts brandy (1 oz./30 ml.)
12 parts hot milk (6 oz./180 ml.)
1 whole egg, separated
Freshly ground nutmeg

Beat the white and the yolk of the
egg separately. Mix them together in
a coffee mug glass. Add the sugar
and beat the egg mixture again.
Pour in the rum and brandy. Add
the hot milk and stir gently. Sprinkle
with nutmeg.

Torreadora Cocktail

4 parts light rum (2 oz./60 ml.)
151-proof rum (1 tbsp.)
2 parts coffee liqueur (1 oz./30 ml.)
1 parts half-and-half (½ oz./15 ml.)

Combine all ingredients, except
rum, with cracked ice in a cocktail
shaker. Shake well and strain into
chilled cocktail glass. Float rum on
top.

Trade Winds

4 parts gold rum (2 oz./60 ml.)
2 parts slivovitz (1 oz./30 ml.)
2 parts fresh lime juice
 (1 oz./30 ml.)
1 part Falernum (½ oz./15 ml.)

Combine all ingredients with
cracked ice in a cocktail shaker.
Shake well and strain into chilled
cocktail glass.

White Lion

4 parts dark rum (2 oz./60 ml.)
2 part fresh lemon juice (1 oz./30 ml.)
1 part Orgeat (almond) syrup
 (½ oz./15 ml.)
Raspberry syrup (¼ tsp.)

Combine all ingredients with
cracked ice in a cocktail shaker.
Shake well and strain into chilled
cocktail glass.

X.Y.Z. Cocktail

4 parts light rum (2 oz./60 ml.)
2 parts white Curaçao (1 oz./30 ml.)
1 part fresh lemon juice
 (½ oz./15 ml.)

Combine ingredients with cracked
ice in a cocktail shaker. Shake
well and strain into chilled cocktail
glass.

Xanadu

4 parts light rum (2 oz./60 ml.)
4 parts guava nectar (2 oz./60 ml.)
4 parts fresh lime juice
 (2 oz./60 ml.)
2 parts Rose's lime juice
 (1 oz./30 ml.)
2 parts half-and-half (1 oz./30 ml.)

Combine ingredients with cracked
ice in a blender. Blend at low speed
until smooth. Pour into chilled
champagne flute.

RUM

Zombie

4 parts dark rum (2 oz./60 ml.)
4 parts light rum (2 oz./60 ml.)
2 parts 151-proof rum (1 oz./30 ml.)
2 parts Triple Sec (1 oz./30 ml.)
Pernod (1 tsp.)
2 parts fresh lime juice
  (1 oz./30 ml.)
2 parts fresh orange juice
  (1 oz./30 ml.)
2 parts pineapple juice
  (1 oz./30 ml.)
2 parts guava nectar (1 oz./30 ml.)
Grenadine (1 tbsp.)
Orgeat (almond) syrup (1 tbsp.)
Fresh mint sprig
Pineapple spear

Combine all ingredients, except mint and pineapple spear, with cracked ice in a blender. Blend until smooth. Pour into chilled collins glass and garnish with pineapple and mint sprig.

Zombie

RYE AND OTHER WHISKEYS

Bourbon and scotch and are not the only distinctive spirits made from fermented grains. Canadian whiskey, Irish whiskey, and rye whiskey are staples in any traditional bar. Rye whiskey, in particular, has long been part of American culture and its production by colonial settlers predates the introduction of Bourbon. American rye whiskey, by law, must be made from a fermented mash that is at least 51% rye grain. Many Canadian whiskeys also contain rye but they are primarily made from corn. Blended Canadian and American whiskeys also make use of other grains, such as wheat, barley malt, and barley. Irish whiskey is made from locally produced malted barley or a mix of unmalted barley and other cereals. American rye whiskey may date to the colonial era but the Irish have perhaps been making whiskey longer than anyone— some credit 6th century Irish monks with inventing whiskey.

Algonquin

3 parts American blended whiskey
  (1½ oz./45 ml.)
1 part dry vermouth (½ oz./15 ml.)
2 parts pineapple juice
  (1 oz./30 ml.)

In a cocktail shaker, combine all
ingredients with ice cubes and
shake well. Strain into a chilled
cocktail glass.

Ballylickey Belt

4 parts Irish whiskey (2 oz./60 ml.)
Honey (¾ tsp.)
Cold sparkling water
Lemon peel

In the bottom of a chilled old-
fashioned glass, muddle the honey
with a little water until it dissolves.
Add the whiskey and ice cubes. Fill
with sparkling water and stir gently.
Twist the lemon peel over the glass
and drop in.

Banff Cocktail

4 parts Canadian whiskey
  (2 oz./60 ml.)
1 part Grand Marnier (½ oz./15 ml.)
1 part kirshwasser (½ oz.;/15 ml.)
Dash Angostura bitters

Combine ingredients with cracked
ice in a cocktail shaker. Shake well.
Strain into chilled cocktail glass.

Black Hawk

4 parts blended whiskey
  (2 oz./60 ml.)
2 parts sloe gin (1 oz./30 ml.)

Stir ingredients in a mixing glass
with cracked ice. Strain into chilled
cocktail glass.

Blackthorn

4 parts Irish whiskey (2 oz./60 ml.)
3 parts dry vermouth
  (1½ oz./45 ml.)
3 – 5 dashes of Pernod
3 – 5 dashes of Angostura bitters

Stir all ingredients in a mixing glass
with cracked ice. Pour into a chilled
old-fashioned glass.

Blinker

4 parts rye (2 oz./60 ml.)
5 parts grapefruit juice
  (2½ oz./75 ml.)
Grenadine (1 tsp.)

Combine all ingredients with
cracked ice in a cocktail shaker.
Shake well and strain into chilled
cocktail glass.

Boilermaker

Boilermaker

Beer (½ pint/250 ml.)
3 parts whiskey of your choice
  (1½ oz./45 ml.)

Pour the whiskey into a shot glass.
Drop shot glass into ½ pint mug of
beer.

Boston Sour

4 parts whiskey (2 oz./60 ml.)
2 parts fresh lemon juice
  (1 oz./30 ml.)
Bar sugar (1 tsp.)
1 egg white (or 1 tbsp. egg white
  substitute)
Lemon slice
Maraschino cherry

Combine all ingredients, except
fruit, in a cocktail shaker with
cracked ice. Shake vigorously.
Strain into chilled sour glass and
garnish with cherry and lemon.

Brighton Punch

4 parts B & B (2 oz./60 ml.)
3 parts bourbon (1½ oz./45 ml.)
2 parts fresh orange juice
  (1 oz./30 ml.)
2 parts fresh lemon juice
  (1 oz./30 ml.)
Sparkling water
Orange slice

Combine all ingredients, except
water and fruit, with cracked ice in
a cocktail shaker. Shake well. Strain
into a chilled highball glass over ice
cubes. Top off with sparkling water
and stir. Garnish with orange.

Cablegram

4 parts blended whiskey
  (2 oz./60 ml.)
1 part fresh lemon juice
  (½ oz./15 ml.)
Bar sugar (½ tsp.)
Ginger ale

Stir all ingredients, except ginger
ale, in a mixing glass with cracked
ice. Strain into chilled highball glass
over ice cubes. Top off with ginger
ale and stir again.

California Lemonade

4 parts blended whiskey
  (2 oz./60 ml.)
2 parts fresh lemon juice
  (1 oz./30 ml.)
2 parts fresh lime juice
  (1 oz./30 ml.)
Bar sugar (1 tsp.)
Sparkling water
Orange slice

Combine whiskey, juices and sugar
in a cocktail shaker with cracked
ice. Shake well. Strain into a chilled
highball glass almost filled with ice
cubes. Top off with sparkling water.
Stir gently and garnish with orange
slice.

Canadian and Campari

3 parts Canadian whiskey
  (1½ oz./45 ml.)
2 parts Campari (1 oz./30 ml.)
1 part dry vermouth (½ oz./15 ml.)
Lemon twist

Stir all ingredients, except lemon
twist, in a mixing glass with cracked
ice. Strain into chilled cocktail glass
and garnish with lemon twist.

Canadian Apple

4 parts Canadian whiskey
  (2 oz./60 ml.)
1 part Calvados (½ oz./15 ml.)
Sugar syrup (1 tsp.)
Fresh lemon juice (1½ tsp.)
Ground cinnamon
Lemon slice

Combine all ingredients, except
lemon slice, in a cocktail shaker
with cracked ice and shake well.
Pour into chilled old-fashioned
glass and garnish with lemon slice.

Canadian Blackberry Cocktail

4 parts Canadian whiskey
  (2 oz./60 ml.)
1 part blackberry brandy
  (½ oz./15 ml.)
1 part fresh orange juice
  (½ oz./15 ml.)
Fresh lemon juice (1 tsp.)
Bar sugar (½ tsp.)

Combine all ingredients with cracked ice in a cocktail shaker and shake well. Strain into a chilled old-fashioned glass.

Canadian Cherry

4 parts Canadian whiskey
  (2 oz./60 ml.)
2 part cherry brandy (1 oz./30 ml.)
Fresh lemon juice (2 tsp.)
Fresh orange juice (2 tsp.)
Bar sugar

Rim a chilled cocktail glass with sugar by pouring one part of the cherry brandy into a saucer and dipping the glass into it. Pour some sugar into another saucer and dip the moistened rim into the sugar. Shake all ingredients in a cocktail shaker with cracked ice and strain into the glass.

Canadian Cocktail

4 parts Canadian whiskey
  (2 oz./60 ml.)
Triple Sec (2 tsp.)
Dash Angostura bitters
Bar sugar (½ tsp.)

Combine all ingredients in a cocktail shaker and shake with cracked ice. Strain into chilled old-fashioned glass.

Canadian Daisy

4 parts Canadian whiskey
  (2 oz./60 ml.)
Brandy (1 tsp.)
1 part fresh lemon juice
  (½ oz./15 ml.)
Raspberry syrup (1 tsp.)
Sparkling water
Fresh raspberries

Combine whiskey, lemon juice and raspberry syrup in a cocktail shaker with ice cubes and shake well. Pour into a chilled highball glass and top off with sparkling water. Float brandy on top and garnish with fresh raspberries.

Canadian Old Fashioned

4 parts Canadian whiskey
  (2 oz./60 ml.)
Triple Sec (1 tsp.)
Dash fresh lemon juice
Dash Angostura bitters
Lemon twist
Orange twist

Combine all ingredients, except twists, in a cocktail shaker with cracked ice. Shake well and pour into chilled old-fashioned glass. Garnish with twists.

Canadian Daisy

Canadian Pineapple

4 parts Canadian whiskey
  (2 oz./60 ml.)
Pineapple juice (1 tbsp.)
Maraschino liqueur (2 tsp.)
Fresh lemon juice (2 tsp.)
Pineapple spear

Combine all ingredients, except
the pineapple spear, in a cocktail
shaker with cracked ice. Shake well.
Strain into chilled cocktail glass
and garnish with pineapple spear.

Coffee Egg Nog

4 parts blended whiskey
  (2 oz./60 ml.)
2 parts coffee liqueur (1 oz./30 ml.)
12 parts milk (6 oz./180 ml.)
2 parts half-and-half (1 oz./30 ml.)
Sugar syrup (1 tsp.)
Instant coffee (½ tsp.)
1 egg
Freshly ground nutmeg

Combine all ingredients, except
nutmeg, with cracked ice in a
blender. Blend until smooth and
pour into chilled collins glass.
Sprinkle with nutmeg.

Commonwealth Cocktail

4 parts Canadian whiskey
  (2 oz./60 ml.)
1 part Grand Marnier (½ oz./15 ml.)
Fresh lemon juice (1 tsp.)
Orange twist

Combine all ingredients, except
orange twist, in a mixing glass with
cracked ice. Stir well. Pour into
chilled cocktail glass and garnish
with orange twist.

Cowboy Cocktail

6 parts rye (3 oz./90 ml.)
Half-and-half (2 tbsp.)

Combine ingredients with cracked ice
in a cocktail shaker and shake well.
Strain into chilled cocktail glass.

Delta

4 parts blended whiskey
  (2 oz./60 ml.)
1 part Southern Comfort
  (½ oz./15 ml.)
1 part fresh lime juice
  (½ oz./15 ml.)
Bar sugar (½ tsp.)
Orange slice
Fresh peach slice

Combine all ingredients, except
fruit, with cracked ice in a cocktail
shaker. Shake well. Pour into chilled
old-fashioned glass and garnish
with fruit.

Dinah

4 parts blended whiskey
  (2 oz./60 ml.)
1 part fresh lemon juice
  (½ oz./15 ml.)
Bar sugar (½ tsp.)
Fresh mint sprig

Shake all ingredients, except mint,
in a cocktail shaker with cracked
ice. Strain into chilled cocktail glass
and garnish with mint sprig.

RYE AND OTHER WHISKEYS

Double Standard Sour

3 parts blended whiskey
(1½ oz./45 ml.)
3 parts gin (1½ oz./45 ml.)
2 parts fresh lemon juice
(1 oz./30 ml.)
Bar sugar (½ tsp.)
Grenadine (1 tsp.)
Maraschino cherry
Orange slice

Combine all ingredients, except fruit,
in a cocktail shaker with cracked
ice. Shake well. Strain into chilled
sour glass and garnish with fruit.

Dry Manhattan

6 parts rye (3 oz./90 ml.)
2 parts dry vermouth (1 oz./30 ml.)
Dash Angostura bitters
Maraschino cherry

Combine all ingredients, except
cherry, in a mixing glass with ice
cubes. Stir well and strain into chilled
cocktail glass. Garnish with cherry.

Earthquake

4 parts blended whiskey
(2 oz./60 ml.)
2 parts gin (1 oz./30 ml.)
2 parts Pernod (1 oz./30 ml.)

Combine all ingredients with
cracked ice in a cocktail shaker.
Shake well and strain into chilled
cocktail glass.

Elk's Own

4 parts rye (2 oz./60 ml.)
2 parts ruby port (1 oz./30 ml.)
1 part fresh lemon juice
(½ oz./15 ml.)
1 egg white
Bar sugar (1 tsp.)
Pineapple spear

Combine all ingredients, except
pineapple spear, with cracked ice
in a cocktail shaker and shake
vigorously. Strain into chilled
cocktail glass.

Everybody's Irish

4 parts Irish whiskey (2 oz./60 ml.)
1 part green Chartreuse
(½ oz./15 ml.)
1 part green crème de menthe
(½ oz./15 ml.)

Stir all ingredients with cracked ice
in a mixing glass. Strain into chilled
cocktail glass.

Fancy Whiskey

4 parts whiskey (2 oz./60 ml.)
Cointreau (½ tsp.)
Bar sugar (½ tsp.)
3 dashes Angostura bitters
Lemon twist

Combine all ingredients, except
lemon twist, with cracked ice in
a cocktail shaker. Shake well and
strain into chilled cocktail glass,
drop lemon twist on top.

Fox River Cocktail

4 parts rye (2 oz./60 ml.)
1 part dark crème de cacao
(½ oz./15 ml.)
3 – 5 dashes Angostura bitters
Lemon twist

Combine all ingredients, except
lemon, in a mixing glass with
cracked ice and stir. Strain into
chilled cocktail glass and garnish
with lemon twist.

Gloom Lifter

4 parts blended whiskey
  (2 oz./60 ml.)
2 parts brandy (1 oz./30 ml.)
Raspberry liqueur (1 tbsp.)
1 part fresh lemon juice
  (½ oz./15 ml.)
Bar sugar (½ tsp.)
½ egg white (or 1 tsp. egg white
  substitute)

Combine all ingredients in cocktail
shaker with cracked ice. Shake
vigorously. Strain into chilled
highball glass over ice cubes.

Habitant Cocktail

4 parts Canadian whiskey
  (2 oz./60 ml.)
2 parts fresh lemon juice
  (1 oz./30 ml.)
1 tsp. maple syrup
Orange slice
Maraschino cherry

Combine all ingredients, except
fruit, in a cocktail shaker with
cracked ice. Shake well and strain
into chilled cocktail glass. Garnish
with fruit.

Halley's Comfort

4 parts Southern Comfort
  (2 oz./60 ml.)
4 parts peach schnapps
  (2 oz./60 ml.)
Sparkling water
Lemon slice

Pour Southern Comfort and
schnapps into a chilled collins
glass filled with ice cubes. Fill with
sparkling water. Stir gently and
garnish with lemon slice.

Heart's Cocktail

4 parts Irish whiskey (2 oz./60 ml.)
2 parts sweet vermouth
  (1 oz./30 ml.)
2 parts Pernod (1 oz./30 ml.)
3 – 5 dashes Angostura bitters

Combine all ingredients in a
cocktail shaker with cracked ice.
Shake well and pour into chilled
old-fashioned glass.

Horse's Neck

4 parts blended whiskey
  (2 oz./60 ml.)
Ginger ale
3 dashes Angostura bitters
Rind of one lemon, peeled in a spiral

Put the lemon spiral in a chilled
collins glass and hand one end over
the rim. Fill with ice cubes and add
whiskey. Fill with ginger ale and stir
well.

Hot Brick Toddy

4 parts blended whiskey
  (2 oz./60 ml.)
2 parts hot water (1 oz./30 ml.)
Bar sugar (1 tsp.)
Butter (1 tsp.)
Ground cinnamon to taste
Boiling water

Dissolve all ingredients, except
whiskey, in hot water in a warmed
coffee mug or punch cup. Add
whiskey and boiling water. Stir well.

Hot Milk Punch

6 parts whiskey (3 oz./90 ml.)
16 parts milk (8 oz./240 ml.)
Bar sugar (1 tsp.)
Cinnamon stick
Freshly ground nutmeg

Heat all ingredients, except nutmeg
and cinnamon stick, in a sauce
pan over low heat. Stir regularly
until mixture is very hot. Pour into
warmed mug and stir with cinnamon
stick. Sprinkle with nutmeg.

RYE AND OTHER WHISKEYS

Irish Coffee

Hunter's Cocktail

4 parts rye (2 oz./60 ml.)
1 part cherry brandy (½ oz./15 ml.)
Maraschino cherry

Pour rye and brandy into a chilled old-fashioned glass filled with ice cubes. Stir well and garnish with cherry.

Imperial Fizz

4 parts blended whiskey
  (2 oz./60 ml.)
2 parts light rum (1 oz./30 ml.)
2 parts fresh lemon juice
  (1 oz./30 ml.)
Bar sugar (½ tsp.)
Sparkling water

Combine all ingredients, except water, with cracked ice in a cocktail shaker. Strain into chilled highball glass and add ice cubes. Fill with sparkling water and stir gently.

Indian River

4 parts blended whiskey
  (2 oz./60 ml.)
1 part raspberry liqueur
  (½ oz./15 ml.)
1 part sweet vermouth
  (½ oz./15 ml.)
2 parts grapefruit juice
  (1 oz./30 ml.)

Combine all ingredients with cracked ice in a cocktail shaker. Shake well and strain into chilled cocktail glass.

Ink Street

4 parts rye (2 oz./60 ml.)
4 parts fresh lemon juice
  (2 oz./60 ml.)
4 parts fresh orange juice
  (2 oz./60 ml.)

Combine all ingredients with cracked ice in a cocktail shaker. Shake well and strain into chilled cocktail glass.

Irish Canadian Sangaree

4 parts Canadian whiskey
  (2 oz./60 ml.)
2 parts Irish mist (1 oz./30 ml.)
2 parts fresh lemon juice
  (1 oz./30 ml.)
2 parts fresh orange juice
  (1 oz./30 ml.)
Freshly grated nutmeg

Pour all ingredients, except nutmeg, into a chilled old-fashioned glass and stir with ice cubes. Sprinkle with nutmeg.

Irish Coffee

4 parts Irish whiskey (2 oz./60 ml.)
Hot black coffee
Whipped cream
Granulated sugar

Rim the cup with sugar and pour in Irish whiskey. Fill the cup to within ½ inch of the rim with coffee. Stir. Top off with whipped cream.

Irish Cow

4 parts Irish whiskey (2 oz./60 ml.)
16 parts hot milk (1 cup or 8 oz.)
Bar sugar (1 tsp.)

Pour the milk into a warmed coffee mug. Add the whiskey and sugar and stir well.

Irish Fix

4 parts Irish whiskey (2 oz./60 ml.)
2 parts Irish mist (1 oz./30 ml.)
1 part fresh lemon juice
  (½ oz./15 ml.)
1 part pineapple juice
  (½ oz./15 ml.)
Lemon slice
Orange slice
Pineapple spear

Combine all ingredients, except fruit, in a blender with cracked ice. Blend until smooth. Pour into chilled old-fashioned glass and garnish with fruit

Irish Kilt

4 parts Irish whiskey (2 oz./60 ml.)
2 parts scotch (1 oz./30 ml.)
2 parts fresh lemon juice
  (1 oz./30 ml.)
2 parts sugar syrup (1 oz./30 ml.)
3 – 5 dashes orange bitters

Combine all ingredients with cracked ice in a cocktail shaker. Shake well and strain into chilled cocktail glass.

Irish Shillelagh

4 parts Irish whiskey (2 oz./60 ml.)
1 part light rum (½ oz./15 ml.)
1 part sloe gin (½ oz./15 ml.)
2 parts fresh lemon juice
  (1 oz./30 ml.)
Bar sugar (½ tsp.)
Fresh peaches, diced
  (¼ cup/60 ml.)
Fresh raspberries

Combine all ingredients, except raspberries, in a blender with cracked ice. Blend until smooth and pour into chilled old-fashioned glass. Garnish with a few raspberries.

Japanese Fizz

4 parts blended whiskey
  (2 oz./60 ml.)
Port (1 tbsp.)
2 parts fresh lemon juice
  (1 oz./30 ml.)
Bar sugar (1 tsp.)
1 egg white (or 1 tbsp. egg white
  substitute)
Sparkling water
Pineapple spear

Combine all ingredients, except sparkling water and pineapple, in a cocktail shaker with cracked ice. Shake vigorously. Strain into chilled highball glass over ice cubes and fill with sparkling water. Stir gently and garnish with pineapple.

RYE AND OTHER WHISKEYS

John Collins

4 parts blended whiskey
  (2 oz./60 ml.)
2 parts fresh lemon juice
  (1 oz./30 ml.)
Bar sugar (1 tsp.)
Sparkling water
Lemon slice
Orange slice
Maraschino cherry

Combine all ingredients, except
sparkling water and fruit, in a
cocktail shaker with cracked ice.
Shake well and strain over ice
cubes into a chilled collins glass.
Fill with sparkling water and stir
gently. Garnish with fruits.

Kerry Cooler

4 parts Irish whiskey (2 oz./60 ml.)
3 parts fino sherry (1½ oz./45 ml.)
2 parts Orgeat (almond) syrup
  (1 oz./30 ml.)
2 parts fresh lemon juice
  (1 oz./30 ml.)
Sparkling water
Lemon slice

Combine all ingredients, except
lemon slice and water, in a cocktail
shaker with cracked ice. Shake
well and strain into chilled highball
glass filled with ice cubes. Fill with
sparkling water and stir gently.

King Cole Cocktail

4 parts blended whiskey
  (2 oz./60 ml.)
Orange slice
Pineapple slice
Sugar (½ tsp.)

Muddle fruit and sugar in an old-
fashioned glass. Add whiskey and
ice cubes. Stir well.

Klondike Cooler

4 parts blended whiskey
  (2 oz./60 ml.)
4 parts sparkling water
  (2 oz./60 ml.)
Bar sugar (½ tsp.)
Ginger ale
Lemon peel spiral

Mix powdered sugar and ginger ale
in a chilled collins glass. Fill glass
with ice cubes and add whiskey. Fill
with sparkling water and stir well.
Garnish with lemon spiral.

Ladies' Cocktail

4 parts blended whiskey
  (2 oz./60 ml.)
Pernod (1 tsp.)
3 – 5 dashes Angostura bitters
Pineapple spear

Combine all ingredients, except
pineapple, in a cocktail shaker with
cracked ice. Shake well and strain
into chilled cocktail glass.

Lawhill Cocktail

4 parts blended whiskey
  (2 oz./60 ml.)
2 part dry vermouth (1 oz./30 ml.)
Pernod (½ tsp.)
Maraschino liqueur (½ tsp.)
Dash Angostura bitters

Combine ingredients with ice cubes
in a mixing glass and stir well.
Strain into chilled cocktail glass.

Leprechaun

4 parts Irish whiskey (2 oz./60 ml.)
2 parts light rum (1 oz./30 ml.)
1 part sloe gin (½ oz./15 ml.)
2 parts fresh lemon juice
  (1 oz./30 ml.)
Bar sugar (½ tsp.)
¼ fresh peach, peeled and diced
Fresh raspberries

Combine all ingredients, except
the raspberries, in a blender
with cracked ice. Blend until
slushy and pour into chilled old-
fashioned glass. Garnish with fresh
raspberries.

Lord Rodney

4 parts blended whiskey
  (2 oz./60 ml.)
2 parts dark rum (1 oz./30 ml.)
White crème de cacao (¼ tsp.)
Coconut syrup (1 tsp.)

Combine all ingredients with
cracked ice in a cocktail shaker.
Shake well and strain into chilled
cocktail glass.

Los Angeles Cocktail

4 parts rye (2 oz./60 ml.)
Sweet vermouth (¼ tsp.)
2 parts fresh lemon juice (1 oz./30 ml.)
Bar sugar (1 tsp.)
1 whole egg

Combine ingredients with cracked
ice in a cocktail shaker. Shake
vigorously and strain into a chilled
sour glass over ice cubes.

Manhasset

4 parts rye (2 oz./60 ml.)
½ part dry vermouth (¼ oz./7.5 ml.)
½ part sweet vermouth
  (¼ oz./7.5 ml.)
Fresh lemon juice (1 tbsp.)
Lemon twist

Combine all ingredients, except
lemon twist, with cracked ice in
a cocktail shaker. Shake well and
strain into chilled cocktail glass.
Garnish with lemon twist.

Manhattan

6 parts rye (3 oz./90 ml.)
2 parts sweet vermouth
  (1 oz./30 ml.)
Dash Angostura bitters
Maraschino cherry

Combine all ingredients, except
cherry, with ice cubes in a mixing
glass. Stir well and strain into
chilled cocktail glass. Garnish with
cherry.

Milk Punch

4 parts blended whiskey
14 parts milk (1 cup or 8 oz.)
Sugar syrup (1 tsp.)
Freshly grated nutmeg

Pour milk into chilled collins glass.
Stir in whiskey and sugar syrup.
Sprinkle nutmeg on top.

Manhasset

RYE AND OTHER WHISKEYS

Mountain Cocktail

4 parts blended whiskey
  (2 oz./60 ml.)
1 part dry vermouth (½ oz./15 ml.)
1 part sweet vermouth
  (½ oz./15 ml.)
1 part fresh lemon juice
  (½ oz./15 ml.)
1 egg white (or 1 tbsp. egg white
  substitute)

Combine all ingredients with
cracked ice in a cocktail shaker and
shake vigorously. Strain into chilled
cocktail glass.

New World

6 parts blended whiskey
  (3 oz./90 ml.)
2 parts fresh lime juice
  (1 oz./30 ml.)
Grenadine (2 tsp.)
Lime twist

Combine all ingredients, except
lime twist, in a cocktail shaker with
cracked ice. Shake well and strain
into chilled cocktail glass. Garnish
with lime twist.

New York Sour

4 parts blended whiskey
  (2 oz./60 ml.)
3 parts fresh lemon juice
  (1½ oz./45 ml.)
Bar sugar (1 tsp.)
Dry red wine (1 tbsp.)

Combine all ingredients, except
wine, with cracked ice in a cocktail
shaker. Shake well and strain into
chilled sour glass. Float wine on top.

Manhattan

New Yorker Cocktail

4 parts blended whiskey
  (2 oz./60 ml.)
2 parts fresh lemon juice
  (1 oz./30 ml.)
Grenadine (½ tsp.)
Sugar syrup (1 tsp.)
Lemon twist

Combine all ingredients, except
lemon twist, with cracked ice in
a cocktail shaker. Shake well and
strain into chilled cocktail glass.
Garnish with lemon twist.

Old Fashioned

4 parts blended whiskey, bourbon,
  or rye (2 oz./60 ml.)
Sugar cube
Dash Angostura bitters
Water (1 tsp.)
Lemon twist

Place a sugar cube in the bottom of
an old-fashioned glass. Add bitters
and water. Muddle until sugar is
dissolved. Add the whiskey and stir.
Add lemon twist and ice cubes.

Old Pal Cocktail

4 parts rye (2 oz./60 ml.)
3 parts Campari (1½ oz./45 ml.)
2 parts sweet vermouth
  (1 oz./30 ml.)

Combine all ingredients with
cracked ice in a cocktail shaker.
Shake well and strain into chilled
cocktail glass.

New Yorker Cocktail

One Ireland

4 parts Irish whiskey (2 oz./60 ml.)
1 part green crème de menthe
  (½ oz./15 ml.)
Small scoop vanilla ice cream

Combine ingredients in a blender.
Blend until smooth and pour into
chilled cocktail glass.

Opening Cocktail

4 parts Canadian whiskey
  (2 oz./60 ml.)
2 parts sweet vermouth (1 oz./30 ml.)
1 part grenadine (½ oz./15 ml.)

Stir ingredients with cracked ice in
a mixing glass. Strain into chilled
cocktail glass.

Oriental

4 parts blended whiskey
  (2 oz./60 ml.)
1 part sweet vermouth
  (½ oz./15 ml.)
1 part white Curaçao (½ oz./15 ml.)
2 parts fresh lime juice
  (1 oz./30 ml.)

Combine all ingredients with
cracked ice in a cocktail shaker.
Shake well and strain into chilled
cocktail glass.

Paddy Cocktail

4 parts Irish whiskey (2 oz./60 ml.)
2 parts sweet vermouth
  (1 oz./30 ml.)
3 – 5 dashes Angostura bitters

Combine all ingredients with
cracked ice in a cocktail shaker.
Shake well and strain into chilled
cocktail glass.

Palmer Cocktail

4 parts rye (2 oz./60 ml.)
Fresh lemon juice (½ tsp.)
Dash Angostura bitters

Stir ingredients with ice cubes in
a mixing glass. Strain into chilled
cocktail glass.

Perfect Manhattan

6 parts rye (3 oz./90 ml.)
1 part dry vermouth (½ oz./15 ml.)
1 part sweet vermouth
  (½ oz./15 ml.)
Maraschino cherry

Combine all ingredients, except
cherry, in a cocktail shaker with
cracked ice. Shake well and strain
into chilled cocktail glass. Garnish
with cherry.

RYE AND OTHER WHISKEYS

Pink Almond

4 parts blended whiskey
  (2 oz./60 ml.)
2 parts amaretto (1 oz./30 ml.)
1 part crème de noyaux
  (½ oz./15 ml.)
1 part kirshwasser (½ oz./15 ml.)
2 parts fresh lemon juice
  (1 oz./30 ml.)
Lemon slice

Combine all ingredients, except
lemon slice, with cracked ice in a
cocktail shaker. Shake well and
pour into a chilled sour glass.
Garnish with lemon slice

Old Fashioned

Preakness Cocktail

4 parts blended whiskey
  (2 oz./60 ml.)
2 parts sweet vermouth
  (1 oz./30 ml.)
Benedictine (1 tsp.)
Dash Angostura bitters
Lemon twist

Combine all ingredients, except
lemon twist, with cracked ice in
a cocktail shaker. Shake well and
strain into chilled cocktail glass.
Garnish with lemon twist.

Québec Cocktail

6 parts Canadian whiskey
  (3 oz./90 ml.)
2 parts Amer Picon (1 oz./30 ml.)
2 parts dry vermouth (1 oz./30 ml.)
1 part maraschino liqueur
  (½ oz./15 ml.)

Combine all ingredients with
cracked ice in a cocktail shaker
and shake well. Strain into chilled
cocktail glass.

Rattlesnake

4 parts blended whiskey
  (2 oz./60 ml.)
1 part fresh lemon juice
  (½ oz./15 ml.)
Sugar syrup (1 tsp.)
1 egg white (or 1 tbsp. egg white
  substitute)
Pernod (¼ tsp.)

Combine all ingredients with
cracked ice in a cocktail shaker.
Shake vigorously and pour into
chilled old-fashioned glass.

New York Sour

RYE AND OTHER WHISKEYS

Rhett Butler

4 parts Southern Comfort
 (2 oz./60 ml.)
1 part fresh lime juice
 (½ oz./15 ml.)
1 part white Curaçao (½ oz./15 ml.)
Fresh lemon juice (1 tsp.)
Lemon twist

Combine all ingredients, except
lemon twist, with cracked ice in
a cocktail shaker. Shake well and
strain into chilled cocktail glass.
Garnish with lemon twist.

Rye Whiskey Cocktail

6 parts rye (3 oz./90 ml.)
Bar sugar (1 tsp.)
Dash Angostura bitters
Maraschino cherry

Combine all ingredients, except
cherry, with cracked ice in a
cocktail shaker. Shake well and
strain into chilled cocktail glass.
Garnish with cherry.

S.F. Sour

4 parts blended whiskey
 (2 oz./60 ml.)
2 parts Benedictine (1 oz./30 ml.)
Fresh lemon juice (1 tsp.)
Fresh lime juice (1 tsp.)
Dash grenadine
Orange slice

Combine all ingredients, except
orange slice, in a cocktail shaker
with cracked ice. Strain into chilled
sour glass and garnish with orange
slice.

Scarlett O'Hara

4 parts Southern Comfort
 (2 oz./60 ml.)
4 parts cranberry juice
 (2 oz./60 ml.)
2 parts fresh lime juice
 (1 oz./30 ml.)

Combine all ingredients with
cracked ice in a cocktail shaker
and shake well. Strain into chilled
cocktail glass.

Seaboard

4 parts blended whiskey
 (2 oz./60 ml.)
2 parts gin (1 oz./30 ml.)
1 part fresh lemon juice
 (½ oz./15 ml.)
Bar sugar (1 tsp.)
Fresh mint sprig

Combine all ingredients, except
mint, with cracked ice in a cocktail
shaker. Shake well and strain into a
chilled old-fashioned glass over ice
cubes. Garnish with mint sprig.

Serpent's Tooth

4 parts Irish whiskey (2 oz./60 ml.)
2 parts sweet vermouth
 (1 oz./30 ml.)
1 part Jagermeister (½ oz./15 ml.)
3 parts fresh lemon juice
 (1½ oz./45 ml.)
3 – 5 dashes Angostura bitters
Lemon twist

Combine all ingredients, except
lemon twist, with cracked ice in
a cocktail shaker. Shake well and
pour into chilled old-fashioned
glass. Garnish with lemon twist.

Seven & Seven

4 parts Seagram's® 7-Crown
  blended whiskey (2 oz./60 ml.)
7-Up®

Pour whiskey into a chilled highball
glass over ice cubes. Fill with 7-Up
and stir gently.

Shamrock

4 parts Irish whiskey (2 oz./60 ml.)
1 part dry vermouth (½ oz./15 ml.)
1 part green crème de menthe
  (½ oz./15 ml.)
Green Chartreuse (1 tsp.)

Combine all ingredients with
cracked ice in a cocktail shaker.
Shake well and strain into chilled
cocktail glass.

Temptation Cocktail

4 parts blended whiskey
  (2 oz./60 ml.)
1 part Cointreau (½ oz./15 ml.)
1 part Dubonnet rouge
  (½ oz./15 ml.)
Pernod (1 tsp.)
Lemon twist

Combine all ingredients, except
lemon twist, with cracked ice in
a cocktail shaker. Shake well and
strain into chilled cocktail glass.
Garnish with lemon twist.

Tennessee

4 parts rye (2 oz./60 ml.)
2 parts maraschino liqueur
  (1 oz./30 ml.)
2 parts fresh lemon juice
  (1 oz./30 ml.)

Combine all ingredients with
cracked ice in a cocktail shaker.
Shake well and strain into chilled
cocktail glass.

Thunderclap

4 parts blended whiskey
  (2 oz./60 ml.)
2 parts brandy (1 oz./30 ml.)
2 parts gin (1 oz./30 ml.)

Combine ingredients with cracked
ice in a cocktail shaker. Shake
well and strain into chilled cocktail
glass.

Tipperary Cocktail

4 parts Irish whiskey (2 oz./60 ml.)
2 parts green Chartreuse
  (1 oz./30 ml.)
1 part sweet vermouth
  (½ oz./15 ml.)

Combine all ingredients with
cracked ice in a cocktail shaker.
Shake well and strain into chilled
cocktail glass.

Trois Rivieres

4 parts Canadian whiskey
  (2 oz./60 ml.)
1 part Dubonnet rouge
  (½ oz./15 ml.)
Cointreau (1 tbsp.)
Orange twist

Combine all ingredients, except
orange twist, in a cocktail shaker
with cracked ice. Shake well and
strain into chilled cocktail glass.
Garnish with orange twist.

Ward Eight

4 parts blended whiskey
  (2 oz./60 ml.)
3 parts fresh lemon juice
  (1½ oz./45 ml.)
Grenadine (1 tsp.)
Bar sugar (1 tsp.)

Combine ingredients with cracked ice in a cocktail shaker. Shake well and strain into chilled wine glass filled with cracked ice.

Whiskey Cocktail

6 parts blended whiskey
  (3 oz./90 ml.)
Sugar syrup (1 tsp.)
Dash Angostura bitters

Combine ingredients with cracked ice in a cocktail shaker. Shake well and strain into chilled cocktail glass.

Whiskey Collins

6 parts whiskey (3 oz./90 ml.)
4 parts fresh lemon juice
  (2 oz./60 ml.)
1 part sugar syrup (½ oz./15 ml.)
Sparkling water
Maraschino cherry
Orange slice

Combine all ingredients, except fruit and sparkling water, in a chilled collins glass filled with ice cubes. Fill with sparkling water and stir gently. Garnish with fruit.

Whiskey Cooler

4 parts blended whiskey
  (2 oz./60 ml.)
Bar sugar (½ tsp.)
Sparkling water
Lemon peel

Mix whiskey with sugar in the bottom of a chilled collins glass. Add ice cubes and fill with sparkling water. Stir gently and garnish with lemon peel.

Whiskey Daisy

6 parts whiskey (3 oz./90 ml.)
2 parts fresh lemon juice
  (1 oz./30 ml.)
Grenadine (1 tbsp.)
Sugar syrup (1 tsp.)
Sparkling water
Orange slice

Combine all ingredients, except orange slice and sparkling water, in a cocktail shaker with cracked ice. Shake well. Pour into chilled highball glass. Top off with sparkling water, stir gently, and garnish with orange slice.

Whiskey Fix

4 parts blended whiskey
  (2 oz./60 ml.)
2 parts fresh lemon juice
  (1 oz./30 ml.)
Bar sugar (½ tsp.)
Orange twist

Combine all ingredients, orange twist, in a cocktail shaker with cracked ice. Shake well and strain into chilled highball glass over ice cubes. Drop orange twist in drink.

Whiskey Milk Punch

6 parts blended whiskey
 (3 oz./90 ml.)
1 cup milk (8 oz./240 ml.)
Sugar syrup (1 tsp.)
Freshly grated nutmeg

Combine all ingredients, except nutmeg, with cracked ice in a cocktail shaker. Shake well and strain into chilled collins glass. Sprinkle with nutmeg.

Whiskey Rickey

4 parts whiskey (2 oz./60 ml.)
2 parts fresh lime juice
 (1 oz./30 ml.)
Sparkling water
Lime slice

Pour whiskey and lime juice into a chilled highball glass over ice cubes. Fill with sparkling water and stir gently. Garnish with lime slice.

Whiskey Sangaree

4 parts blended whiskey
 (2 oz./60 ml.)
Ruby port (1 tbsp.)
Bar sugar (½ tsp.)
Water (1 tsp.)
2 parts sparkling water
 (1 oz./30 ml.)

In the bottom of a chilled old-fashioned glass, dissolve sugar in water, add blended whiskey and stir. Fill glass with ice cubes and sparkling water. Float port on top.

Whiskey Sling

4 parts blended whiskey
 (2 oz./60 ml.)
1 part fresh lemon juice
 (½ oz./15 ml.)
Water (1 tsp.)
Bar sugar (1 tsp.)
Orange twist

In the bottom of a mixing glass, dissolve sugar in water and lemon juice. Add whiskey and stir. Pour over ice cubes into a chilled old-fashioned glass and garnish with orange twist.

Whiskey Sour

4 parts blended whiskey
 (2 oz./60 ml.)
2 parts fresh lemon juice
 (1 oz./30 ml.)
Sugar syrup (1 tsp.)
Maraschino cherry
Orange slice

Combine liquid ingredients with cracked ice in a cocktail shaker. Shake well and strain into chilled cocktail glass. Garnish with fruit.

SCOTCH

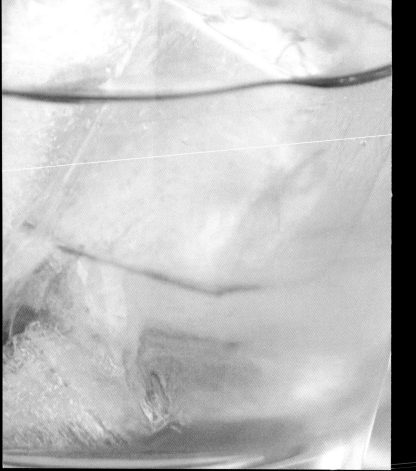

Scotland is the home of scotch, although whiskeys are also made just across the North Channel in Ireland. The word "whiskey" comes from Gaelic, and means "water of life." Most scotch drinkers would agree with that. Scotch whiskey is distilled from barley malt and aged in oaken casks for at least five years and as long as fifty. Generally speaking, the older the scotch, the better and smoother it is. Single malt scotch is made from one distillery pot; blended scotch is made with whiskeys from different distillations. The drink's peaty, rich flavor can vary from distillery to distillery. True scotch aficionados can tell you the geographic origin of a whiskey simply by tasting it. Is it from the Isle of Islay? The Isle of Mull? The Highlands? Have a scotch tasting party and see if you can tell the difference!

Bairn

4 parts scotch (2 oz./60 ml.)
2 parts Cointreau (1 oz./30 ml.)
3 – 5 dashes orange bitters

Mix all ingredients in a cocktail shaker with cracked ice. Shake well. Strain into chilled cocktail glass.

Balmoral Cocktail

4 parts scotch (2 oz./60 ml.)
1 part Dubonnet rouge
  (½ oz./15 ml.)
1 part Dubonnet blanc
  (½ oz./15 ml.)
3 dashes Angostura bitters

Combine all ingredients in mixing glass with ice cubes. Stir well. Strain into chilled cocktail glass.

Beadlestone

4 parts scotch (2 oz./60 ml.)
3 parts dry vermouth
  (1½ oz./45 ml.)

Stir ingredients with ice cubes in a mixing glass and strain into chilled cocktail glass.

Blood and Sand

2 parts scotch (1 oz./30 ml.)
1 part kirshwasser (½ oz./15 ml.)
1 part sweet vermouth
  (½ oz./15 ml.)
1 part fresh orange juice
  (½ oz./15 ml.)

Shake all ingredients with cracked ice in a cocktail shaker. Strain into chilled cocktail glass.

Blue Blazer for Two

10 parts scotch or blended whiskey
  (5 oz./150 ml.)
10 parts boiling water
  (5 oz./150 ml.)
Bar sugar (2 tsp.)
2 lemon peels

Warm the coffee mugs by filling them with boiling water and letting them sit for about 5 minutes. Discard water. Pour the scotch into one mug and the boiling water into the other. Ignite the whiskey. While the whiskey is blazing, mix it with the water by carefully pouring them back and forth between the two mugs. Extinguish the flames and serve in two mugs. Add 1 tsp. of sugar and lemon peel to each drink. With some practice, this can be a very dramatic presentation, giving the appearance of liquid fire.

Bobby Burns

4 parts scotch (2 oz./60 ml.)
2 parts sweet vermouth
  (1 oz./30 ml.)
Benedictine (1 tsp.)
Lemon twist

Stir liquid ingredients with cracked ice in a mixing glass. Strain into chilled cocktail glass and garnish with lemon twist.

Charmer

3 parts scotch (1½ oz./45 ml.)
1 part blue Curaçao (½ oz./15 ml.)
Dash dry vermouth
Dash orange bitters

Mix all ingredients with cracked ice in a cocktail shaker. Strain into chilled cocktail glass.

SCOTCH

Charmer

Derby Fizz

4 parts scotch (2 oz./60 ml.)
Triple Sec (1 tsp.)
1 part fresh lemon juice
  (½ oz./15 ml.)
Bar sugar (½ tsp.)
Sparkling water

Combine all ingredients, except
water, with cracked ice in a cocktail
shaker and shake vigorously. Pour
over ice cubes into a chilled collins
glass. Fill with sparkling water and
stir gently.

Flying Scotsman

4 parts scotch (2 oz./60 ml.)
2 parts sweet vermouth
  (1 oz./30 ml.)
Bar sugar (¼ tsp.)
3 – 5 dashes Angostura bitters

Combine all ingredients with
cracked ice in a blender and blend
at low speed until slushy. Pour into
chilled old-fashioned glass.

Glasgow

4 parts scotch (2 oz./60 ml.)
Dry vermouth (1 tsp.)
Fresh lemon juice (1 tbsp.)
Almond extract (1 tsp.)

Combine all ingredients with
cracked ice in a cocktail shaker.
Shake well and strain over ice into a
chilled old-fashioned glass.

Godfather

4 parts scotch (2 oz./60 ml.)
2 parts amaretto (1 oz./30 ml.)

Pour ingredients into a chilled
old-fashioned glass filled with ice
cubes. Stir well.

Highland Cooler

4 parts scotch (2 oz./60 ml.)
4 parts sparkling water
  (2 oz./60 ml.)
Bar sugar (1 tsp.)
Ginger ale
Lemon twist

In a chilled collins glass, dissolve
the sugar in the water. Add scotch
and ice cubes. Fill with ginger ale
and stir gently. Garnish with lemon
twist.

Highland Fling

4 parts scotch (2 oz./60 ml.)
2 parts sweet vermouth
  (1 oz./30 ml.)
3 – 5 dashes orange bitters
Spanish olive

Stir liquid ingredients with cracked
ice in a mixing glass. Strain into
chilled cocktail glass and drop in
the olive.

SCOTCH

Hole-in-One

4 parts scotch (2 oz./60 ml.)
1 part dry vermouth (½ oz./15 ml.)
Fresh lemon juice (½ tsp.)
Dash orange bitters

Combine all ingredients with cracked ice in a cocktail shaker and shake well. Strain into chilled cocktail glass.

Hoot Mon

4 parts scotch (2 oz./60 ml.)
1 part Lillet blanc (½ oz./15 ml.)
1 part sweet vermouth
  (½ oz./15 ml.)

Combine all ingredients with cracked ice in a cocktail shaker. Shake well and strain into chilled cocktail glass.

Linstead Cocktail

4 parts scotch (2 oz./60 ml.)
Pernod (¼ tsp.)
4 parts pineapple juice
  (2 oz./60 ml.)
Fresh lemon juice (¼ tsp.)
Bar sugar (½ tsp.)

Combine all ingredients in a cocktail shaker with cracked ice. Shake well and strain into chilled cocktail glass.

Loch Lomond

6 parts scotch (3 oz./90 ml.)
1 part sugar syrup (½ oz./15 ml.)
3 – 5 dashes Angostura bitters

Combine all ingredients with cracked ice in a cocktail shaker. Shake well and strain into chilled cocktail glass.

Mamie Taylor

6 parts scotch (3 oz./90 ml.)
2 parts fresh lime juice
  (1 oz./30 ml.)
Ginger ale
Lime slice

Pour scotch and lime juice into a chilled collins glass over ice cubes. Fill with ginger ale and stir gently. Garnish with lime slice.

Miami Beach Cocktail

4 parts scotch (2 oz./60 ml.)
3 parts dry vermouth
  (1½ oz./45 ml.)
4 parts grapefruit juice
  (2 oz./60 ml.)

Combine all ingredients with cracked ice in a cocktail shaker. Shake well and strain into a chilled old-fashioned glass over ice cubes.

Mint Sunrise

3 parts scotch (1½ oz./45 ml.)
1 part brandy (½ oz./15 ml.)
1 part Curaçao, any kind
  (½ oz./15 ml.)
Lemon slice
Mint sprig

Pour all ingredients, except for lemon and mint, into a chilled highball glass over ice cubes. Stir gently. Garnish with lemon slice and mint sprig.

Mint Sunrise

Modern Cocktail

5 parts scotch (2½ oz./75 ml.)
Dark rum (1 tsp.)
Pernod (1 tsp.)
Fresh lemon juice (1 tsp.)
3 – 5 dashes orange bitters
Maraschino cherry

Combine all ingredients, except
cherry, with cracked ice in a
cocktail shaker. Shake well and
pour into chilled old-fashioned
glass. Garnish with cherry.

Morning Glory Fizz

6 parts scotch (3 oz./90 ml.)
1 part Pernod (½ oz./15 ml.)
2 parts fresh lemon juice
 (1 oz./30 ml.)
Bar sugar (½ tsp.)
1 egg white (or 1 tbsp. egg white
 substitute)
Dash Angostura bitters
Sparkling water

Combine all ingredients, except
sparkling water, in a cocktail shaker
with cracked ice. Shake well and
strain over ice cubes into a chilled
highball glass. Fill with sparkling
water and stir gently.

Prince Edward

4 parts scotch (2 oz./60 ml.)
1 part Lillet blanc (½ oz./15 ml.)
1 part Drambuie (½ oz./15 ml.)
Orange slice

Combine all ingredients, except
orange slice, with cracked ice in
a cocktail shaker. Shake well and
pour into chilled old-fashioned
glass. Garnish with orange slice.

Remsen Cooler

6 parts scotch (3 oz./90 ml.)
Sugar syrup (1 tsp.)
Sparkling water
Lemon twist

Pour scotch and syrup into a chilled
collins glass filled with ice cubes.
Fill with sparkling water and stir
gently. Garnish with lemon twist.

Rob Roy

Rob Roy

6 parts scotch (3 oz./90 ml.)
2 parts sweet vermouth
 (1 oz./30 ml.)
Dash Angostura bitters
Maraschino cherry

Combine all ingredients, except
cherry, with ice cubes in a mixing
glass. Stir well and strain into
chilled cocktail glass. Garnish with
cherry.

SCOTCH

Rusty Nail

4 parts scotch (2 oz./60 ml.)
2 parts Drambuie (1 oz./30 ml.)

Pour ingredients into a chilled old-fashioned glass over ice cubes and stir.

Scotch Cobbler

4 parts scotch (2 oz./60 ml.)
1 part honey (½ oz./15 ml.)
1 part white Curaçao (½ oz./15 ml.)
Fresh mint sprig

Combine all ingredients, except mint, with cracked ice in a cocktail shaker. Shake well and strain into chilled old-fashioned glass over ice cubes. Garnish with mint sprig.

Scotch Cooler

6 parts scotch (3 oz./90 ml.)
1 part white crème de menthe (½ oz./15 ml.)
Sparkling water

Pour scotch and crème de menthe into chilled highball glass over ice cubes. Fill with sparkling water and stir gently.

Scotch Holiday Sour

4 parts scotch (2 oz./60 ml.)
2 parts cherry Heering (1 oz./30 ml.)
2 parts fresh lemon juice (1 oz./30 ml.)
1 part sweet vermouth (½ oz./15 ml.)
Lemon slice

Combine all ingredients with cracked ice in a cocktail shaker. Shake well and strain into chilled sour glass. Garnish with lemon slice.

Rusty Nail

Scotch Mist

6 parts scotch (3 oz./90 ml.)
Lemon twist

Pour scotch into a chilled old-fashioned glass filled with crushed ice. Garnish with lemon twist.

Scotch Orange Fix

4 parts scotch (2 oz./60 ml.)
Triple Sec (1 tbsp.)
2 parts fresh lemon juice (1 oz./30 ml.)
Bar sugar (½ tsp.)
Orange twist

Combine all ingredients, except Triple Sec and orange twist, in a cocktail shaker with cracked ice. Shake well and strain into chilled highball glass over ice cubes. Drop orange twist in drink and float Triple Sec on top.

SCOTCH

Scotch Sour

Scotch Sangaree

4 parts scotch (2 oz./60 ml.)
Honey (1 tsp.)
Lemon twist
Sparkling water
Freshly grated nutmeg

Muddle the honey with a little
sparkling water in the bottom of
a chilled highball glass until the
honey is dissolved. Add the scotch,
lemon twist and ice cubes. Fill with
sparkling water and stir gently.
Sprinkle nutmeg on top.

Scotch Smash

6 parts scotch (3 oz./90 ml.)
Honey (1 tbsp.)
8 fresh mint leaves
Dash orange bitters
Fresh mint sprig

Muddle mint leaves with honey in
the bottom of a chilled highball
glass. Fill the glass with crushed ice
and add the scotch. Stir well and
top off with bitters and mint sprig.

Scotch Sour

4 parts scotch (2 oz./60 ml.)
2 parts fresh lemon juice
 (2 oz./60 ml.)
Sugar syrup (1 tsp.)
Maraschino cherry
Orange slice

Combine liquid ingredients with
cracked ice in a cocktail shaker.
Shake well and strain into chilled
cocktail glass. Garnish with fruit.

Secret

4 parts scotch (2 oz./60 ml.)
White crème de menthe (½ tsp.)
Sparkling water

Combine scotch and liqueur with
cracked ice in a cocktail shaker
and shake well. Strain into chilled
highball glass over ice cubes and fill
with sparkling water. Stir gently.

Stone Fence

4 parts scotch (2 oz./60 ml.)
Dash Angostura bitters
Sparkling apple cider

Pour scotch and bitters into a
chilled highball glass over ice
cubes. Fill with cider and stir.

Thistle Cocktail

4 parts scotch (2 oz./60 ml.)
3 parts sweet vermouth
 (1½ oz./45 ml.)
3 dashes Angostura bitters

Combine ingredients with ice cubes
in a mixing glass. Stir and strain
into chilled cocktail glass.

Walters

6 parts scotch (3 oz./90 ml.)
1 part fresh lemon juice
 (½ oz./15 ml.)
1 part fresh orange juice
 (½ oz./15 ml.)

Combine ingredients with cracked
ice in a cocktail shaker. Shake
well and strain into chilled cocktail
glass.

Woodward

4 parts scotch (2 oz./60 ml.)
1 part dry vermouth (½ oz./15 ml.)
1 part grapefruit juice (½ oz./15 ml.)

Combine ingredients with cracked
ice in a cocktail shaker. Shake
well and strain into chilled cocktail
glass.

SCOTCH

TEQUILA

T equila is an American original, or rather an Americas original, and no other high-proof spirit has a greater mythology surrounding it. It is made from the fermented juice of the agave, a family of succulents that is native to the southwestern United States, Mexico, and Central America. Agave has been cultivated in Mexico for at least 10,000 years, and tequila, in one form or another, has been distilled from its sap for just as long. Most tequila is made in the area surrounding the town of Tequila in the Mexican state of Jalisco, and, by law, it must be made from the blue agave in order to be called tequila. White tequila is the youngest. Its flavor is rough, and it is best used in mixed drinks. Gold tequila, also called anejo, is aged in wooden barrels, and its richness should be savored alone in a shot glass (perhaps accompanied by the time-honored salt and lime) or mixed in a cocktail where tequila is the top note. Mezcal, the one with the worm in the bottle, is a related drink, also produced from Mexican agave plants, but it is not tequila. And, yes, you should eat the worm.

Acapulco Clam Digger

3 parts silver tequila (1½ oz./45 ml.)
6 parts tomato juice (3 oz./90 ml.)
6 parts clam juice (3 oz./90 ml.)
White horseradish (¾ tbsp.)
Tabasco® sauce to taste
Worcestershire sauce to taste
Splash of fresh lemon juice
Slice of lemon or lime

Mix all ingredients in an old-fashioned glass with cracked ice. Garnish with slice of lemon or lime.

NOTE: Clamato® juice (6 oz./180 ml.) may be substituted for the tomato and clam juices.

All That

4 parts silver tequila (2 oz./60 ml.)
1 part Falernum (½ oz./15 ml.)
1 part cherry liqueur (½ oz./15 ml.)
1 part fresh lemon juice
  (½ oz./15 ml.)
Club soda
Maraschino cherry

Combine all ingredients with cracked ice in a cocktail shaker, except club soda and cherry. Shake well. Strain into highball glass over ice cubes and fill with club soda. Stir gently. Top off with cherry.

Aztec Punch

Silver tequila (2 qt. or 64 oz./2 l.)
Grapefruit juice (2 qt. or 64 oz./2 l.)
8 parts white Curaçao
  (½ cup or 4 oz./120 ml.)
Cold strong black tea
  (1 qt. or 32 oz./1 l.)
8 parts fresh lemon juice
  1 cup or 4 oz./120 ml.)
Orgeat (almond) syrup
  (¾ cup or 6 oz./180 ml.)
1 part orange bitters (½ oz./15 ml.)
Ground cinnamon (2 tsp.)

Mix all ingredients well in large punch bowl with block of ice. Serves 40.

Banana Leaky

4 parts gold tequila (2 oz./60 ml.)
Fresh orange juice (½ cup or 4 oz.)
Fresh lime juice (½ tsp.)
½ banana, sliced

Combine all ingredients with cracked ice in a blender and blend until smooth. Pour into chilled wine glass.

Berta's Special

4 parts gold tequila (2 oz./60 ml.)
Honey (1 tsp.)
1 egg white (or 1 tbsp. egg white
  substitute)
5 – 7 dashes orange bitters
Juice of one lime
Sparkling water
Lime slice

Combine all ingredients, except lime slice and sparkling water, in a cocktail shaker. Shake vigorously. Pour over into a chilled collins glass filled with ice cubes and top off with sparkling water. Garnish with lime slice.

Blue Margarita

4 parts silver tequila (2 oz./60 ml.)
2 parts blue Curaçao (1 oz./30 ml.)
Triple Sec (1 tbsp.)
3 parts fresh lime juice
  (1½ oz./45 ml.)
Coarse salt (2 tsp.)
Lime wedge

Spread the salt in a saucer. Rub the rim of a cocktail glass with the lime wedge and dip the glass into the salt to coat the rim. Save lime for garnish. Combine all liquid ingredients in a cocktail shaker with cracked ice and shake well. Strain into salted cocktail glass and garnish with lime wedge.

TEQUILA

Blue Margarita

Brave Bull

4 parts silver tequila (2 oz./60 ml.)
2 parts coffee liqueur (1 oz./30 ml.)
Lemon twist

Pour liquid ingredients into a chilled old-fashioned glass with ice cubes. Stir and garnish with lemon twist.

Bunny Bonanza

4 parts gold tequila (2 oz./60 ml.)
2 parts Calvados (1 oz./30 ml.)
1 part fresh lemon juice
  (½ oz./15 ml.)
Maple syrup (¾ tsp.)
3 dashes Triple Sec
Lemon slice

Combine all ingredients, except lemon slice, in a cocktail shaker with cracked ice. Shake well. Strain into chilled old-fashioned glass and garnish with lemon slice.

Carolina

6 parts gold tequila (3 oz./90 ml.)
2 parts half-and-half (1 oz./30 ml.)
Grenadine (1 tsp.)
Vanilla extract (1 tsp.)
1 egg white (or 1 tbsp. egg white
  substitute)
Ground cinnamon
Maraschino cherry

Combine all ingredients, except cinnamon and cherry, in a cocktail shaker with cracked ice. Shake vigorously. Strain into chilled cocktail glass. Sprinkle with cinnamon and top with cherry.

Changuirongo

4 parts silver tequila (2 oz./60 ml.)
Ginger ale
Lime wedge

Pour tequila and soda into a chilled collins glass filled with ice cubes. Stir and garnish with lime wedge.

Chapala

4 parts gold tequila (2 oz./60 ml.)
1 part Triple Sec (½ oz./15 ml.)
4 parts fresh orange juice
  (2 oz./60 ml.)
2 parts fresh lime juice
  (1 oz./30 ml.)
1 part grenadine (½ oz./15 ml.)

Combine all ingredients in a cocktail shaker and shake well. Pour into a chilled highball glass half-filled with cracked ice and stir.

Chupacabra

4 parts gold tequila (2 oz./60 ml.)
2 parts chartreuse (1 oz./30 ml.)
1 tsp. grenadine

Combine all ingredients, except grenadine, in a cocktail shaker with cracked ice. Shake well. Pour into a chilled cocktail glass and slowly drizzle the grenadine into the mixture.

Coco Loco

1 fresh coconut with coconut water
Crushed ice (1 cup/240 ml.)
4 parts silver tequila (2 oz./60 ml.)
2 parts gin (1 oz./30 ml.)
2 parts light rum (1 oz./30 ml.)
4 parts pineapple juice
 (2 oz./60 ml.)
Sugar syrup (1 tsp.)
½ lime

Open a fresh coconut by sawing off the top. Do not discard the water inside. Add the crushed ice to the coconut and pour in all liquid ingredients. Squeeze the lime half over the drink and drop it in. Stir well.

Coco Loco

Cowgirl's Prayer

4 parts gold tequila (2 oz./60 ml.)
Homemade fresh lemonade
2 parts fresh lime juice
 (1 oz./30 ml.)
Lemon slice
Lime slice

Pour the tequila and lime juice over ice cubes in a chilled collins glass. Fill with lemonade and stir. Garnish with lemon and lime slices.

Frostbite

4 parts silver tequila (2 oz./60 ml.)
1 part white crème de cacao
 (½ oz./15 ml.)
2 parts blue Curaçao (1 oz./30 ml.)
4 parts half-and-half (2 oz./60 ml.)

Combine all ingredients in a cocktail shaker with cracked ice and shake well. Pour into chilled sour glass.

Frozen Margarita

4 parts silver tequila (2 oz./60 ml.)
1 parts Triple Sec (½ oz./15 ml.)
2 parts fresh lime juice
 (1 oz./30 ml.)
Lime slice

Combine all ingredients, except lime slice, with ½ cup of cracked ice in a blender. Blend at low speed until slushy and pour into chilled cocktail glass. Garnish with lime slice.

Frozen Margarita

Frozen Matador

4 parts gold tequila (2 oz./60 ml.)
4 parts pineapple juice
 (2 oz./60 ml.)
1 part fresh lime juice
 (½ oz./15 ml.)
Lime slice

Combine all ingredients, except lime slice, with ½ cup of cracked ice in a blender. Blend until smooth. Pour into cocktail glass. Garnish with lime slice.

Gentle Ben

4 parts silver tequila (2 oz./60 ml.)
2 parts vodka (1 oz./30 ml.)
2 parts gin (1 oz./30 ml.)
Fresh orange juice (½ cup or
 4 oz./120 ml.)
Sloe gin (1 tsp.)
Orange slice

Combine all liquid ingredients, except sloe gin and orange slice, in a cocktail shaker with cracked ice. Pour into a chilled highball glass and float sloe gin on top. Garnish with orange slice.

Gentle Bull

4 parts silver tequila (2 oz./60 ml.)
2 parts coffee liqueur (1 oz./30 ml.)
3 parts half-and-half
 (1½ oz./45 ml.)

Combine all ingredients with cracked ice in a cocktail shaker and shake well. Strain into chilled cocktail glass.

Grapeshot

4 parts gold tequila (2 oz./60 ml.)
1 part white Curaçao (½ oz./15 ml.)
3 parts white grape juice
 (1½ oz./45 ml.)

Combine all ingredients with cracked ice in a cocktail shaker. Shake well and strain into chilled cocktail glass.

Gringo Swizzle

4 parts silver tequila (2 oz./60 ml.)
1 part crème de cassis
 (½ oz./15 ml.)
2 parts fresh lime juice
 (1 oz./30 ml.)
2 parts fresh orange juice
 (1 oz./30 ml.)
2 parts pineapple juice
 (1 oz./30 ml.)
Ginger ale

Combine all ingredients, except ginger ale, in a cocktail shaker with cracked ice. Shake well and pour into chilled collins glass. Fill with cold ginger ale and stir gently.

TEQUILA

Hot Pants

4 parts silver tequila (2 oz./60 ml.)
1 part peppermint schnapps
  (½ oz./15 ml.)
1 part grapefruit juice (½ oz./15 ml.)
Bar sugar (½ tsp.)

Rim a chilled old-fashioned glass
with salt. Combine all ingredients
with ice cubes in a cocktail shaker
and shake well. Pour into salted
glass.

Margarita

6 parts silver or gold tequila
  (3 oz./90 ml.)
2 parts Triple Sec (1 oz./30 ml.)
4 parts fresh lime juice
  (2 oz./60 ml.)
Coarse salt
Lime wedge

Rim a large cocktail glass by
rubbing the rim with the lime wedge
and dipping it into a saucer of
coarse salt. Combine remaining
ingredients in a cocktail shaker with
cracked ice. Shake well and strain
into the chilled, salted cocktail
glass.

Margarita

Matador

4 parts gold tequila (2 oz./60 ml.)
1 part Triple Sec (½ oz./15 ml.)
6 parts pineapple juice
  (3 oz./90 ml.)
2 parts fresh lime juice
  (1 oz./30 ml.)

Combine all ingredients with
cracked ice in a cocktail shaker.
Shake well and strain into chilled
sour glass.

Mexican Coffee

4 parts gold tequila (2 oz./60 ml.)
1 part coffee liqueur (½ oz./15 ml.)
Hot black coffee
Whipped cream

Mix tequila and liqueur in a coffee
mug. Pour in hot coffee and stir
again. Top off with whipped cream.

Mexicana

4 parts silver tequila (2 oz./60 ml.)
4 parts pineapple juice
  (2 oz./60 ml.)
2 parts fresh lime juice
  (1 oz./30 ml.)
Grenadine (¼ tsp.)

Combine all ingredients with
cracked ice in a cocktail shaker.
Shake well and strain over ice
cubes into a chilled highball glass.

Mexicola

4 parts silver tequila (2 oz./60 ml.)
Cola
Lime wedge

Pour tequila into a chilled collins
glass over ice cubes. Fill with cola
and squeeze lime over drink. Stir
gently and garnish with lime.

Montezuma

4 parts gold tequila (2 oz./60 ml.)
2 parts Madeira (1 oz./30 ml.)
Coddled egg

Combine ingredients with cracked
ice in a blender and blend until
smooth. Pour into chilled cocktail
glass.

Olé

4 parts white tequila (2 oz./60 ml.)
2 parts coffee liqueur (1 oz./30 ml.)
Sugar syrup (1 tsp.)
Half-and-half (1 tbsp.)

Stir all ingredients, except half-and-
half, in a mixing glass. Pour into a
chilled cocktail glass over crushed
ice. Float half-and-half on top.

Peach Margarita

4 parts silver tequila (2 oz./60 ml.)
1 part peach liqueur (½ oz./15 ml.)
Triple Sec (1 tbsp.)
4 parts fresh lime juice
  (2 oz./60 ml.)
Coarse salt
Lime wedge
Fresh peach slice

Rim a chilled cocktail glass with
salt by rubbing the lime wedge
along the rim and dipping it in a
saucer of coarse salt. Combine
remaining ingredients, except peach
slice, with cracked ice in a cocktail
shaker. Shake well and pour into
salt-rimmed cocktail glass. Garnish
with peach slice.

Piña

4 parts gold tequila (2 oz./60 ml.)
6 parts pineapple juice
  (3 oz./90 ml.)
2 parts fresh lime juice
  (1 oz./30 ml.)
Honey (1 tsp.)
Lime slice

Combine all ingredients, except lime
slice, with cracked ice in a cocktail
shaker. Shake well and pour into
chilled old-fashioned glass. Garnish
with lime slice.

Piñata

4 parts gold tequila (2 oz./60 ml.)
2 parts crème de bananes
  (1 oz./30 ml.)
3 parts fresh lime juice
  (1½ oz./45 ml.)

Combine all ingredients with
cracked ice in a cocktail shaker.
Shake well and strain into chilled
cocktail glass.

Prado

4 parts silver tequila (2 oz./60 ml.)
2 parts fresh lime juice
  (1 oz./30 ml.)
Maraschino liqueur (1 tbsp.)
Grenadine (1 tsp.)
1 egg white (or 1 tbsp. egg white
  substitute)
Lime slice

Combine all ingredients in a
cocktail shaker with cracked ice.
Shake vigorously and strain into a
chilled sour glass. Garnish with lime
slice.

TEQUILA

Rosita

4 parts white tequila (2 oz./60 ml.)
4 parts Campari (2 oz./60 ml.)
1 part dry vermouth (½ oz./15 ml.)
1 part sweet vermouth
 (½ oz./15 ml.)
Lemon twist

Combine all ingredients, except lemon twist, in a mixing glass with cracked ice. Stir well and pour into chilled old-fashioned glass. Garnish with lemon twist.

Royal Matador

8 parts gold tequila (4 oz./120 ml.)
3 parts raspberry eau de vie
 (1½ oz./45 ml.)
Amaretto (1 tbsp.)
4 parts fresh lime juice
 (2 oz./60 ml.)
One whole, ripe pineapple

Cut the top off the pineapple and save it. Scoop out the pineapple, being careful not to damage the shell. Put pineapple chunks in blender, and liquefy. Strain the pineapple juice and put it back in the blender. Add remaining ingredients and cracked ice, blend until slushy, and pour into pineapple shell. Add more ice if necessary. Replace pineapple "lid" and serve with straws. Serves 2.

Silk Stockings

4 parts silver tequila (2 oz./60 ml.)
2 parts white crème de cacao
 (1 oz./30 ml.)
4 parts half-and-half (2 oz./60 ml.)
Dash grenadine
Ground cinnamon

Combine all ingredients, except cinnamon, with cracked ice in a cocktail shaker. Shake well and strain into chilled cocktail glass. Sprinkle with cinnamon.

Sloe Tequila

4 parts silver tequila (2 oz./60 ml.)
2 parts sloe gin (1 oz./30 ml.)
1 part fresh lime juice
 (½ oz./15 ml.)
Cucumber slice

Combine all ingredients, except cucumber, with cracked ice in a blender. Blend until slushy and pour into chilled old-fashioned glass. Add more ice if necessary and garnish with cucumber.

Spanish Moss

6 parts white tequila (3 oz./90 ml.)
2 parts coffee liqueur (1 oz./30 ml.)
1 part green crème de menthe
 (½ oz./15 ml.)

Combine ingredients with cracked ice in a cocktail shaker. Strain into chilled old-fashioned glass over ice cubes.

Steaming Bull

4 parts white tequila (2 oz./60 ml.)
6 parts beef bouillon (3 oz./90 ml.)
6 parts tomato juice (3 oz./90 ml.)
Tabasco® sauce to taste
Worcestershire sauce (¼ tsp.)
1 part fresh lime juice
 (½ oz./15 ml.)
Celery salt to taste
Freshly ground pepper to taste

Combine all ingredients, except tequila, in a saucepan. Heat well but do not boil. Pour tequila into heated coffee mug and fill with bouillon mixture. Stir.

Strawberry Margarita

4 parts silver tequila (2 oz./60 ml.)
Triple Sec (1 tbsp.)
1 part strawberry syrup
  (½ oz./15 ml.)
4 parts fresh lime juice
  (2 oz./60 ml.)
Fresh strawberry
Coarse salt
Lime wedge

Rim a chilled cocktail glass with coarse salt by rubbing the lime wedge along the rim and dipping it into a saucer of coarse salt. Combine the remaining ingredients with cracked ice in a cocktail shaker and shake well. Strain into a chilled cocktail glass and garnish with fresh strawberry.

Submarino

4 parts white tequila (2 oz./60 ml.)
Beer

Fill chilled mug ¾ full with beer. Pour tequila into shot glass. Drop the shot glass into the beer.

Tequila Cocktail

6 parts gold tequila (3 oz./90 ml.)
2 parts fresh lime juice
  (1 oz./30 ml.)
Grenadine (¼ tsp.)
Dash Angostura bitters

Combine all ingredients in a cocktail shaker with cracked ice. Shake well and strain into chilled cocktail glass.

Submarino

Tequila Collins

4 parts silver tequila (2 oz./60 ml.)
2 parts fresh lemon juice
  (1 oz./30 ml.)
Sugar syrup (1 tsp.)
Sparkling water
Maraschino cherry

Pour tequila into a chilled collins glass over ice cubes. Add lemon juice and syrup. Stir well and add sparkling water. Stir gently and garnish with cherry.

Tequila Fizz

6 parts white tequila (3 oz./90 ml.)
2 parts fresh lime juice
  (1 oz./30 ml.)
2 parts grenadine (1 oz./30 ml.)
1 egg white (or 1 tbsp. egg white
  substitute)
Ginger ale

Combine all ingredients, except ginger ale, with cracked ice in a cocktail shaker. Shake vigorously. Strain into chilled collins glass over ice cubes and fill with ginger ale. Stir gently.

Tequila Ghost

4 parts silver tequila
 (2 oz./60 ml.)
2 parts Pernod (1 oz./30 ml.)
1 part fresh lemon juice
 (½ oz./15 ml.)

Combine ingredients with cracked ice in a cocktail shaker. Shake well and strain into chilled cocktail glass.

Tequila Gimlet

6 parts silver tequila (3 oz./90 ml.)
2 parts Rose's lime juice
 (1 oz./30 ml.)
Lime slice

Pour tequila and lime juice into an old-fashioned glass filled with ice cubes. Stir and garnish with lime wedge.

Tequila Manhattan

6 parts gold tequila (3 oz./90 ml.)
2 parts sweet vermouth
 (1 oz./30 ml.)
Fresh lime juice (1 tsp.)
Maraschino cherry
Orange slice

Combine all ingredients, except fruit, with cracked ice in a cocktail shaker. Shake well and strain into a chilled old-fashioned glass over ice cubes. Garnish with fruit.

Tequila Maria

4 parts white tequila (2 oz./60 ml.)
8 parts tomato juice (4 oz./120 ml.)
1 part fresh lime juice
 (½ oz./15 ml.)
White horseradish (1 tsp.)
Tabasco® sauce to taste
3 – 5 dashes Worcestershire sauce
Ground black pepper to taste
Celery salt to taste
Pinch of cilantro
Lime wedge

Combine all ingredients, except lime wedge, with cracked ice in a mixing glass. Pour into chilled old-fashioned glass and garnish with lime wedge.

Tequila Mockingbird

Tequila Martini 🍸

4 parts gold tequila (2 oz./60 ml.)
1 part or less dry vermouth
  (½ oz./15 ml.)
Spanish olive

Combine ingredients, except olive, with cracked ice in a cocktail shaker. Shake well. Pour into chilled cocktail glass and garnish with olive.

Tequila Shot

Tequila Mockingbird 🍸

4 parts silver tequila (2 oz./60 ml.)
2 parts white crème de menthe
  (1 oz./30 ml.)
2 parts fresh lime juice
  (1 oz./30 ml.)

Combine all ingredients with cracked ice in a cocktail shaker. Shake well and strain into chilled cocktail glass.

Tequila Old-Fashioned

4 parts gold tequila (2 oz./60 ml.)
Bar sugar (1 tsp.)
3 – 5 dashes Angostura bitters
Sparkling water
Maraschino cherry

Combine sugar, water and bitters in the bottom of a chilled old-fashioned glass. Fill glass with ice cubes and add tequila. Stir well and garnish with cherry.

Tequila Shot

4 parts finest anejo tequila of your
  choice (2 oz./60 ml.)
Lemon wedge
Salt

Pour tequila into a shot glass. Moisten hand between thumb and forefinger and put salt on it. Lick the salt, down the shot, and suck on the lemon.

Tequila Singer 🍸

4 parts gold tequila (2 oz./60 ml.)
2 parts white crème de menthe
  (1 oz./30 ml.)

Combine ingredients with cracked ice in a cocktail shaker. Shake well and strain into chilled cocktail glass.

Tequila Sour

4 parts silver tequila (2 oz./60 ml.)
3 parts fresh lemon juice
  (1½ oz./45 ml.)
Bar sugar (1 tsp.)
Lemon slice
Maraschino cherry

Combine all ingredients, except
fruit, with cracked ice in a cocktail
shaker. Shake well and strain into
chilled sour glass. Garnish with
fruit.

Tequila Sunrise

4 parts silver tequila (2 oz./60 ml.)
Fresh orange juice
2 parts grenadine (1 oz./30 ml.)

Pour tequila into chilled highball
glass over ice cubes. Fill glass
with orange juice, leaving a little
room on top and stir. Slowly pour in
grenadine.

Tequini

6 parts silver tequila (3 oz./90 ml.)
1 part dry vermouth (½ oz./15 ml.)
Dash Angostura bitters
Lemon twist

Stir all ingredients, except lemon
twist, with ice cubes in a mixing
glass. Strain into chilled cocktail
glass and garnish with lemon twist.

Tequonic

4 parts silver tequila (2 oz./60 ml.)
3 parts fresh lime juice
  (1½ oz./45 ml.)
Tonic water
Lime wedge

Pour tequila into chilled highball
glass over ice cubes. Add juice and
stir. Fill with tonic water and garnish
with lime wedge.

Twist-and-Shout

2 parts tequila (1 oz./30 ml.)
4 parts cranberry juice
  (2 oz./60 ml.)
1 splash lemon juice

Mix ingredients over ice in a
cocktail shaker and strain into shot
glass.

Viva Villa

4 parts silver tequila (2 oz./60 ml.)
4 parts fresh lime juice
  (2 oz./60 ml.)
Bar sugar (1 tsp.)
Lime wedge
Coarse salt

Rim a chilled old-fashioned glass
with salt by moistening the rim
of the glass with the lime wedge
and dipping the glass into the
salt. Discard the lime. Combine
remaining ingredients with cracked
ice in a cocktail shaker. Shake well
and strain into chilled old-fashioned
glass over ice cubes.

VODKA

I t is impossible to pinpoint the birthplace of vodka. It is best known as a Russian spirit—its name means "little water" in Russian—and Russian distillers have been perfecting this ethereal spirit since the early Middle Ages. However, Sweden, Finland, and Poland all have legitimate claims to the origin of this clear, virtually tasteless liquor as well.

Some think that potatoes make the best vodka; others swear that only rye grain will do; still others will only drink vodka distilled from wheat. Today, you can even find vodkas distilled from grapes. In fact, as long as the result is a clear, colorless, tasteless liquid filtered through charcoal, any grain can be used to make vodka.

Flavored vodkas occupy a lot of real estate behind the bar these days. Vodka's neutral taste is the perfect medium for conveying the essence of a fruit or spice. Centuries ago, Northern Europeans flavored their vodkas with honey, or even sweet clover. If you haven't tried some of the newer flavored vodkas, such as vanilla, raspberry, or citrus, experiment! A word of advice—chocolate vodka is wonderful, but kiwi was never meant to flavor this Slavic spirit.

Absolute Martini

5 parts vodka (2½ oz./75 ml.)
1 part Triple Sec (½ oz./15 ml.)
2 parts fresh lemon juice
  (1 oz./30 ml.)
Dash orange bitters

Combine all ingredients in a cocktail shaker with cracked ice and shake well. Strain into chilled cocktail glass.

Algonquin Bloody Mary

4 parts vodka (2 oz./60 ml.)
8 parts tomato juice (4 oz./120 ml.)
Salt to taste
Pepper to taste (freshly ground)
Juice of half a lime
Worcestershire sauce (1½ tsp.)
6 - 8 dashes Tabasco® sauce
1 lime wedge

Combine all ingredients, except the lime wedge, in a cocktail shaker filled with ice. Shake quickly (about 9 to 10 times, as not to cause the tomato juice to separate). Strain into a highball glass over ice. Drop in the lime wedge.

Alternatini

6 parts orange vodka (3 oz./90 ml.)
½ tsp. sweet vermouth
½ tsp. dry vermouth
1 tsp. white crème de cacao
Sweetened cocoa powder
Hershey's® Kiss

Rim a chilled cocktail glass with sweetened cocoa powder. Combine liquid ingredients with cracked ice in a cocktail shaker and shake well. Strain into a cocktail glass and garnish with Hershey's Kiss.

Anna's Banana

4 parts vodka (2 oz./60 ml.)
2 parts fresh lime juice
  (1 oz./30 ml.)
½ small banana, peeled and
  sliced thin
Honey (1 tsp.) (almond syrup may
  also be used)
Slice of lime

Combine all ingredients, except for lime slice, in a blender with 4 ounces of cracked ice. Blend at medium speed for 10 - 15 seconds. Pour into chilled white wine glass and garnish with lime.

Apple Martini

6 parts vodka (3 oz./90 ml.)
1 part Calvados (½ oz./15 ml.)
1 tsp. bar sugar (optional)
Apple slice

Shake vodka and Calvados (and sugar) with ice. Pour into chilled cocktail glass and garnish with apple slice.

Apple Martini II

6 parts apple vodka (3 oz./90 ml.)
1 part apple liqueur (½ oz./15 ml.)
Lemon twist

Vigorously shake vodka and liqueur with ice. Strain into chilled cocktail glass and garnish with lemon twist.

Apple Pie

6 parts vanilla vodka (3 oz./90 ml.)
1 part Calvados (½ oz./15 ml.)
1 part dry vermouth (½ oz./15 ml.)
Apple slice

Combine liquid ingredients with cracked ice in a cocktail shaker and shake well. Strain into a chilled highball glass over ice and garnish with a thin slice of apple.

Aqueduct Cocktail   Y

4 parts vodka (2 oz./60 ml.)
White Curaçao (1½ tsp.)
Apricot brandy (1 tsp.)
Fresh lime juice (1 tsp.)
Fresh lemon juice (1 tsp.)
Lemon twist

Combine all ingredients, except lemon twist, with cracked ice in a cocktail shaker. Shake well. Strain into chilled cocktail glass and garnish with lemon twist.

Armada Martini   Y

6 parts orange vodka (3 oz./90 ml.)
1 part amontillado sherry
 (½ oz./15 ml.)
Orange twist

Combine liquid ingredients in a mixing glass with cracked ice and stir well. Strain into a cocktail glass and garnish with twist.

Barbed Wire   Y

6 parts vodka (3 oz./90 ml.)
1 tsp. sweet vermouth
½ tsp. Pernod
½ tsp. Chambord
Lemon twist

Combine liquid ingredients with cracked ice in a cocktail shaker and shake well. Strain into a chilled cocktail glass and garnish with lemon twist.

Beer Buster

Bottle of ice-cold beer
4 parts frozen 100-proof vodka
 (2 oz./60 ml.)
Tabasco® sauce to taste

Pour all ingredients into frosted beer mug and stir gently.

Belmont Stakes   Y

4 parts vodka (2 oz./60 ml.)
2 parts gold rum (1 oz./30 ml.)
1 part strawberry liqueur
 (½ oz./15 ml.)
1 part fresh lime juice
 (½ oz./15 ml.)
Grenadine (1 tsp.)
Lime wedge
Orange slice

Combine all liquid ingredients in a cocktail shaker with cracked ice and shake well. Strain into chilled cocktail glass and garnish with fruit.

Berry-tini   Y

6 parts berry vodka (3 oz./90 ml.)
1 part crème de cassis
 (½ oz./15 ml.)
Fresh berries

Combine liquid ingredients in a cocktail shaker with cracked ice and shake well. Strain into chilled cocktail glass and garnish with berries.

Bloody Mary

Black and White Martini

6 parts vanilla vodka (3 oz./90 ml.)
1 part dark crème de cacao
  (½ oz./15 ml.)
Splash of Pernod
Black and white licorice candies

Combine liquid ingredients in a cocktail shaker and shake well with cracked ice. Strain into chilled cocktail glass and garnish with candies.

Black Magic

4 parts vodka (2 oz./60 ml.)
2 parts coffee liqueur (1 oz./30 ml.)
1 – 2 dashes fresh lemon juice

Stir all ingredients in a mixing glass. Strain into a chilled old-fashioned glass over ice cubes.

Black Russian

4 parts vodka (2 oz./60 ml.)
2 parts coffee liqueur (1 oz./30 ml.)

Pour into chilled old-fashioned glass over ice cubes. Stir.

Bloody Brew

4 parts vodka (2 oz./60 ml.)
6 parts beer (3 oz./90 ml.)
8 parts tomato juice
  (½ cup or 4 oz./120 ml.)
Salt to taste
Dill pickle spear

Mix all ingredients, except pickle, in chilled highball glass with ice. Garnish with pickle.

Bloody Bull

4 parts vodka (2 oz./60 ml.)
8 parts tomato juice (4 oz./120 ml.)
8 parts chilled beef bouillon
  (4 oz./120 ml.)
1 part lime juice (½ oz./15 ml.)
Tabasco® sauce to taste
Freshly ground pepper to taste
Lime wedge

Combine all ingredients, except pepper and lime wedge, with cracked ice in a cocktail shaker and shake well. Strain over ice cubes into chilled highball glass. Grind pepper over drink and garnish with lime wedge.

Bloody Mary

4 parts vodka (2 oz./60 ml.)
12 parts tomato juice
  (6 oz./180 ml.)
Fresh lemon juice (½ tsp.)
Worcestershire sauce (½ tsp.)
White horseradish (½ tsp.)
Tabasco® sauce to taste
Freshly ground pepper to taste
Salt to taste
Lime wedge

Combine all ingredients, except lime wedge, in a cocktail shaker with cracked ice. Shake gently. Strain into chilled highball glass and garnish with lime wedge. Adjust seasonings to taste.

Blowtorch

2 parts vodka (1 oz./30 ml.)
5 dashes Tabasco® sauce
1 tsp. lime juice

Mix all ingredients together in a shot glass, adding Tabasco sauce to taste. Serve immediately.

Blue Lagoon

4 parts vodka (2 oz./60 ml.)
2 parts blue Curaçao (1 oz./30 ml.)
4 parts pineapple juice
  (2 oz./60 ml.)
3 - 5 dashes Triple Sec
Pineapple spear

Combine all ingredients, except
pineapple spear, with cracked ice in
a cocktail shaker. Shake well. Strain
into chilled cocktail glass and
garnish with pineapple.

Blue Lagoon

Blue Monday

4 parts vodka (2 oz./60 ml.)
2 parts Cointreau (1 oz./30 ml.)
1 part blue Curaçao (½ oz./15 ml.)

Stir all ingredients with cracked ice
in a mixing glass. Strain into chilled
cocktail glass.

Blue Shark

4 parts vodka (2 oz./60 ml.)
4 parts white tequila (2 oz./60 ml.)
Several dashes blue Curaçao

Combine all ingredients with
cracked ice in a cocktail shaker.
Shake well and strain into chilled
old-fashioned glass.

Boardwalk Martini

6 parts peach vodka (3 oz./90 ml.)
1 part red vermouth (½ oz./15 ml.)
½ tsp. fresh lime juice
Lemon twist

Shake liquid ingredients with
cracked ice in a cocktail shaker.
Strain into a chilled cocktail glass
and garnish with twist.

Bohemian

4 parts citrus vodka (2 oz./60 ml.)
2 parts pineapple juice
  (1 oz./30 ml.)
1 part passion fruit nectar
  (½ oz./15 ml.)
1 part cranberry juice (½ oz./15 ml.)
Fresh raspberries

Mix all liquid ingredients with ice.
Strain into a cocktail glass and
garnish with raspberries.

Buddy's Bloody Mary

4 parts vodka (2 oz./60 ml.)
12 parts V-8 juice (6 oz./180 ml.)
Fresh lime juice (½ tsp.)
Several dashes Worcestershire
  sauce
Several dashes Tabasco® sauce
White horseradish (1 tsp.)
Freshly ground pepper to taste
Celery salt to taste
Lime wedge

Combine V-8 juice, lime juice,
Worcestershire sauce, Tabasco
sauce and horseradish in a cocktail
shaker. Shake well. Fill a chilled
highball glass with ice cubes. Grind
pepper and shake celery salt into
the glass to make seasoned ice
cubes. Pour the juice mixture into
the highball glass and stir gently.
Squeeze the lime slice over the
drink and drop in.

Bull Shot

4 parts vodka (2 oz./60 ml.)
8 parts cold beef bouillon
 (4 oz./120 ml.)
Fresh lemon juice (1 tsp.)
Several dashes Worcestershire
 sauce
Tabasco® sauce to taste
Celery salt to taste
Freshly ground pepper to taste

Mix all ingredients in a chilled
highball glass with ice cubes.

Bullfrog

4 parts vodka (2 oz./60 ml.)
Triple Sec (1 tsp.)
Limeade
Lime slice

Pour vodka and Triple Sec over ice
cubes into a chilled highball glass.
Stir. Top off with limeade. Stir again
and garnish with slice of lime.

Bunker Buster

1 part vodka (½ oz./15 ml.)
1 part strawberry schnapps
 (½ oz./15 ml.)
Draft Beer

Mix ingredients in a shot glass.
Shoot the shot and follow with a
draft beer.

Cajun Martini

6 parts pepper vodka (3 oz./90 ml.)
Dash of dry vermouth
Large slice of pickled jalapeño
 pepper

Combine vodka and vermouth in a
mixing glass with cracked ice and
stir well. Strain into cocktail glass.
Drop in the jalapeño.

NOTE: For a Cajun martini with extra
kick, steep pickled jalapeños in the
vodka for at least an hour in the
freezer before preparing the drink.

Caipiroska

6 parts vodka (3 oz./90 ml.)
2 parts fresh limejuice
 (1 oz./30 ml.)
Granulated sugar (1 tbsp.)
Lime rinds

Combine all ingredients in a
cocktail shaker with cracked ice.
Shake well. Strain into chilled old-
fashioned glass over ice cubes.

Cape Codder

4 parts vodka (2 oz./60 ml.)
12 parts cranberry juice
 (6 oz./180 ml.)
Lime wedge

Stir vodka and juice in a chilled
highball glass with ice cubes.
Squeeze the lime wedge over the
drink and drop it in.

Cape Codder

Chiquita

4 parts vodka (2 oz./60 ml.)
1 part banana liqueur (½ oz./15 ml.)
1 part fresh lime juice
  (½ oz./15 ml.)
¼ cup sliced bananas
Orgeat (almond) syrup (1 tsp.)

Combine all ingredients in a mixing
glass with cracked ice and stir
well. Pour into chilled deep-saucer
champagne glass.

Chocolate Banana Martini

6 parts chocolate vodka
  (3 oz./90 ml.)
1 part crème de bananas
  (½ oz./15 ml.)

Combine ingredients in cocktail
shaker with ice cubes. Shake well
and strain into chilled cocktail
glass.

Chocolate Martini

6 parts chocolate vodka
  (3 oz./90 ml.)
1 part chocolate liqueur
  (½ oz./15 ml.)
Chocolate curl

Combine liquid ingredients in a
mixing glass with ice cubes and
stir. Strain into a cocktail glass and
garnish with chocolate curl.

Chocolate Mudslide

4 parts chocolate vodka
  (2 oz./60 ml.)
3 parts coffee liqueur
  (1½ oz./45 ml.)
3 parts Irish cream liqueur
  (1½ oz./45 ml.)

Combine all ingredients with
cracked ice in a cocktail shaker.
Shake well and strain into chilled
cocktail glass.

Chocolate Orange Martini

4 parts chocolate vodka
  (2 oz./60 ml.)
1 part orange vodka (½ oz./15 ml.)
1 tbsp. orange liqueur
Orange peel

Combine vodkas and liqueur in a
cocktail shaker with cracked ice
and shake well. Strain into cocktail
glass and garnish with orange peel.

Climax

2 parts vanilla vodka (1 oz./30 ml.)
1 part Amaretto (½ oz./15 ml.)
1 part white crème de cacao
  (½ oz./15 ml.)
1 part Triple Sec (½ oz./15 ml.)
Splash of half-and-half

Combine all ingredients in a
cocktail shaker. Shake well and
pour over cracked ice into a cocktail
glass.

Cock n' Bull Shot

4 parts vodka (2 oz./60 ml.)
4 parts chicken bouillon
  (2 oz./60 ml.)
4 parts beef bouillon (2 oz./60 ml.)
1 part fresh lemon juice
  (½ oz./15 ml.)
Tabasco® sauce to taste
Worcestershire sauce to taste
Freshly ground pepper to taste
Celery salt to taste

Combine all ingredients in a mixing
glass with cracked ice. Stir well.
Pour into chilled old-fashioned
glass.

Cold and Clammy Bloody Mary

4 parts iced vodka (2 oz./60 ml.)
12 parts Clamato® juice
 (6 oz./180 ml.)
Fresh lime juice (½ tsp.)
Worcestershire sauce (½ tsp.)
Several dashes Tabasco® sauce
Freshly ground pepper to taste
Salt to taste
Slice of green onion

Combine all ingredients, except onion, in cocktail shaker with cracked ice. Shake well. Strain over ice cubes into chilled highball glass. Garnish with green onion. Adjust seasonings if necessary.

Cool Yule Martini

6 parts vodka (3 oz./90 ml.)
1 part dry vermouth (½ oz./15 ml.)
1 tsp. peppermint schnapps
Miniature candy cane

Combine liquid ingredients with cracked ice in a cocktail shaker and shake well. Strain into a chilled cocktail glass.

Cosmopolitan

Cosmopolitan

4 parts vodka (2 oz./60 ml.)
2 parts Triple Sec (1 oz./30 ml.)
2 parts cranberry juice
 (1 oz./30 ml.)
1 part fresh lime juice
 (½ oz./15 ml.)

Combine ingredients with cracked ice in a cocktail shaker. Shake well. Pour into chilled cocktail glass.

Cossack

4 parts vodka (2 oz./60 ml.)
2 parts cognac (1 oz./30 ml.)
2 parts fresh lime juice
 (1 oz./30 ml.)
Bar sugar (½ tsp.)

Combine all ingredients in a cocktail shaker with cracked ice. Shake well. Strain into chilled cocktail glass.

Count Stroganoff

4 parts vodka (2 oz./60 ml.)
2 parts white crème de cacao
 (1 oz./30 ml.)
1 part fresh lemon juice
 (½ oz./15 ml.)

Combine all ingredients with cracked ice in a cocktail shaker and shake well. Strain into chilled cocktail glass.

Creamy Screwdriver

4 parts vodka (2 oz./60 ml.)
2 parts vanilla vodka (1 oz./30 ml.)
Bar sugar (½ tsp.)
12 parts fresh orange juice
 (6 oz./180 ml.)

Combine all ingredients with cracked ice in a blender and blend until smooth. Pour into chilled collins glass over ice cubes.

East Wing

6 parts vodka (3 oz./90 ml.)
2 parts cherry brandy (1 oz./30 ml.)
1 part Campari (½ oz./15 ml.)
Lemon twist

Combine liquid ingredients with cracked ice in a cocktail shaker and shake well. Strain into a chilled cocktail glass and garnish with lemon twist.

Flaming Joe

3 parts vodka (1½ oz./45 ml.)
1 part coffee liqueur (½ oz./15 ml.)

Pour the liqueur first, finishing with the vodka on top. Light the mix and let it burn out (about 10 seconds), then shoot.

Flying Grasshopper

4 parts vodka (2 oz./60 ml.)
1 part green crème de menthe
 (½ oz./15 ml.)
1 part white crème de menthe
 (½ oz./15 ml.)

Combine all ingredients with cracked ice in a blender and blend at low speed until slushy. Pour into a chilled old-fashioned glass.

Fuzzy Martini

4 parts vanilla vodka (2 oz./60 ml.)
1 part coffee vodka (½ oz./15 ml.)
1 tsp. peach schnapps
Fresh peach slice

Combine liquid ingredients in a cocktail shaker with cracked ice and shake well. Strain into a chilled cocktail glass and garnish with a fresh peach slice.

Fuzzy Navel

4 parts vodka (2 oz./60 ml.)
2 parts peach schnapps
 (1 oz./30 ml.)
16 parts fresh orange juice
 (8 oz./240 ml.)
Orange slice

Combine all ingredients, except orange slice, with cracked ice in a cocktail shaker. Shake well and pour into chilled collins glass and garnish with orange slice.

Genoa Vodka

4 parts vodka (2 oz./60 ml.)
2 parts Campari (1 oz./30 ml.)
6 parts fresh orange juice
 (3 oz./90 ml.)

Combine all ingredients with cracked ice in a cocktail shaker and shake well. Pour into chilled old-fashioned glass.

Fuzzy Navel

Georgia Peach

4 parts vodka (2 oz./60 ml.)
2 parts peach brandy (1 oz./30 ml.)
Fresh lemon juice (1 tsp.)
Peach preserves (1 tsp.)
1 wedge peeled fresh peach,
  chopped fine (about 2 oz./60 ml.)

Combine all ingredients with
cracked ice in a blender. Blend
until smooth and pour into chilled
highball glass.

Gingersnapper

6 parts citrus vodka (3 oz./90 ml.)
Ginger Ale
Slice of candied ginger

Pour vodka over ice into chilled
highball glass. Fill with ginger ale.
Stir gently and drop in candied
ginger.

Ginza Mary

4 parts vodka (2 oz./60 ml.)
3 parts sake (1½ oz./45 ml.)
4 parts tomato juice (2 oz./60 ml.)
1 part fresh lemon juice
  (½ oz./15 ml.)
3 – 5 dashes Tabasco® sauce
2 dashes soy sauce
Freshly ground pepper to taste

Combine all ingredients with
cracked ice in a mixing glass. Stir
well and pour into chilled old-
fashioned glass.

Godmother

4 parts vodka (2 oz./60 ml.)
2 parts amaretto (1 oz./30 ml.)

Pour ingredients into a chilled
old-fashioned glass filled with ice
cubes. Stir well.

Golden Frog

2 parts vodka (1 oz./30 ml.)
2 parts Falernum (1 oz./30 ml.)
2 parts Strega (1 oz./30 ml.)
2 parts fresh lemon juice
  (1 oz./30 ml.)

Combine all ingredients with
cracked ice in a blender and blend
until slushy. Pour into chilled
cocktail glass.

Good and Plenty

2 parts chocolate vodka
  (1 oz./30 ml.)
2 parts coffee liqueur (1 oz./30 ml.)
2 parts vanilla vodka (1 oz./30 ml.)
Dash Pernod
½ scoop vanilla ice cream

Combine all ingredients in a
blender. Blend for a few seconds
at low speed. Pour into chilled red
wine glass.

Gotham's Bellini Martini

4 parts Stoli Oranj or equivalent
  orange-flavored vodka
  (2 oz./60 ml.)
2 parts peach puree (1 oz./30 ml.)
Peach liqueur (1 tbsp.)
Prosecco (Italian sparkling wine)

Combine vodka, peach puree, and
peach liqueur in a cocktail shaker
with ice. Shake vigorously and
strain into chilled cocktail glass.
Top with Prosecco.

Hair Raiser Cocktail

4 parts vodka (2 oz./60 ml.)
1 part rock and rye (½ oz./15 ml.)
2 parts fresh lemon juice
  (1 oz./30 ml.)

Combine all ingredients with
cracked ice in a cocktail shaker
and shake well. Strain into chilled
cocktail glass.

Hairy Navel

3 parts vodka (1½ oz./45 ml.)
2 parts peach schnapps
 (1 oz./30 ml.)
10 parts fresh orange juice
 (5 oz./150 ml.)

Stir ingredients together in a mixing glass, and then pour into a highball glass over ice cubes.

Harvey Wallbanger

4 parts vodka (2 oz./60 ml.)
2 parts Galliano (1 oz./30 ml.)
10 parts orange juice
 (5 oz./150 ml.)

Pour vodka and orange juice over ice cubes in chilled collins glass. Stir. Float Galliano on top.

Hep Cat

6 parts berry vodka (3 oz./90 ml.)
1 part dry vermouth (½ oz./15 ml.)
Dash sweet vermouth
Dash Cointreau

Combine all ingredients with cracked ice in a mixing glass and stir well. Strain into a chilled cocktail glass.

Hot and Dirty Martini

6 parts pepper vodka (3 oz./90 ml.)
1 part dry vermouth (½ oz./15 ml.)
1 tsp. olive brine
Spanish olive stuffed with pickled
 jalapeño
Pepper

Stir liquid ingredients with cracked ice in a cocktail shaker and shake well. Strain into a chilled cocktail glass and garnish with olive.

Huntsman Cocktail

4 parts vodka (2 oz./60 ml.)
2 parts dark rum (1 oz./30 ml.)
2 parts fresh lime juice
 (1 oz./30 ml.)
Bar sugar (½ tsp.)

Combine all ingredients with cracked ice in a cocktail shaker. Shake well and strain into chilled cocktail glass.

Ice Pick

4 parts vodka (2 oz./60 ml.)
Iced tea
Lime wedge

Pour vodka and iced tea into a chilled collins glass filled with ice cubes. Squeeze the lime wedge over drink and drop in. Stir.

Island Hopper

2 parts vanilla vodka (1 oz./30 ml.)
2 parts pineapple juice
 (1 oz./30 ml.)
1 splash grenadine syrup

Mix vanilla vodka and pineapple juice together in a shot glass. Add a splash of grenadine and serve.

Jolly Pop

2 parts citrus (1 oz./30 ml.)
1 part raspberry liqueur
 (½ oz./15 ml.)
1 part cranberry juice (½ oz./15 ml.)

Mix all ingredients over ice in a shaker. Strain into a chilled shot glass and serve.

Jungle Jimmy

4 parts currant vodka (2 oz./60 ml.)
4 parts crème de bananes
  (2 oz./60 ml.)
4 parts milk (2 oz./60 ml.)

Combine all ingredients with cracked ice in a blender and blend until smooth. Pour into chilled old-fashioned glass.

Kamikaze

6 parts vodka (3 oz./90 ml.)
Triple Sec (½ tsp.)
Fresh lime juice (½ tsp.)
Lime wedge

Combine all ingredients, except lime wedge, in a cocktail glass with cracked ice and shake well. Strain into chilled cocktail glass and garnish with lime wedge.

Kangaroo

4 parts vodka (2 oz./60 ml.)
2 parts dry vermouth (1 oz./30 ml.)
Lemon twist

Stir the vodka and vermouth in a mixing glass with ice cubes. Strain over ice cubes into a chilled old-fashioned glass. Twist lemon over drink and drop in.

Kempinsky Fizz

4 parts vodka (2 oz./60 ml.)
2 parts crème de cassis
  (1 oz./30 ml.)
Fresh lemon juice (2 tsp.)
Bitter lemon soda (ginger ale or
  seltzer may be substituted)

Pour all ingredients, except soda, into a chilled highball glass filled with ice cubes. Fill with soda and stir.

Kremlin Cocktail

4 parts vodka (2 oz./60 ml.)
3 parts crème de cacao
  (1½ oz./45 ml.)
3 parts half-and-half
  (1½ oz./45 ml.)

Combine ingredients in a blender with cracked ice. Blend until smooth and pour into chilled cocktail glass.

Kretchma Cocktail

4 parts vodka (2 oz./60 ml.)
3 parts white crème de cacao
  (1½ oz./45 ml.)
2 parts fresh lemon juice
  (1 oz./30 ml.)
2 dashes grenadine

Combine all ingredients with cracked ice in a cocktail shaker. Shake well and strain into chilled cocktail glass.

Lemon Drop Original

4 parts frozen vodka (2 oz./60 ml.)
Bar sugar
Lemon wedge

Pour vodka into a shot glass. Dampen the space between your thumb and forefinger and coat with sugar. Suck the sugar off your hand, drink the shot in one swallow, and then bite and suck on the lemon.

Lemon Drop II

6 parts lemon or citrus vodka
  (3 oz./90 ml.)
1 part fresh lemon juice
  (½ oz./15 ml.)
Bar sugar
Lemon twist

Rim a chilled cocktail glass with bar sugar. Shake vodka and lemon juice with ice in a cocktail shaker. Strain into chilled cocktail glass and garnish with twist.

Long Island Iced Tea

4 parts vodka (2 oz./60 ml.)
2 parts gin (1 oz./30 ml.)
2 parts white tequila (1 oz./30 ml.)
2 parts white rum (1 oz./30 ml.)
1 part white crème de menthe
  (½ oz./15 ml.)
4 parts fresh lemon juice
  (2 oz./60 ml.)
Bar sugar (1 tsp.)
Lime wedge
Cola

Combine all ingredients, except lime and cola, in a cocktail shaker with cracked ice. Shake well and strain into chilled collins glass over ice cubes. Fill with cola and stir gently. Garnish with lime wedge.

Macaroon

6 parts vodka (3 oz./90 ml.)
1 part chocolate liqueur
  (½ oz./15 ml.)
1 part amaretto (½ oz./15 ml.)
Orange twist

Combine liquid ingredients in a cocktail shaker with cracked ice and strain into a chilled cocktail glass. Garnish with orange twist.

Madras

4 parts vodka (2 oz./60 ml.)
6 parts cranberry juice
  (3 oz./90 ml.)
6 parts fresh orange juice
  (3 oz./90 ml.)

Combine ingredients with cracked ice in a mixing glass and stir. Strain over ice cubes into a chilled highball glass.

Madras Shorts

4 parts melon vodka (2 oz./60 ml.)
2 parts currant vodka (1 oz./30 ml.)
4 parts cranberry juice
  (2 oz./60 ml.)
6 parts fresh orange juice
  (3 oz./90 ml.)

Combine ingredients with cracked ice in a mixing glass and stir. Strain over ice cubes into a chilled highball glass.

Melon Ball

4 parts vodka (2 oz./60 ml.)
4 parts melon liqueur (2 oz./60 ml.)
8 parts pineapple juice
  (½ cup or 4 oz.)
Slice of honeydew or cantaloupe

Combine all ingredients, except melon slice, with cracked ice in a mixing glass and stir. Strain over ice cubes into a chilled highball glass and garnish with melon.

Long Island Iced Tea

Melon Ball Deluxe

4 parts melon vodka (2 oz./60 ml.)
4 parts melon liqueur (2 oz./60 ml.)
8 parts pineapple juice
 (4 oz./120 ml.)
Slice of summer melon

Combine all ingredients, except melon slice, with cracked ice in a mixing glass and stir. Strain over ice cubes into a chilled highball glass and garnish with melon.

Melon Meltdown

3 parts melon vodka (1½ oz./45 ml.)
1 part melon liqueur (½ oz./15 ml.)

Mix the melon vodka and melon liqueur in a shaker with ice cubes. Shake briefly and strain into an old-fashioned glass and serve.

Midnight Sun

4 parts citrus vodka (2 oz./60 ml.)
2 parts grapefruit juice
 (1 oz./30 ml.)
Grenadine (¼ tsp.)
Orange slice

Combine all ingredients, except orange slice, with cracked ice in a cocktail shaker. Shake well and strain into chilled cocktail glass. Garnish with orange slice.

Mocha Martini

3 parts chocolate vodka
 (1½ oz./45 ml.)
3 parts coffee vodka
 (1½ oz./45 ml.)
1 part chocolate liqueur
 (½ oz./15 ml.)
3 chocolate covered coffee beans

Shake ingredients together with ice in a cocktail shaker. Strain into chilled cocktail glass and garnish with chocolate covered coffee beans.

Moscow Mule

6 parts vodka (3 oz./90 ml.)
Fresh lime juice (1 tbsp.)
Ginger beer
Lime wedge

Pour vodka and lime juice into a chilled beer mug over ice cubes. Fill with ginger beer and stir gently. Garnish with lime wedge.

Mudslide

3 parts vodka (1½ oz./45 ml.)
3 parts coffee liqueur
 (1½ oz./45 ml.)
3 parts Irish cream liqueur
 (1½ oz./45 ml.)

Combine all ingredients with cracked ice in a cocktail shaker. Shake well and strain into chilled cocktail glass.

Ninotchka

4 parts vodka (2 oz./60 ml.)
2 parts white crème de cacao
 (1 oz./30 ml.)
1 part fresh lemon juice
 (½ oz./15 ml.)

Combine all ingredients with cracked ice in a cocktail shaker. Shake well and strain into chilled cocktail glass.

Osaka Dry

6 parts vodka (3 oz./90 ml.)
1 part sake (½ oz./15 ml.)
Pickled plum

Combine liquid ingredients with cracked ice in a cocktail shaker. Strain into a chilled cocktail glass and garnish with plum.

Passion Cup

4 parts vodka (2 oz./60 ml.)
4 parts orange juice (2 oz./60 ml.)
2 parts passion fruit juice
  (1 oz./30 ml.)
1 part coconut milk (½ oz./15 ml.)
1 part pineapple juice
  (½ oz./15 ml.)
Maraschino cherry

Combine all ingredients, except
cherry, in a cocktail shaker with
cracked ice. Shake well and strain
into chilled red wine glass. Garnish
with cherry.

Peach Buck

4 parts vodka (2 oz./60 ml.)
2 parts peach brandy (1 oz./30 ml.)
2 parts fresh lemon juice
  (1 oz./30 ml.)
Ginger ale
Fresh peach slice

Combine all ingredients, except
ginger ale and peach slice, with
cracked ice in a cocktail shaker.
Shake well and pour into chilled
highball glass. Fill with ginger ale
and stir gently. Garnish with peach
slice.

Pineapple Lemonade

4 parts vodka (2 oz./60 ml.)
6 parts pineapple juice
  (3 oz./90 ml.)
Fresh lemonade

Pour vodka and pineapple juice
into a chilled collins glass over ice
cubes. Fill with lemonade and stir.

Pink Lemonade

4 parts vodka (2 oz./60 ml.)
2 parts maraschino liqueur
  (1 oz./30 ml.)
Fresh lemonade

Pour vodka and liqueur into a
chilled collins glass over ice cubes.
Fill with lemonade and stir.

Pink Panther

4 parts vodka (2 oz./60 ml.)
2 parts dry vermouth (1 oz./30 ml.)
1 part crème de cassis
  (½ oz./15 ml.)
2 parts orange juice (1 oz./30 ml.)
½ egg white (or 1 tbsp. egg white
  substitute)

Combine all ingredients with
cracked ice in a cocktail shaker.
Shake vigorously. Strain into chilled
cocktail glass.

Polynesian Cocktail

4 parts vodka (2 oz./60 ml.)
2 parts cherry brandy (1 oz./30 ml.)
1 part fresh lime juice (½ oz./15 ml.)
1 part fresh lemon juice
  (½ oz./15 ml.)
Lime wedge
Bar sugar

Rim a chilled cocktail glass with
sugar by rubbing the rim of the
glass with the lime wedge and
dipping it in the sugar. Discard
the lime. Combine remaining
ingredients with cracked ice in a
cocktail shaker and shake well.
Strain into the cocktail glass.

Polynesian Pepper Pot

4 parts vodka (2 oz./60 ml.)
2 parts gold rum (1 oz./30 ml.)
8 parts pineapple juice
  (½ cup or 4 oz.)
1 part Orgeat (almond) syrup
  (½ oz./15 ml.)
Fresh lemon juice (1 tsp.)
3 – 5 dashes Tabasco® sauce
Cayenne pepper (¼ tsp. or to taste)
Curry powder

Combine all ingredients, except the
curry powder, in a cocktail shaker
with cracked ice. Shake well and
pour into chilled highball glass.
Sprinkle curry powder on top.

Princess Pink Lemonade

4 parts peach vodka (2 oz./60 ml.)
2 parts maraschino liqueur
  (1 oz./30 ml.)
Fresh pink lemonade

Pour vodka and liqueur into a chilled collins glass over ice cubes. Fill with lemonade and stir.

Purple Passion

4 parts vodka (2 oz./60 ml.)
8 parts purple grape juice
  (½ cup or 4 oz./120 ml.)
8 parts grapefruit juice
  (½ cup or 4 oz./120 ml.)

Combine ingredients with cracked ice in a cocktail shaker. Shake well and strain into a chilled collins glass over ice cubes.

Red Snapper

4 parts vodka (2 oz./60 ml.)
6 parts tomato juice (3 oz./90 ml.)
3 – 5 dashes Worcestershire sauce
Salt to taste
Freshly ground black pepper to taste
Cayenne pepper to taste
Dash lemon juice
Celery rib

Combine all ingredients, except vodka, tomato juice and celery, in a cocktail shaker. Shake well. Add ice cubes, vodka and tomato juice and shake again. Pour into chilled highball glass; garnish with celery rib.

Rock and Rye Cooler

4 parts vodka (2 oz./60 ml.)
3 parts rock and rye (1½ oz./45 ml.)
2 parts fresh lime juice
  (1 oz./30 ml.)
Bitter lemon soda
Lime slice

Combine all ingredients, except soda and lime slice, with cracked ice in a cocktail shaker. Strain into a chilled collins glass over ice cubes and fill with bitter lemon soda. Stir gently and garnish with lime slice.

Russian Bear

4 parts vodka (2 oz./60 ml.)
2 parts dark crème de cacao
  (1 oz./30 ml.)
1 part half-and-half (½ oz./15 ml.)

Combine all ingredients with cracked ice in a cocktail shaker. Shake well and strain into a chilled cocktail glass.

Russian Cocktail

4 parts vodka (2 oz./60 ml.)
3 parts gin (1½ oz./45 ml.)
3 parts white crème de cacao
  (1½ oz./45 ml.)

Combine ingredients with cracked ice in a cocktail shaker. Shake well and strain into chilled cocktail glass.

Russian Quaalude

4 parts vodka (2 oz./60 ml.)
2 parts Frangelico (1 oz./30 ml.)
2 parts Irish cream liqueur
  (1 oz./30 ml.)

Combine ingredients with cracked ice in a cocktail shaker. Shake well and pour into chilled old-fashioned glass.

Salty Dog

Russian Rose

6 parts strawberry vodka
  (3 oz./90 ml.)
1 part dry vermouth (½ oz./15 ml.)
1 part grenadine (½ oz./15 ml.)
Dash orange bitters

Combine all ingredients with ice in
a mixing glass and stir. Strain into a
chilled cocktail glass.

Salty Dog

4 parts vodka (2 oz./60 ml.)
Grapefruit juice
Coarse salt
Granulated sugar
Lime wedge

Mix salt and sugar together in a
saucer. Moisten rim of chilled old-
fashioned glass with lime wedge.
Dip the rim into the salt/sugar
mixture. Discard lime. Fill glass with
ice cubes and pour in vodka and
grapefruit juice. Stir.

Sangrita

32 parts tomato juice
  (1 pint or 16 oz./480 ml.)
16 parts fresh orange juice
  (1 cup or 8 oz./240 ml.)
10 parts pepper vodka
  (5 oz./150 ml.)
6 parts fresh lime juice
  (3 oz./90 ml.)
½ jalapeno pepper, seeded and
  chopped fine
Tabasco® sauce (1 tbsp.)
Worcestershire sauce (2 tsp.)
White pepper (¼ tsp.)
Celery salt to taste
4 parts silver tequila per person
  (2 oz./60 ml.)

Pour all ingredients, except tequila,
in a large pitcher. Chill for at least
one hour (the longer you chill this,
the spicier it gets). When ready to
serve, strain into a fresh pitcher.
Pour the tequila into one shot glass;
the sangrita into another. Drink the
tequila in one swallow and chase it
with a shot of sangrita. Serves 14.

Screwdriver

4 parts vodka (2 oz./60 ml.)
Fresh orange juice
Orange slice

Pour vodka and orange juice into
chilled highball glass over ice
cubes. Stir and garnish with orange
slice.

Sea Breeze

4 parts vodka (2 oz./60 ml.)
4 parts cranberry juice
  (2 oz./60 ml.)
Grapefruit juice

Pour vodka and cranberry juice into
a chilled highball glass filled with
ice cubes. Fill with grapefruit juice
and stir.

Sex on the Beach

4 parts vodka (2 oz./60 ml.)
3 parts peach schnapps
 (1½ oz./45 ml.)
6 parts cranberry juice
 (3 oz./90 ml.)
6 parts pineapple juice
 (3 oz./90 ml.)
Maraschino cherry

Pour all ingredients, except cherry,
into a chilled highball glass filled
with ice cubes and stir well. Garnish
with cherry.

Sexy Devil

4 parts vodka (2 oz./60 ml.)
2 parts cranberry vodka
 (1 oz./30 ml.)
1 part dry vermouth (½ oz./15 ml.)
Fresh strawberry
Lemon peel

Combine liquid ingredients with
cracked ice in a cocktail shaker
and shake well. Strain into a chilled
cocktail glass and garnish with
lemon peel and strawberry.

Shark Attack

Shark Attack

6 parts vodka (3 oz./90 ml.)
3 parts lemonade (1½ oz./45 ml.)
2 dashes grenadine

Pour ingredients into a collins glass
filled with ice cubes, and stir.

Shelley's Sweet &
Fruity

4 parts currant vodka (2 oz./60 ml.)
6 parts pineapple juice
 (3 oz./90 ml.)
1 tsp. Rose's lime juice

Combine all ingredients in a
cocktail shaker with cracked ice
and shake. Strain into a highball
glass over ice cubes.

Screwdriver

Sloe Comfortable Screw

4 parts vodka (2 oz./60 ml.)
2 parts Southern comfort
  (1 oz./30 ml.)
1 part sloe gin (½ oz./15 ml.)
Fresh orange juice

Combine all ingredients, except orange juice, in a cocktail shaker with cracked ice. Strain into a chilled highball glasses over ice cubes and fill with orange juice. Stir well.

Smokin' Texas Mary

6 parts vodka (3 oz./90 ml.)
1 part fresh lime juice
  (½ oz./15 ml.)
1 part barbecue sauce
  (½ oz./15 ml.)
Tabasco® sauce to taste
3 – 5 dashes Worcestershire sauce
Freshly ground pepper
Tomato juice
Pickled jalapeno pepper
Lime slice

Combine all ingredients, except tomato juice, jalapeno and lime slice, in a cocktail shaker with cracked ice. Shake well and pour into chilled highball glass. Fill with tomato juice and stir. Garnish with jalapeno and lime slice.

Soviet Cocktail

6 parts vodka (3 oz./90 ml.)
2 parts Manzanilla sherry
  (1 oz./30 ml.)
1 part dry vermouth (½ oz./15 ml.)
Lemon twist

Combine all ingredients, except lemon twist, with cracked ice in a cocktail shaker. Shake well and pour into chilled old-fashioned glass over ice cubes. Garnish with lemon twist.

St. Petersburg

6 parts vodka (3 oz./90 ml.)
Orange bitters (½ tsp.)
Orange slice

Pour vodka and bitters into a mixing glass with cracked ice. Stir well and strain into chilled old-fashioned glass over ice cubes. Garnish with orange slice.

Tahoe Julius

4 parts vodka (2 oz./60 ml.)
8 parts fresh orange juice
  (4 oz./120 ml.)
2 parts half-and-half (1 oz./30 ml.)
Sugar syrup (1 tsp.)

Combine all ingredients in a blender and blend until smooth. Pour into chilled wine glass.

Velvet Hammer

Tovarisch Cocktail

6 parts vodka (3 oz./90 ml.)
3 parts Jagermeister (1½ oz./45 ml.)
2 parts fresh lime juice
  (1 oz./30 ml.)

Combine ingredients with cracked ice in a cocktail shaker. Shake well and strain into chilled cocktail glass.

Velvet Hammer

6 parts vodka (3 oz./90 ml.)
2 parts dark crème de cacao
  (1 oz./30 ml.)
2 parts half-and-half (1 oz./30 ml.)

Combine ingredients with cracked ice in a cocktail shaker. Shake well and strain into chilled cocktail glass.

Vodka and Tonic

6 parts vodka (3 oz./90 ml.)
Tonic water
Lime wedge

Pour vodka into a chilled collins glass over ice cubes. Fill with tonic and stir gently. Garnish with lime wedge.

Vodka Citrus Sour

4 parts citrus vodka (2 oz./60 ml.)
3 parts fresh lemon juice
  (1½ oz./45 ml.)
Bar sugar (1 tsp.)
Lemon slice
Maraschino cherry

Combine all ingredients, except fruit, with cracked ice in a cocktail shaker. Shake well and strain into chilled sour glass. Garnish with fruit.

Vodka Collins

6 parts vodka (3 oz./90 ml.)
4 parts fresh lemon juice
  (2 oz./60 ml.)
1 part sugar syrup (½ oz./15 ml.)
Sparkling water
Maraschino cherry
Orange slice

Combine all ingredients, except fruit and sparkling water, in a chilled collins glass filled with ice cubes. Fill with sparkling water and stir gently. Garnish with fruit.

Vodka Cooler

4 parts vodka (2 oz./60 ml.)
Bar sugar (½ tsp.)
Sparkling water
Lemon peel

Mix vodka with sugar in the bottom of a chilled collins glass. Add ice cubes and fill with sparkling water. Stir gently and garnish with lemon peel.

Vodka Daisy

6 parts vodka (3 oz./90 ml.)
2 parts fresh lemon juice
  (1 oz./30 ml.)
Grenadine (1 tbsp.)
Sugar syrup (1 tsp.)
Sparkling water
Orange slice

Combine all ingredients, except orange slice and sparkling water, in a cocktail shaker with cracked ice. Shake well. Pour into chilled highball glass. Top off with sparkling water, stir gently, and garnish with orange slice.

Vodka Gimlet

6 parts vodka (3 oz./90 ml.)
2 parts Rose's lime juice
 (1 oz./30 ml.)
Lime slice

Pour vodka and lime juice into an old-fashioned glass filled with ice cubes. Stir and garnish with lime wedge.

Vodka Grasshopper

4 parts vodka (2 oz./60 ml.)
4 parts green crème de menthe
 (2 oz./60 ml.)
4 parts white crème de cacao
 (2 oz./60 ml.)

Combine all ingredients with cracked ice in a cocktail shaker and shake well. Strain into chilled cocktail glass.

Vodka Martini

6 parts iced vodka (3 oz./90 ml.)
Dry vermouth (⅛ – ¼ tsp.)
Spanish olive

Combine vodka and vermouth with cracked ice in a mixing glass. Stir well and strain into chilled cocktail glass. Garnish with olive.

Vodka Sling

4 parts vodka (2 oz./60 ml.)
1 part fresh lemon juice
 (1 oz./30 ml.)
Water (1 tsp.)
Bar sugar (1 tsp.)
Orange twist

In the bottom of a mixing glass, dissolve sugar in water and lemon juice. Add vodka and stir. Pour over ice cubes into a chilled old-fashioned glass and garnish with orange twist.

Vodka Sour

4 parts vodka (2 oz./60 ml.)
3 parts fresh lemon juice
 (1½ oz./45 ml.)
Bar sugar (1 tsp.)
Lemon slice
Maraschino cherry

Combine all ingredients, except fruit, with cracked ice in a cocktail shaker. Shake well and strain into chilled sour glass. Garnish with fruit.

Vodka Stinger

4 parts vodka (2 oz./60 ml.)
2 parts white crème de menthe
 (1 oz./30 ml.)

Combine ingredients with cracked ice in a cocktail shaker. Shake well and strain into chilled cocktail glass.

Volga Boatman

4 parts vodka (2 oz./60 ml.)
2 parts kirshwasser (1 oz./30 ml.)
2 parts fresh orange juice
 (1 oz./30 ml.)
Maraschino cherry

Combine all ingredients, except cherry, with cracked ice in a cocktail shaker. Strain into chilled cocktail glass and garnish with cherry.

Waikiki Beachcomber

4 parts vodka (2 oz./60 ml.)
1 part raspberry liqueur
 (½ oz./15 ml.)
2 parts fresh lime juice
 (1 oz./30 ml.)
10 parts guava juice (5 oz./150 ml.)

Combine all ingredients, except liqueur, with cracked ice in a cocktail shaker. Pour into chilled collins glass and float liqueur on top.

White Russian

4 parts vodka (2 oz./60 ml.)
2 parts coffee liqueur (1 oz./30 ml.)
2 parts half-and-half (1 oz./30 ml.)

Combine ingredients with cracked ice in a cocktail shaker. Shake well and pour into chilled old-fashioned glass.

White Spider

4 parts vodka (2 oz./60 ml.)
2 parts white crème de menthe
 (1 oz./30 ml.)

Combine ingredients with cracked ice in a cocktail shaker. Shake well and strain into chilled cocktail glass.

Woman Warrior

6 parts vodka (3 oz./90 ml.)
2 parts blue Curaçao (1 oz./30 ml.)
2 parts fresh lime juice

Combine ingredients with cracked ice in a cocktail shaker. Shake well and strain into chilled cocktail glass.

Woo-Woo

4 parts vodka (2 oz./60 ml.)
4 parts peach schnapps
 (2 oz./60 ml.)
8 parts cranberry juice
 (4 oz./120 ml.)

Pour ingredients into chilled highball glass over ice cubes. Stir.

Yorsh

4 parts vodka (2 oz./60 ml.)
Beer

Fill a mug ¾ full with beer. Pour the vodka into the beer and drink it.

Index of Recipes

B

B-52, 133
Babbie's Special Cocktail, 65
Baby Bellini, 161
Bachelor's Bait, 88
Backhoe, 170
Bahama Mama, 170
Bairn, 221
Bali Hai, 170
Ballylickey Belt, 203
Balmoral cocktail, 221
Bamboo Cocktail, 133
Banana Daiquiri, 170
Banana Leaky, 229
Banana Milk Shake, 170
Banana Rum Frappe, 170
Banff Cocktail, 203
Banshee, 133
Barbados Planter's Punch, 171
Barbarella, 133
Barbary Coast, 171
Barbed Wire, 242
Barton Special, 65
Batida de Piña, 171
Bayard Fizz, 89
Bayou Bomb, 171
Beach Bum, 171
Beachcomber, 161
Beachcomber's Gold, 171
Beadlestone, 221
Beauty Spot, 89
Bee's Kiss, 171
Bee's Knees, 172
Beer Buster, 242
Behind Bars, 133
Bellini, 133
Belmont Stakes, 242
Belmont, 89
Bennett, 89
Bentley Cocktail, 65
Bermuda Bouquet, 89
Bermuda Highball, 89
Bermuda Rose, 89
Berry Bomb, 134
Berry-tini, 242
Berta's Special, 229

Betsey Ross, 65
Between the Sheets, 66
Between the Streets, 66
Beverly Hills, 134
Big Apple, 66
Bijon Cocktail, 90
Billy Taylor, 90
Bird of Paradise Cooler, 90
Biscayne Bay Cocktail, 90
Bishop, 134
Bittersweet Cocktail, 134
Black and Tan, 161
Black and White Martini, 243
Black Devil, 172
Black Dog, 53
Black Hawk, 203
Black Jack, 66
Black Magic, 243
Black Maria, 172
Black Russian, 243
Black Stripe, 172
Black Velvet, 134
Blackthorn, 203
Blanche, 134
Blended Comfort, 53
Blinker, 203
Blizzard, 53
Blood and Sand, 221
Bloodhound, 90
Bloody Brew, 243
Bloody Brew, 243
Bloody Mary, 243
Blow Me Down, 172
Blowtorch, 243
Blue Angel, 66
Blue Blazer for Two, 221
Blue Devil, 90
Blue Grass Cocktail, 54
Blue Hawaiian, 172
Blue Lady, 134
Blue Lagoon, 244
Blue Margarita, 229
Blue Monday, 244
Blue Moon, 90
Blue Mountain, 173
Blue Shark, 244

G

N

O

P

Q

R

T

U

V

W

Index of Ingredients

A

Aguardiente, 170

Ale, 47, 153, 158

Almonds, 87, 142

Amaretto, 60, 66, 75, 85, 126, 127, 131, 132, 134, 135, 141-143, 148, 157, 175, 179, 215, 222, 235, 246, 249, 252

Amber ale, 47

Amer Picon, 91, 112, 132, 150, 154, 215

Anisette, 150

Aperitifs, liqueurs, and wines, 130-159

Apple brandy. *See* Brandy, apple; Applejack; Calvados.

Apple cider. *See* Cider, apple.

Apple juice, 64, 66, 152, 166

Applejack, 63, 64, 76, 77

Apples, 63, 72, 75, 126, 169, 241

Applesauce, 66

Apricot, 67

Apricot brandy. *See* Brandy, apricot.

Apricot liqueur. *See* Liqueur, apricot.

Apricot nectar, 164

Aquavit, 74, 117, 142

Au Bar, 8

Avocado, 163

B

Banana, 137, 162, 166, 170, 171, 182, 239, 241, 246

Banana liqueur. *See* Liqueur, banana.

Bar basics, 13-16

Bar oddities, 11-12

Barbecue sauce, 258

Bars at home, 12-17

Bartending at home, 8-11

Basics for a full bar, 14-16

Basics for a small bar, 13

Beer, 47-49, 140, 154, 203, 236, 242, 243, 245, 261

Beer guide, 47-49

Beer, dark, 76

Benedictine, 57, 61, 75, 76, 79, 88, 118, 119, 133, 138, 152, 154, 215, 216, 221

Benedictine and Brandy (B & B), 204

Berk, Sally Ann, 12

Berries, 242

Bitter ale, 47

Blackberries, 117

Blackberry brandy. *See* Brandy, blackberry.

Blond ale, 47

Bock beer, 47

Bouillon, beef , 162, 176, 235, 243, 245, 246

Bouillon, chicken, 162, 246

Bourbon, 53-61, 159, 171, 186, 204, 213

Brandy, 62-85, 89, 95, 113, 124, 127, 132, 134, 138-140, 142, 143, 147, 150, 151, 154, 155, 158, 159, 174, 180, 196-200, 205, 208, 217, 223. *See also* Cognac.

Brandy, apple, 63-66, 73-79, 81-85, 88, 95, 107, 118

Brandy, apricot, 58, 59, 63-65, 67, 70, 73, 78-80, 82, 84, 88, 89, 91-93, 95-98, 102, 103, 108, 113, 115, 118-120, 123, 125, 127, 128, 141, 157, 169, 177, 178, 183, 185, 190, 242

W

Y

Notes

Notes